NEGOTIATE TO
WIN

To Josh,

Happy Haggling!

NEGOTIATE TO
WIN

*The 21 Rules for
Successful Negotiation*

JIM THOMAS

Collins

An Imprint of HarperCollinsPublishers

Negotiate to Win is a registered service mark of CGS, Inc. for classes, seminars, and workshops in the field of management and business skill training.

HarperCollins books may be purchased for educational, business, or sales promotional use. For information please write: Special Markets Department, HarperCollins Publishers, 10 East 53rd Street, New York, NY 10022.

Designed by Ellen Cipriano

Library of Congress Cataloging-in-Publication Data
Thomas, Jim, 1949–
Negotiate to win : the 21 rules for successful negotiation /
Jim Thomas.—1st ed.
p. cm.
ISBN 0-06-078106-8
1. Negotiation. I. Title.
BF637.N4T45 2005
302.3—dc22

2005045711
ISBN-13 978-0-06-078106-4
11 12 13 DIX/RRD 10 9 8 7

To my parents

CONTENTS

PART THREE:
THE PRACTICE OF NEGOTIATING

ACKNOWLEDGMENTS

In writing *Negotiate to Win,* I've been blessed with the unsparing assistance of family, friends, students, clients, and top-drawer negotiators. It's said that our best thoughts come from others; most of the credit for this book belongs to them.

So many of my negotiating and legal colleagues contributed that I cannot possibly list, let alone thank, all of them. I am deeply grateful for their priceless help. Thanks also to the tens of thousands of students with whom I have had the pleasure of working in *Negotiate to Win* seminars around the world. They have given me countless invaluable insights.

Special thanks go to my clients—my early clients, in particular. Thomas Edison once said, "I have not failed. I've just found 10,000 ways that won't work." The number of mistakes one can make in negotiating is very large. I know this because I have made so many of them myself. Trial and error is a brutally inefficient, incredibly costly way to learn how to negotiate. It was at my clients' expense that I learned my craft, but it is because of them that I can offer you an alternative.

I wish to thank my children, Alex, Kelly, and Ryan, for their sacrifice of a lot of irreplaceable daddy-time during the writing of this book. For his suggestions about real estate negotiating, I thank my friend Bob Brown. For believing in me and guiding me through the process, I thank my amazing agent Bonnie Tandy Leblang, who got the show on the road. For his unfailing objectivity, good humor, advocacy, advice, patience, and confidence, I thank my editor, Herb Schaffner.

INTRODUCTION

Many books have been written about negotiating. *Negotiate to Win* is about *how* to negotiate. Its purpose is to make you a better negotiator, as quickly and painlessly as possible. If you're a beginner, it will show you, step by step, how to negotiate with confidence and skill. If you're more experienced, it will help you become a better negotiator than you ever imagined.

Here's the plan. When you boil down all the bromides, clichés, theories, and folklore about negotiating, you wind up with a handful of techniques that actually work. Those techniques—the **21 Rules of Negotiating**—are the heart and soul of *Negotiate to Win* and the focus of each of its three parts. **Part One** gets you ready for the Rules, **Part Two** gives you the Rules, and **Part Three** helps you use the Rules more effectively. When you know the Rules, you'll know negotiating.

Part One, The World Is a Big Blue Negotiating Table, takes a big-picture look at the topic. In **Chapter 1, Haggling Is Hot,** we consider some of the trends behind the growing, worldwide importance of better negotiating. In **Chapter 2, Trashing the Hallowed Halls of Haggling,** we detail the surprising shortage of practical information about bargaining that inspired this book. A quick spin around the planet in **Chapter 3, Why Johnny and Janey Can't Negotiate,** reveals that Americans are among the worst—if not the worst—negotiators on Earth. We look at some cultures in which people bargain well, and some reasons why Americans don't. In **Chapter 4, Concessions Speak Louder Than Reasons,** we mark the all-important boundary between persuasion and negotiation. Often used interchangeably, these terms describe vastly different processes; proficient negotiators must know when to use one technique or the other, and why. The final stop before the Rules is **Chapter 5, Win-Win Negotiating.** There, we explain how humans come prewired with a deep-seated need to save face, and, when we don't, a burning desire to retaliate. Win-win negotiating is, by and large, a function of human evolution: If you vanquish the other side, they'll retaliate.

The heart of the book is **Part Two, The 21 Rules of Negotiating,** where the Rules are explained in detail. The seven **Critical Rules** are covered in **Chapter 6,** the four **Important but Obvious Rules** in **Chapter 7,** and the ten **Nice to Do Rules** in **Chapter 8. Part Two** concludes with **Chapter 9, Putting It All Together,** in which each of the Rules is demonstrated in a hypothetical negotiation.

In **Part Three, The Practice of Negotiating,** the Rules meet the real world. **Chapter 10, Ethics,** takes on the thorny subject of ethical negotiating. We identify some bargaining moves that are clearly ethical, some that clearly aren't, and some that aren't so clear, along with guidelines to help you recognize and avoid ethical traps. Globalism is making **Chapter 11, International Negotiating,** more important every day. Opportunities abroad are immense, but dealing with the negotiating styles of other countries—especially those where bargaining is commonplace—requires special care and attention. **Chapter 12, Quickies,** offers specific tips on how to successfully handle everyday negotiations with bosses, children, car dealers, contractors, auto mechanics, and many others. We wrap up with a key-points review and some final words of advice in **Chapter 13, Concluding Thoughts,** and **Chapter 14, Thomas's Truisms.**

Let's set a few ground rules before we begin:

- I am living proof that God has a sense of humor. My cornucopia of flaws includes being an incurable wise guy. No matter how solemn the occasion, I can't be deadpan for more than about five minutes at a stretch. Many things in the following pages are said in jest. I mean no disrespect or offense, and I offer heartfelt apologies, in advance, for any that might inadvertently be given.

- *Negotiate to Win* is the product of experience, not research. You won't find the abundant references and footnotes common to more scholarly works. This approach maintains the long-standing disconnect between me and anything that could remotely be called "scholarly," while simultaneously making room for stuff that somebody actually might read.

- Many of my examples depict people bargaining over some imaginary order of widgets, doodads, or gizmos. I use such examples only because they can be illustrated quickly and grasped easily, and in no way to minimize the importance of the countless negotiations that have nothing to do with buying, selling, numbers, or tangible things.

- The moment you write about somebody, sex becomes an issue. In English, anyway. That's because English doesn't have a gender-neutral, third-person-singular pronoun. In English, everybody has to be *he* or *she*. I try to finesse this, first, by proudly using the forbidden third person plural *(they/them/their)* whenever I think I can get away with it; and, second, by alternating between male- and female-gendered pronouns. Neither solution is ideal—the alternating pronouns, in particular, can make for some awkward going at first—but they're a start.

- The party on the other side of a negotiation is often called "the opponent." "Opponent" sounds hostile and combative to me, like someone to be vanquished. I view good negotiating as more of a joint problem-solving enterprise than a battle, so I use neutral or positive terms like "the other side," "counterpart," "fellow negotiator," and "colleague" instead.

- Canadians, Latin Americans, and everybody else residing on the American Continent may rightly be called "Americans." However, in *Negotiate to Win*, "Americans" refers only to people from the United States.

- *Negotiate to Win* lionizes an imaginary "Japanese" negotiator and bargaining style as the standard of excellence. Our superhuman Japanese bargainer is a literary device. *Nobody*—from Japan or anywhere else—negotiates that well. Like all stereotypes, positive ones included, he is one-dimensional and inherently unrealistic.

- Over the years I've jotted down various adages about negotiating, often having just experienced their validity firsthand. These sayings have become known as Thomas's Truisms. You'll find 50 of them scattered throughout the book and collected at the end.

    Thomas's Truisms can help make important bargaining principles compact and portable, but like all maxims, they must be used carefully. Some of them are flat-out bargaining dogma, but most are in the nature of commentary and observation. Some are deliberate oversimplifications. Others are not applicable in all circumstances. A few are even directly contradictory—and valid nonetheless—requiring the negotiator to balance their competing advice.

PART ONE

THE WORLD IS
A BIG BLUE
BARGAINING TABLE

1

Haggling Is Hot

We are all going to die. Aside from that, it's negotiable.

Among animals, only humans negotiate. We negotiate unceasingly, from our first cry to our last breath. We dicker with bosses, subordinates, colleagues, customers, vendors, parents, spouses, children, merchants, laborers, craftspeople, bureaucrats, policemen, lovers, friends, and enemies. We haggle with individuals and groups, at home and at work, day and night, rain and shine. Negotiating is part of practically every human activity. Any time two or more of us *confer for agreement*—about anything—we could be negotiating.

If you think a lot of haggling is going on *now*, just wait. Society is being hammered by revolutionary social, political, and economic changes that will sharply raise the stakes on skillful negotiating.

New economic realities. It's not just your imagination—things *really are* getting tougher. It's harder than ever to manage a business, make a profit, raise a child, balance a family budget, or run a government. And the tougher things get, the more important *good negotiating* becomes.

As I write this, the average net after-tax profit margin of S&P 500 companies is a razor-thin 4%. 4%! Margins of 10 to 20% and more used to be typical; only grocery chains and a few other high-volume businesses had 4% margins. Yes, in some years margins will get better. And in others, they'll get worse. They constantly fluctuate with economic cycles. But, on average, they've been steadily shrinking for the past half-century. I'm no economist, but this looks like a trend to me.

What happens when the sellers and buyers in a company with a 4% net after-tax margin start negotiating 1% better? Just 1%? That 1% drops straight to the bottom line—increasing profit by 25%! Imagine the effect on the price of that company's stock.

Scarcity is the mother of better bargaining. When times are good and margins are fat, you can get away with a little sloppy negotiating now and then. When margins are 4%, you can't. The economic landscape has changed, probably forever. We share a future of constrained resources—of 4% margins—in which ever-smaller advantages will determine who succeeds and who doesn't; a future in which better negotiating can make all the difference.

New globalism. The doors to the Mother of All Bazaars are open. Electronically exchanged information and capital are quickly making international borders irrelevant. We are all citizens of—and competitors in—a wired, global state.

An obvious consequence of our connected world is a huge upsurge in transactions between individuals and organizations with vastly different cultural backgrounds. Westerners just entering the international marketplace are often shocked to discover that *the rest of the world negotiates like crazy!* New globalism requires successful negotiators to quickly adapt to the ways of other cultures. **Chapter 10, International Negotiating** examines these issues and highlights some of the shortcomings of the traditional American "one size fits all" approach to cross-cultural negotiating.

New management and work styles. Today's organizations are smaller, flatter, faster, and increasingly dependent upon capable negotiating. Corporate pyramids topped by shouting, imperial bosses have been replaced by unstructured, collaborative enterprises. Today's employees, more self-interested and nomadic than their careerist forebears, have little tolerance for dictatorial treatment. Good "office negotiation" skills have become almost indispensable to managerial success.

The rapid growth of strategic alliances between companies has been another boon to bargaining. Members of these alliances trade their traditionally predatory relationships for shared forecasts and technology, pooled financial and human resources, and joint design and production decisions. Maintaining the health of these alliances requires the constant renegotiation of delicately balanced burdens, benefits, rights, and responsibilities.

New frugality. Yet another trend helping make negotiation a growth industry is the "new frugality" movement in America. Many Americans have joined a subtle but widespread retreat from unrestrained conspicuous consumption in favor of simpler pleasures, thriftier ways, and more practical lifestyles. Besides bag lunches, bulk buying, and recycling, negotiating is *de rigueur* for growing numbers of "new frugality" adherents. Even in day-to-day retail dealings, they're rejecting the traditional American taboo against bargaining.

You ain't seen nothin' yet. The future will test our negotiating skills as never before. Haggling is hot, and it's getting hotter all the time.

2

Trashing the Hallowed Halls of Haggling

Seven hundred years ago, an unknown, penniless Franciscan friar named William of Ockham had a notion that changed the world. "The best answer to a question," he said, "is the simplest answer that explains the facts." In modern vernacular, "Keep it simple, stupid!" *

Upon a fourteenth-century society that believed everyday events were governed by mystical forces beyond human reckoning, his proposition—today known as Ockham's Razor—fell like a bombshell. Suddenly, everything was open to question. Unfortunately for Ockham, "everything" included the Catholic Church, which promptly branded him a heretic and tossed him into the slammer.

His idea, however, refused to be unthought. The first faint glimmers of Renaissance brilliance—kindled, in part, by Ockham's notion—soon illuminated the Dark Ages. Ockham's Razor would help to change modern thinking.

---

* Another modern restatement of Ockham's rule—*attributed both to Albert Einstein and Yogi Berra*—is "Keep things as simple as possible, but no simpler."

It changed *my* thinking about negotiating.

Many years ago, a client requested that I give a short briefing on negotiating techniques. The client was determined to improve the negotiating skills of his people, and had tried everything—every bargaining book and seminar he could find—to no avail. Nothing worked.

The client's instructions were very specific: "I don't want any theory. I don't want to hear about Maslow's Hierarchy of Needs. Just give me the stuff that works. If you have any doubt about something, leave it out."

In short, take Ockham's Razor to the subject of negotiating.

I read everything I could find on the topic. And the more I read, the more frustrated I became. Practically nothing passed the Razor test. Much of the material was naively theoretical, or focused on physical trappings (table shape, clothing, seating protocol, and the like), or preached intimidating or unethical behavior, or worse. Newer works rehashed earlier ones. Instead of nuts-and-bolts guidance, I found theory, folklore, trivia, clichés, and war stories. Here's a brief, Razor-eye view of some of negotiation's "accepted wisdom":

The academic approach. For years, respected and influential scholars have rejected ordinary (they call it "hard" or "positional") bargaining in favor of a more inclusive or "principled" style. A central tenet of this approach is the importance of focusing on the true needs and interests *behind* the other side's stated position, rather than the position itself.

> **BUYER:** I want a 10% price rollback. *Now.*
> **SELLER:** I hear what you're saying about a 10% price rollback. But what are we really talking about? Is this a recognition thing for you? An empowerment thing? Do you feel that my company hasn't treated you with enough respect in the past? Let's be honest with each other.

In the above example, it's altogether possible that the buyer will respond with a thoughtful, revealing answer, and the parties will go on to form a lasting agreement. However, I wouldn't bet on it. This is *much* more likely:

> **BUYER:** Thanks, pal, but if I'd wanted psychotherapy, I woulda' called a shrink. I'm here to talk about pricing. And I'm in a hurry. What's it gonna be?

When adults haggle—especially at work—you can bet your patootie that most of the time our stated positions are going to be seriously close, if not identical, to our real interests. On those rare occasions when they aren't, we'll be absolutely *delighted* to make our underlying interests abundantly clear, along with the many wonderful ways they can be satisfied. You won't be able to shut us up about our interests.

Negotiations fail because of conflicting values, perceptions, and beliefs. They fail because of insufficient resources, fear, timidity, and clashing personalities. The interest-based, academic approach rarely works because conflicting interests are rarely the problem. And when, as is frequently the case, one side is adversarial or more powerful than the other, it's almost completely useless. It's elegant and well intentioned, and it doesn't pass the Razor test.

Folklore. The subject of negotiating abounds with folklore, much of it about the trappings of the bargaining venue or the bargainers themselves. We're advised that the person in the "power seat" (head of the table, back to the window, facing the door) is likely to prevail. We're coached on the best days and times for negotiating, the preferred table shape, whose "turf" we should bargain on, and what biorhythms insure haggling success. We're urged to wear "power colors" (dark blue, gray, and black). Picture this:

As the blue-suited negotiator strides confidently into the room, her counterpart anxiously whispers to an assistant, "No! She's wearing the blue suit! We're toast! Whenever she wears that suit, I give away the ranch! I just can't help myself! What's the point of going on? Why don't we just give up right now?"

Wouldn't that be great? This would be the shortest negotiating book of all time: "Wear blue. And keep it to yourself. It'll be our little secret."

There's not a shred of empirical evidence behind this stuff. It just gets repeated, gaining undeserved credibility with each retelling. I have never heard of, let alone witnessed, a negotiation that was significantly influenced by when or where it took place, what the participants wore, where they sat, or the shape of the table (if any) they used. In fact, after almost 30 years in this business, I can honestly say that I don't know of any physical factor that has so much as a *measurable effect* on negotiated outcomes. Not one. When you Razor-cut it, much of negotiation's folklore turns out to be fiction.

Body language. Some negotiating pundits insist that an individual's posture and gestures can be "read" to reveal what he or she is thinking. Everyday nonverbal gestures—an opened palm, a tilted head, a stroked chin—are given elaborate interpretations. Folded arms show skepticism and resistance. An unbuttoned jacket signals openness and readiness to reach agreement.

Then again, maybe it signals that the wearer's hot. Or needs some air. Or has put on some weight. And maybe those arms are folded because their owner is freezing. Or shy. Or thinks it makes the biceps look bigger. Or any one of a thousand other reasons.

It all fails the Razor test. An insurmountable obstacle will always frustrate the development of any reliable, systematic analysis of body language: *Everybody's different.* A gesture or cluster of gestures that convey a specific meaning when exhibited by a particular person in a particular culture at a particular time can easily have an altogether different meaning—or no meaning at all—for another person, or within another culture, or at another time.

Now, don't get me wrong. I freely admit that a vast amount of important communication takes place without words, and in no way am I suggesting that you ignore nonverbal cues. What I'm suggesting is that you're a body-language guru *right now*. Since you were a kid, you've been reading the other side's body language like a highway sign. You know when they're excited, happy, sad, angry, interested, resistant, or bored. You know that when they stand up, the meeting's probably over. You don't have to think about it. You just *know* it.

If you're consciously thinking about body language, you're giving it too much attention. And you're distracting yourself from more important things you *should* be thinking about.

Strategies. *While looking through his desk, the new Manager of Labor Relations finds four envelopes. The first is labeled "Strategy 1," the next "Strategy 2," and the third "Strategy 3." The fourth is labeled "Open Me First," which he does. Inside is a letter from his predecessor that says: "Welcome aboard! These envelopes contain my best negotiating strategies. If you ever run up against a problem you can't solve, use* Strategy 1 *first, then* Strategy 2, *then* Strategy 3."

The new manager smiles at his predecessor's thoughtfulness, puts the envelopes back in the desk, and forgets about them.

Six months later the union goes on strike, shutting the company down. It's losing money fast. After a long night of hostile negotiating with the union, the manager remembers the envelopes. As instructed, he opens the "Strategy 1" envelope. Inside is a note that says, "Blame your predecessor for everything."

It works. The strike ends and his job is saved.

A few months later, there's another strike. The union is even more adversarial than before, and its demands are outrageous. After hours of fruitless bargaining, the manager goes to his desk and opens the "Strategy 2" envelope. The note reads, "Blame the government for everything."

It works like a charm. Once again, the strike ends and his job is saved.

A month later the union declares yet another strike. This time, its demands are simply preposterous. It refuses to compromise on anything. Desperate, the manager runs to his desk, tears open the last envelope, and reads the note. It says: "Prepare four new envelopes . . ."

The literature of negotiation is packed with literally hundreds of so-called "strategies." Often carrying faux-dramatic names like "salami" and "surprise," they offer an uneven patchwork of advice that ranges from worthwhile to wrongheaded to downright unethical.

The "forbearance" strategy, for example, advises the negotiator to patiently "wait out" the other side. In Rule 15, Be patient, we'll show why patience in negotiation—when practicable—is a fine idea. But it's hardly a strategy, a carefully devised plan of action. Without the host of other elements that animate the negotiation—offers, counteroffers, concessions, and more—forbearance alone accomplishes almost nothing.

The "bland withdrawal" strategy suggests that the negotiator simply leave the discussions—perhaps without so much as an explanation to the other participants:

Where did Bill go? He was here a minute ago. He was going to give us his position on the offshore tax structure. You say he just wandered off? Does this happen a lot? I hope he's O.K.

This is no strategy; it's just loony behavior. And it's no way to reach an agreement.

The *fait accompli* strategy is often illustrated by the sending of a check for less than the agreed amount. Not only isn't this a negotiating *strategy*, it isn't even *negotiating*. The negotiation ends when the parties agree on the number. What's being suggested by this technique is *chiseling*. Or fraud. It's blatantly unethical, highly offensive, and a virtual guarantee of reprisal.

When you've only got a hammer, everything is a nail. The Achilles heel of all negotiating strategies is that they try to solve inherently dynamic problems with inherently static solutions. Every negotiation—and every negotiator—is unique and must be handled differently. You can't do this with a handful of canned strategies. Even if you could, the exasperating unpredictability of the process would quickly render even the best-planned strategy obsolete.

Strategies fail the Razor test, not because they aren't simple enough, but because they're *too* simple. Strategies alone will never make you a good negotiator. You must know *how* to negotiate.

Intimidation. There's something strangely fascinating about intimidation in negotiation. It's juvenile, rude, unprofessional, and ineffective but, like the proverbial train wreck, we're mesmerized by it. We love to hear about how somebody gave away the ranch because of a sweltering room, a wobbly chair, a blinding light, a noxious smell, or the other side's obnoxious behavior.

The concept is simple enough: By behaving antagonistically, irrationally, or offensively, you can intimidate, upset, or confuse the other side into making generous concessions.

Here's a scenario. You arrive at the appointed time, only to learn that the meeting has been delayed. After an hour's wait in the reception area, you're ushered into your counterpart's office and motioned to a small, soft, stuffed chair. You sit, quickly sinking up to your waist in pillow-soft padding. Your counterpart's desk—easily the biggest desk you've ever seen—sits on a low platform in front of a huge window. You can just make out his head and shoulders from your sunken vantage point.

Shortly after the talks begin, the sun appears from behind an adjacent building. A brilliant sunbeam centers itself perfectly on the back of your counterpart's head. Now, looking at him is like looking at a solar eclipse: Incandescent rays emanate from the black dot that used to be his face. Tears stream down your cheeks. The room is hotter than a sauna. His calls aren't being held, so the telephone rings constantly. A stream of visitors interrupt the meeting. Implements of war decorate the walls: axes, maces, bows and arrows, guns, spears, knives, animal heads. There isn't a square inch of unused flat surface, so you have to hold your paperwork in your lap—but it keeps falling on the floor because one of your chair's legs is an inch shorter than the other three and you're uncontrollably rocking back and forth. This aggravates your nausea from the noxious blend of fumes from your counterpart's rancid cigar and cheap cologne.

Got the picture? Good. Now, how do you feel? Conciliatory? Flexible? Generous? More specifically, do you feel like making concessions to the person behind the big desk?

No? Precisely. If you're like most people, concessions are about the last thing on your mind right now. People who are treated like this don't get generous, they get *angry.* Or at the very least, defensive. They make fewer, not more, concessions. Aside from insulting or screaming at the other side, it would be hard to dream up behavior less likely than this to elicit concessions. It just doesn't work.

And it's a good thing it doesn't, because it would be even worse if it did.

Here's what would happen. Let's make our imaginary victim a complete bargaining neophyte in his very first formal negotiation. He walks into the above-described den of horrors, he panics and he gives away the ranch. In the vernacular of the trade, it's called "a hosing.*" Stay with me on this.

---

* From **hose** (*hoz*) vt. In negotiating, to obtain a highly favorable, one-sided agreement. Probably derived from the Canadian slang "hoser" popularized by the Bob and Doug Mackenzie skits on SCTV: *"I can't wait to hose those tree-hugging geeks."* **Hosed** (*hozed*) adj. In negotiating, to be bargained into a highly unfavorable, one-sided agreement. *"We were totally hosed in that negotiation. And it's your fault."* See also **dehose, rehose, hoser, hosee.**

The unsuspecting hosee returns to his office and dutifully presents the deal to his boss. At first, the boss is merely incredulous: "This is a joke, right?" he says. "You're a comedian." When the true enormity of the debacle sinks in, the boss is apoplectic: "This is the stupidest deal I've ever seen! Have you taken leave of your senses?"

With luck, the hosee will keep his job. But he'll never forget who put him in this humiliating, career-threatening position. As he drifts off to sleep that night, his last thoughts will be of the person behind the big desk—the hoser. And he'll quietly vow eternal revenge against him, his organization, his family, and his lineage unto the last generation.

Some day, the hoser's and hosee's paths will cross again.† And when they do, I'll bet the hoser gets an unforgettable lesson in the true cost of win-lose negotiating.

THOMAS'S TRUISMS

**What goes around comes around. Sooner or
later, you have to pay for your sins.**

THOMAS'S TRUISMS

Pestering. A tawdry variant of the "negotiation by intimidation" approach advocates, in essence, negotiating by being a pest: bugging people until they give in. Prescribed techniques include deliberately wasting the other side's time, making a scene, raising your voice, and complaining endlessly.

Pestering passes the Razor test because, unlike intimidation, it actually works sometimes. But like intimidation, it's tacky and win-lose. And if you use this approach, have no illusion about the reason you're getting whatever the other side gives you:

To get rid of you.

All of this brings us back to my little briefing. It was now

---

† The Bargaining Gods will insist on it. There's been a hosing, the accounts are out of balance, and the Bargaining Gods are offended. They'll arrange a rematch.

painfully clear that I wasn't going to be able to cut and paste a presentation out of conventional wisdom. I was going to have to start from scratch. And so, with my client's instructions ("Just give me the stuff that works") firmly in mind, I began. I didn't know it then, but I was writing *Negotiate to Win*.

3

Why Johnny and Janey Can't Negotiate

When it comes to negotiating, Americans have a *biiiiig* problem. How big? Let's take a quick spin around the planet and see how Americans measure up, bargaining-wise, to the rest of the world.*

Japan, home to the finest negotiators on Earth, is the perfect place to start. You'd be hard-pressed to find much of anything wrong in the way the Japanese negotiate. Their skill at bargaining comes from two fundamental Japanese social imperatives: saving face, and maintaining the *wa*, or harmony, of the group. Here's the formula: If a deal is unfair, someone will lose face; and if someone loses face, the *wa* of the whole group will be undermined.

If anybody gets hosed, *everybody's* hosed.

You can see the importance of face-saving to the Japanese in something as simple as the way they say "no." Blunt language is scrupulously avoided; a straightforward "no" would be unthinkable.

---

* **Disclaimer:** The "cultural descriptions" in this chapter are deliberate, extreme oversimplifications. We'll take a far more thoughtful look at cultural differences in Chapter 11, International Negotiating.

Among the various gambits that let the Japanese say "no" without causing offense is a little maneuver known affectionately as a "Japanese No."

A Japanese No is simply a "yes" with an "if" attached—an "if" so extravagant it's almost certain to be rejected by the other side:

AMERICAN: I want X, Y, and Z.

JAPANESE: Certainly! We are delighted and honored to give you X, Y, and Z! [ten-second pause] In exchange, however, we will require your firstborn child. Is that agreeable?

Except for the sorry handful of you who screamed "It's a deal!" the proposed trade has the practical effect of a flat "no." Its emotional effect, however, is altogether different. A simple "no" is an edict; it precludes discussion; its recipient is a bystander. A Japanese No is a choice; it requires discussion; its recipient *must* participate:

AMERICAN: Firstborn child? Hmmmm. Interesting, but for now, I'm gonna have to pass. Thanks for asking, though!

Hobsonian or not, any choice is better than none. I'll take a Japanese No over the regular kind any day.

How do the Japanese say "yes"? The same way! They just lighten up on the "if"! For the Japanese, the only difference between a yes and a no is the size of the "if." To say no they crank the "if" up, and to say yes they crank it down.

THOMAS'S TRUISMS

For the Japanese, the only difference between a yes and a no is the size of the "if."

THOMAS'S TRUISMS

Yes or no, there's always an "if." No honorable Japanese negotiator would make a concession without one.

Leaving Japan and moving west, we find competent negotiating throughout Asia. Further west, the Russians are legendary for their bargaining skills, and their Eastern and Central European neighbors are home to some fine hagglers as well.

Unfortunately, the wheels fall off when we get to Western Europe. Germany enjoys the unique distinction of having Europe's largest economy and its worst negotiators. This isn't surprising, since Germans worship the very things that negotiation so famously lacks: logic and efficiency. The British, who look down on the whole process as a sign of bad breeding, aren't much better. The French easily outbargain the Brits; the Italians top the French; the Greeks outdo the Italians; and the Turks whip the Greeks.

Interestingly, there seems to be a lot more negotiating outside of Western Europe and North America than inside. Why? Supply and demand. Our very own incredibly efficient economies have made negotiating slackers out of us. We don't bargain at the Wal-Mart because there's a Target just down the street. When Target has a lower price, it's goodbye Wal-Mart. They burn the midnight oil at Wal-Mart until they figure out how to beat Target's price, and when they do, it's goodbye Target! Why don't we negotiate in the West? *Because we have feet!*

I'll grant you that much of the heavy lifting in Western commerce is handled very capably by market forces. But even the most efficient market forces will only drive prices to market *levels*. To beat the market—especially a highly competitive market—requires skillful negotiating. The results—an extra quarter-percent here, an extra half-percent there—won't be particularly dramatic. But when viewed over the course of a career, or when multiplied by the colossal scale of routine Western transactions, these little adjustments can become huge, potentially decisive advantages.

And completely aside from commercial negotiations, what about the infinite variety of bargaining encounters that aren't market-driven? Like what movie we'll see, or when a project will be done, or where we'll eat, or what we'll name the puppy, or when we'll go on vacation, or what Junior's bedtime will be? Supply and demand won't help you here. There aren't any market forces to hide behind. Bargaining skills—not economics—will determine these outcomes.

But I digress. Next stop on our tour is the Middle East, legendary home of colorful bazaars and wily merchants. Here, haggling is both social interaction and entertainment, and as common a daily activity as eating. Indeed, refusing to bargain is considered rude in the Middle East—much like refusing a handshake in the West.

Africa, with its dozens of nations and hundreds of languages, religions, and cultures, is a land of incredible diversity. Everywhere on the continent, however, talented bargainers and spirited negotiating are commonplace.

Jumping to the Western Hemisphere, our next stop is Canada—a vast country of wonderful people who mostly can't negotiate worth a maple leaf. In fairness, however, Eastern Canadians (with a little more French influence, *peut-être*) are better hagglers than the hapless Westerners.

Latin Americans, on the other hand, are marvelous bargainers. A Latin American negotiation is like an elaborate, highly stylized dance. Each step must be observed. First, we get acquainted in a seemingly endless round of hugs, kisses, dinners, drinking, gift-giving, and discussions about history, politics, and above all, family. These lengthy pleasantries are followed by negotiations that are—by North American standards, at least—*interminable.* And if a deal is struck, it's celebrated with more hugs, kisses, small talk, drinking, eating, and gift-giving.

One last westward jump brings us to the Land Down Under. Australians and New Zealanders are forging unique national identities from their many peoples, cultures, and religions. Unfortunately, their bloody awful bargaining proves they're still British to their bootstraps.

I skipped the States.

America is a cultural icon, the envy of the modern world, the largest economy, the oldest democracy, and the lone superpower. And Americans are wonderful people: generous, brave, clean, cheerful, thrifty, and reverent. But when it comes to negotiating, we're among the worst—if not *the* worst—on the face of the Earth.

It pains me to say this, but I assure you it's true. We're neck-and-neck with the Germans for dead last.

Americans *hate* to negotiate. We find it embarrassing and tacky, something *just not done* in polite society. We're bottom-line people. We're partial to phrases like "Let's stop beating around the bush," "Here's the bottom line," "Let's get down to brass tacks," "Let's cut to the chase," "Let's lay our cards on the table," and that perennial American favorite, "Do we have a deal, or *what?*"

We negotiate like John Wayne. Unfortunately, *John Wayne didn't negotiate.*

Where did we go wrong? How did we get to be like this? Why do we flock to "no-haggle" Saturn dealers? Why does the mere thought of bargaining for some cheap trinket in a Caribbean straw market send us into a panic?

There is no shortage of theories. Our negotiophobia could stem from our Puritan ethic, our low population density, or our material abundance. It could be the result of our geographical isolation, our military strength, or our need to be liked. It might even be an Old World v. New World thing, the long-forgotten "cultural distancing" of earlier immigrants who tried to Americanize themselves by renouncing the "Old Country" habits—haggling, in particular—that made them most conspicuous.

Lots of theories, but few answers.

I have my own theory about why Americans don't haggle. I call it Thomas's Immigrant Theory of Negotiation in America. What did people back in the Old Country do if they couldn't work a deal where they were? They left. Yep, they split.

And they came *here.*

That's the theory. America is a nation of *self-selected non-negotiators.* We're the homeland of the People Who Split. "You won't let me practice my religion? I'm outta' here!" "You won't let me vote? I'm outta' here!" "You won't let me own land? I'm outta' here! I'm going to America!" From all over the world, the "I'm outta' here" people came to America. Our national motto shouldn't be "In God We Trust"; it should be "I'm outta' here!"

Wait, wait, that's not all. Where did all of these people settle? New York! The entire planet's "I'm outta' here" people hung around New York, trying to make a deal. And if they couldn't make a deal in New York? They left! Using the old "I'm outta' here" strategy, these Johnny Haggleseeds headed west, leaving the better negotiators behind them as they went. St. Louis? "I'm outta' here!" Denver? "I'm outta' here!" Salt Lake City? "I'm outta' here!" At long last, the wretched refuse of the original "I'm outta here!" people—and their descendants—settled in California, having run out of real estate.

According to Thomas's Immigrant Theory of Negotiation in America:

- The overall skill level of American negotiators should be rather poor, seeing as how we're the direct descendants of the accumulated "I'm outta' here" people of the planet Earth.
- New Yorkers should be the best negotiators in the country, and Californians should be the worst.

And you know what? That's exactly the way it is! My theory may be a joke, but it's the only one that explains the data!

New York City is the last bastion of hard-core haggling in America. It's perfectly acceptable, even admirable, for a New Yorker to walk into a camera store on 47th Street, spot a particularly attractive Nikon behind the counter, and launch into a spiel like this:

Yo, Vinnie, c'mere. Come ovah here. Gimme a price on dis' camera. Gimme another price. C'mon, help me out, here. How much? I can't hear you! I still can't hear you! Vinnie, talk to me! You're bustin' my chops! You're killin' me! I'm dyin' *over here! Whata' you, crazy? I thought we were* friends!

Try pulling that on Rodeo Drive in Beverly Hills. They'll think you're from Mars. They'll call security on you.

Negotiating skills are not yet an American birthright. Americans become more supportive of negotiation every day, but we still have a long way to go. And while the following chapters should alleviate much of your anxiety about negotiating, a little stress will almost inevitably remain. A couple of butterflies, flying in formation, might just be a healthy sign that you're taking things seriously.

4

Concessions Speak Louder Than Reasons

The heart has its reasons of which reason knows nothing.
Blaise Pascal (1623–62),
French philosopher and scientist

Persuasion and Negotiation

There are two ways to get people to voluntarily do something. You can persuade them to do it, or you can negotiate with them to do it. Often used interchangeably, persuasion and negotiation are actually very different processes. To become a successful negotiator you must know the difference, and by the end of this chapter, you will.

Let's start with our old buddy, the undisputed heavyweight champ of behavior modification, *persuasion*. Persuasion is the process of getting someone to do something by convincing him that it's the logical and reasonable thing to do. We persuade each other constantly, vastly more often than we negotiate with each other. Many of our most familiar activities—convincing, requesting, arguing, flirting, coaxing, advertising, debating, buying, selling, nagging, flattering, and criticizing, to name just a few—are rooted in persuasion. Since infancy, we've persuaded, and been persuaded, countless times. It's second nature to us. We're *really good* at it.

Thanks, in part, to our history, nobody loves persuasion more than Americans. America is a child of the Age of Reason,* the eighteenth-century celebration of science, order, and logic. Some of our foremost revolutionaries—Thomas Paine, Thomas Jefferson, and Benjamin Franklin among them—were leading proponents of the Age of Reason's then-unorthodox central tenet: Truth will be found through rational thinking. Age of Reason themes—the common people are fundamentally wise; with free speech and a free press they'll know the truth; when they know the truth they'll make the right decisions—suffuse our Declaration of Independence and our Constitution. Way down deep, Americans believe that with a good enough argument, presented well enough, we can persuade *anybody*.

Persuasion isn't very complicated: Give somebody a bunch of reasons why they should do something; if they're convinced, they'll do it.

> **YOU:** Here's my position. Here are facts and reasons support-
> ing it. So, do we have a deal, or what?
> **THEM:** Sure!

To be fair, persuasion doesn't always work quite so effortlessly. The other side may have an objection, or *lots* of objections, to your argument. With more logic and reason, you mow down every objection like grass.

> **THEM:** But the price is too high!
> **YOU:** I understand your concern, and you'll be happy to
> know it's unfounded balderdash! Here are facts and rea-
> sons that prove my product would be cheap at *twice* the
> price. Now, do we have a deal, or what?
> **THEM:** Sure!

---

* Also known as *the Enlightenment.*

Persuasion usually works. Sometimes it works quickly. Sometimes—impeded by objections—it works more slowly.

But sometimes it doesn't work at all.

"If *Only* I Could Make You Understand!"

Let's change the scenario. What if the other side's response to your incontrovertible argument is a bit less enthusiastic?

> **YOU:** So, do we have a deal, or what?
> **THEM:** Nope.

What if they *aren't persuaded*? What're you going to do now? If you're like most people—utterly confident of the power of persuasion and the inevitable triumph of logic—I'll bet you a zillion dollars what you're going to do now. You're going to *repeat your argument!*

> **YOU:** Let's go over this again. I'll go more slowly. Try to stay with me. Ready? O.K., here's my position. Remember it from before? Excellent! And here are my reasons. Remember them? There're some new ones in there, too. Still with me? Great! Now, do we have a deal, or what?
> **THEM:** No, we don't. And *please* don't repeat yourself again. I understood you perfectly the first time. I didn't agree with you then, and I don't agree with you now.

Can we all agree that, in this case, persuasion probably won't work? The other side has heard, considered, and *firmly rejected* your argument. Twice! What're you going to do now? Of course—*repeat your argument!*

> **Insanity is doing the same thing over and over
> and expecting a different result.**
>
> —Chinese proverb

Once we start persuading, it's hard for us to stop. We're fools for logic. We've all succumbed to persuasion's seductive, pernicious fallacy: *Understanding must beget agreement.* From this delusion flow such familiar laments as "If only I could make them understand!" and "I'm just not getting through to them!" The idea is that the other side doesn't agree with us simply because they don't *understand* us—that is, we haven't "gotten through" to them. And the moment we do, they will, so what are we waiting for? We must explain ourselves again—*unmistakably,* this time, and without delay!

I have some good news and some bad news for you on this. The good news is that you got through to them. They understand your position. You can stop repeating yourself.

The bad news is that they don't *agree* with it, and never will. Welcome to Persuasion Hell.

Bubba Meets Beelzebub

Ever since hostilities erupted in the Middle East in 1948, a parade of eager, hopeful U.S. "peace envoys"—including every president since Jimmy Carter—have struggled fruitlessly to bring peace to the region. Bill Clinton's turn at Middle East peacemaking arrived with special urgency. The scandals that had scarred his administration raised the stakes on success from mere foreign policy triumph to legacy lifesaver. A deal would instantly transform Clinton from rake to statesman. It would be his crowning achievement, the defining event of his presidency. It might even win him a Nobel Prize.

Like every good American, Clinton carried an unshakable faith in his ability to convince anybody to do anything. And with good reason. Say what you will about Bill Clinton, he could persuade the chrome off a trailer hitch. Since childhood, his intelligence, charisma, persuasive skills, and aw-shucks grin had rarely failed him. As he presented his peace plan to Palestinian leader Yasser Arafat and Israeli Prime Minister Ehud Barak, he had no reason to think those skills would fail him now. Clinton eagerly looked forward to watching Arafat and Barak do the diplomatic equivalent of slapping themselves on the forehead as they proclaimed, "Bill! That's it! That's the answer! Why didn't we think of it before? How could we have been so stupid? How can we ever thank you?"

But Bill Clinton wasn't going to Oslo for the Peace Prize. He was going to *Persuasion Hell! Ahhhhhahahahahahaha!!!!*

To Clinton's astonishment, what Arafat and Barak *actually* said was something like, "Go jump in a lake." Disappointed but undaunted, Clinton made one increasingly desperate attempt after another to explain how his plan would resolve this ancient, deadly conflict. But even his vast persuasive powers proved no match for the bitter, unyielding reality of Middle Eastern politics, and in the end he accomplished exactly what his predecessors had: nothing.

If understanding had been the impediment to peace in the Middle East, David and Goliath would have been old drinking buddies. Arafat and Barak understood Clinton's plan just fine. After thousands of years of Middle East conflict, *everybody* understands what the solutions are. Like their predecessors, Arafat and Barak rejected Clinton's plan because they didn't *like* it. Give both sides a plan they like—that is, one that offers something clearly better than what they already have—and they'll be all over it like a cheap suit. You won't be able to hold them back!

There are few places on Earth where persuasion is *less* likely to produce agreement than the Middle East. Broad visions and bold statements will never change the minds of millions of Arabs for whom the very existence of Israel is an affront to God, or millions of Israelis who believe they have a covenant with that same God making Jerusalem their eternal capital. If peace in the Middle East is ever to be achieved, it will be through concessions—costly, painful concessions—from all parties. Not talk.

The Middle East dispute may be one of Persuasion Hell's more infamous denizens, but it's certainly not alone. Care to place odds on China persuading Taiwan to reunify? India convincing Pakistan to forsake Kashmir? North Korea working out a merger with South Korea? Turkey persuading Greece to accept a divided Cyprus? England convincing Argentina that the Falkland Islands will never, ever be *Las Islas Malvinas?*

Persuasion Hell, everywhere you look.

Know When to Fold 'Em

Hard-core persuaders (and that probably includes you) are a bit like compulsive gamblers. Gambling addicts are sure they're just one bet away from the "big win." Devoted persuaders are totally confident that the other side will change its mind—and not eventually, but *at any moment!* Shut up and deal! This could be the big one!

Psssst! Wanna' sure thing? Sometimes persuasion doesn't work. Understanding *may*—and often *does*—beget agreement, but it certainly doesn't have to. It can also beget rejection. Humans are entirely capable of understanding something perfectly while, at the same time, disagreeing with it vehemently. Not only capable, but proficient.

If your argument failed to persuade the other side the first few times you trotted it out—at the absolute pinnacle of its novelty and vigor—why might it suddenly succeed on the fourth, or tenth, or fiftieth repetition? Because it took that long to get through the other side's thick skull? Because they had to translate it into their native language, Erdu? Because they were distracted by thoughts of Bora Bora, or chocolate, or their first kiss? Trust me on this: *It's not going to work.* After the first couple of repetitions, your argument has a chance of success somewhere between slim and fat. By then, the other side won't even be listening any more. They'll just be waiting for you to shut up so they can repeat *their* argument—the one that *you* aren't listening to any more.

This, by the way, is a pretty fair description of your Standard Spousal Discussion. Your better half will patiently listen to one or two iterations of your feeble case. Any subsequent remonstrations by you—passion and eloquence notwithstanding—will be inaudible.

THOMAS'S TRUISMS

> How do you get agreement when
> persuasion doesn't work? You negotiate.

THOMAS'S TRUISMS

When persuasion works, it usually works pretty quickly. After one good, solid presentation—and an encore for insurance—the other side will almost certainly understand your argument. If they haven't been convinced by then, they'll probably never be convinced. Persuasion-wise, it's time to fold your cards and go home. If you continue to argue your position thereafter, you won't just be wasting time, you'll be annoying the *bejeezus* out of the other side. Each repetition will only crank up the volume on an already unmistakable message: Your counterpart is obtuse, weak-willed, or both. While you and your counterpart are still on speaking terms, stop persuading and start negotiating.

Buy 'Em When You Can't Sell 'Em

Persuasion

UNITED STATES: You must resign. Your regime is cruel and your people are suffering.

DICTATOR: Who let you in here? Guards!

Negotiation

UNITED STATES: You must resign. Your regime is cruel and your people are suffering. If you'll go into exile, we'll let you keep your ill-gotten billions and give you the keys to a magnificent Swiss chateau where, at our expense, you and your family can live out your days in obscene luxury.

DICTATOR: Now you're talking! Throw in a case of Macanudos and you've got yourself a deal!

The difference between persuasion and negotiation? *Concessions.* Negotiating is the process of getting someone to do something, even if they disagree with it, by giving them enough concessions to make it worth their while. When you can't win the other side's agreement with the compelling power of your argument, you can usually *buy* it with concessions.

THOMAS'S TRUISMS

When you can't sell 'em, you can usually buy 'em.

THOMAS'S TRUISMS

Persuaders give *reasons.* Negotiators give *concessions.* The other side may or may not like your reasons, but *everybody* likes concessions. Always persuade first. Put your heart into it. Persuasion is faster, easier, more comfortable, and, above all, *cheaper* than negotiation. The agreements you can't win through persuasion you'll have to negotiate with concessions, and concessions are expensive. In the following pages I'll be showing how to make the concessions that are required—no more, no less—to negotiate your way to the agreements you couldn't achieve through persuasion.

THOMAS'S TRUISMS

Always persuade first. Negotiate only when persuasion fails.

THOMAS'S TRUISMS

5

Win-Win Negotiating

We ride through life on the beast within us.
Luigi Pirandello (1867–1936),
Italian playwright

The Beast Within

We are, each of us, the miraculous product of four billion years of evolution. We still carry a few leftovers from our distant evolutionary past. Some of them aren't pretty.

Did you know you've got the brain of a reptile? Yes, you. It sits at the top of your spinal column, and it's the oldest and most primitive structure in your head. Over millions of years, humans developed higher-level mental functions—logic, memory, creative thought, language—but they've never *replaced* our reptilian brain. They've just added to it.

Our lizard brain is the source of our most basic instincts and emotions, also known as the four F's: feeding, fighting, fleeing, and, uh, sexual behavior. And the lizard brain is *tough*. It easily dominates our rational brain. When the lizard brain is aroused, logic goes out the window.

It's activated when we feel threatened. Threats to our self-esteem work just like physical threats. Whenever we "lose face"—when we're humiliated, insulted, demeaned, embarrassed, or treated unjustly—our lizard brain takes charge. And in lizard-think, there's only one way to respond to a loss of face: revenge.

What does this have to do with bargaining? Everything. The lizard brain—that little clump of cells between the hippocampus and the amygdala—is the genesis of win-win negotiating.

Global Thermonuclear War

People are naturally skeptical about this lizard-brain face-losing revenge business. For the students in my negotiating seminars, proof comes in a game called *Global Thermonuclear War*.

The Global Thermonuclear War exercise places students in an imaginary conflict between a distant planet's two superpowers. Their instructions are simple: *End the War*. The class is divided into two groups with equal numbers of imaginary missiles and imaginary people. The groups are separated and, every few minutes, required to decide whether or not to launch missiles at the other side. Each group may voluntarily destroy any quantity of its own missiles at any time. Negotiations occur at regular intervals, and larger and larger attacks are permitted as the exercise progresses. The result? Nine times out of ten, every imaginary soul on one or both sides is killed.

Here's what happens. At some point in the exercise, one side comes to have more missiles than the other. Neither the size of the disparity, nor how it came about, are important. The disparity itself is what counts, and it's the turning point in the exercise. The imbalance transforms equals into top dog and underdog. The underdog loses face. And losing face *looses the lizard*.

The underdog demands that the top dog immediately destroy enough of its missiles to bring the sides back into parity. The top dog replies:

Thanks, but we're going to hold off on parity for now. Let's see how things go. Sure, we'll be a few missiles ahead, but so what? The numbers aren't important. You can trust us. Let's talk about parity later, when things settle down.

Translation: In your face! The gloves are off now! The top dog refuses to relinquish its advantage. The underdog is hopping mad. Serious face has been lost. The underdog decides that, since the top dog won't voluntarily equalize the arsenals, it will have to take matters into its own hands. Its small surprise attack provides not just parity but a small numerical advantage in missiles. Underdog has become top dog.

The new underdog—completely unaware that *its own behavior* caused the loss of face that led to the attack—is furious:

So we were ahead by a couple of missiles. Does that justify nuking us? You must be insane!

The new underdog demands immediate missile parity. Not surprisingly, the new top dog is unreceptive:

I'm having a déjà vu thing here. Remember what you said when I asked you for parity? "In your face," I believe it was. Well, my answer's the same. Parity is out of the question. There's no way we're destroying anything!

Apoplectic with rage, the new underdog launches a full-scale attack. Simultaneously, the new top dog—having decided that the only *safe* underdog is a *dead* underdog—launches its own all-out strike. Everybody dies.

In less than an hour, a roomful of decent, intelligent, principled people has been reduced to a bunch of bloodthirsty, genocidal maniacs. Male, female, young, old, gay, straight, liberal, conservative, the demographics don't matter. It's the *species*. They're all Homo sapiens. They all lost face. And they all nuked.

There's an important lesson here. Face is humankind's third rail. Touch it and die.

Face is humankind's third rail. Touch it and die.

A Little Geopolitical History

Regrettably, the importance of face-saving is a lesson rarely learned in the classroom. Let's go back to 1919. World War I had just ended. Woodrow Wilson was President. Wilson believed that lasting world peace could best be achieved through law, justice, and fair dealings between nations. He was one of the founders of the League of Nations (a forerunner of the United Nations, which, to Wilson's embarrassment, Congress refused to let the U.S. join). Wilson went to the British and French and said, in essence, "Now that we've vanquished the Hun, we have a unique chance to bring peace to the world. Let's embrace our former enemies. Let's let bygones be bygones. Let's make the Germans a full partner in our new world community."

The British and French weren't feeling so magnanimous. "Woodrow," they said, "are you crazy? And what kind of name is *Woodrow*, anyway? We just lost a whole generation of our kids in the mud of Belgium and France, beating these guys. Ten million people are dead. Europe is devastated. All thanks to the Germans. Help them out? No thanks. We're going to help *ourselves*. We're going to grab anything of value we can find over there, crate it up, and ship it home. End of story, Woodrow."

Wilson lost that negotiation, and on a beautiful June day in 1919, in the Hall of Mirrors of the Palace of Versailles, the Treaty of Versailles was signed and World War I officially ended.

> We will get everything out of her that you can squeeze out
> of a lemon and a bit more. . . . I will squeeze her until you
> can hear the pips squeak.
>
> Sir Eric Geddes (1875–1937), British politician,
> on German war reparations, June 1919

By any calculation, the Treaty of Versailles ranks as one of the greatest negotiating slam-dunks of all time. It hosed Germany up one side and down the other. She was disarmed. Her borders were redrawn, her colonies were seized, and the confiscated territory was divided up among the victorious allies. Her industrial heartland, the Saar Valley and the Rhineland, was put under foreign control. She was compelled to pay massive reparations. Her currency became worthless. And her people—the envy of Europe just a few years earlier—found themselves unemployed, poor, and hungry.

Into this chaos came a guy named Hitler. He made the humiliated, filthy, starving German people an irresistible offer: "Vote for me, and I'll tear up the Treaty of Versailles." Their reply, as with one voice: "Adolph, *you the man!*"

Adolph Hitler might have been born in Austria, but he was conceived on the bargaining table at Versailles. He didn't take power in Germany by force. Thanks to the Versailles Treaty, he didn't have to. He was *elected*. He was the most popular leader in German history. The German people adored him. For a few heady years, he gave them back everything the Versailles Treaty had taken away: their pride, their dignity, *their face.*

Fast-forward to the summer of 1945. Germany and Japan were defeated. The United States was the biggest top dog ever. We had all the cards—the biggest army, the biggest navy, the biggest air force, the only atomic weapons. We could have done whatever we wanted to Germany and Japan. We could have made the Versailles Treaty look like a trip to the beach.

But we didn't. Instead of hanging Emperor Hirohito for war crimes, we let him keep his throne (a figurehead, to be sure, but a *live* figurehead). We even let him keep his divinity for a little while. Not until 1946 did we insist that Hirohito admit he wasn't actually divine. Japanese war reparations were nominal and war crimes trials relatively few. Postwar Japan enjoyed a new constitution, free elections, and generous economic assistance.

In Germany, occupation forces were quickly withdrawn and self-government was restored before the end of the decade. More than a billion dollars in Marshall Plan financial aid from America helped soothe the sting of defeat.

What kind of behavior was this? What about "To the victor go the spoils"?

The United States was well aware that World War II was, in part, a tragic consequence of the Versailles Treaty's gluttony. We were determined not to repeat the mistake. Instead of the revenge that victors since time immemorial have always taken, the United States and our allies did something virtually unprecedented in the long, sad history of human conflict: We let our vanquished enemies save face.

Today, only the economy of the United States is larger than those of Japan and Germany. Both nations are our dedicated military, economic, and political partners. And there's been peace among the world powers ever since—the longest continuous global peace since the Roman Empire. It worked.

We're almost done. Jump ahead to October 1962, when Jack Kennedy discovered short-range Soviet ballistic missiles in Cuba. In response, he mobilized the American military, put a naval blockade around Cuba, raised the U.S. defense posture to DEFCON 2— one step short of nuclear war, a level not seen before or since—and delivered to Nikita Khrushchev what was only the second nuclear ultimatum in history.* Pull those missiles out of Cuba or we're going to war.

To fully appreciate what happened next, you need some back-

---

* The first was delivered to the Japanese government by Harry Truman immediately after the attack on Hiroshima. To the everlasting sorrow of the people of Nagasaki, it was ignored.

ground information. Both leaders knew that Khrushchev had significantly fewer intercontinental ballistic missiles than Kennedy. They knew that Khrushchev's navy looked like a coastal defense force next to Kennedy's big, blue-water fleet. And they knew that if the United States decided to invade Cuba, Russian troops wouldn't be there to stop them: It was too far away for Khrushchev's airplanes, and his ships couldn't pierce the American blockade.

Kennedy's ultimatum called Khrushchev's hand, and Khrushchev's military circumstances left him only one option: fold. He packed up his missiles and shipped them back to Russia. Kennedy was the hero, Khrushchev was the goat, the Cuban missile crisis was over, and we lived happily ever after. The end. Right?

If only it were so. Unlike fairy tales, there is no "happily ever after" in human events. We can't just close the book and put it away. Human events *keep unfolding.* Just like the Energizer Bunny, they keep going and going and going. Act I of the Cuban missile crisis—"High Noon in Havana"—was over. Act II—"Midnight in Moscow"—was about to begin.

Shortly after withdrawing his missiles from Cuba, Khrushchev was summoned before an irate Soviet Central Committee. "Nikita," he was told, "sit down. We need to talk. That teenager in Washington. The one with the hair? He tore your face off, Nikita. You were *hosed.* You disgraced the Workers' Paradise before the entire world. We'd like you to turn in your Party card, please, Nikita. You're fired."

Khrushchev was canned because of the Cuban missile crisis. The militarists, led by Leonid Brezhnev, took over and promptly launched the biggest arms buildup in world history. The Soviets never forgot how their military weakness let the United States humiliate them in Cuba, and they vowed it would never happen again. Before the crisis, the Soviets were a relatively limited threat to the United States. Less than a decade later, they would be the most powerful military force on Earth and a mortal danger to every American.

The Bunny Never Stops

Win-win negotiating is mandatory. Why? Because the other side doesn't *die* when the negotiation ends. They survive the talks. That changes everything. If they just croaked, you could hose them with impunity. Their survival means that whatever impression they take away from the discussions will be visited on you in the future. In short, they'll get you if you hose them.

THOMAS'S TRUISMS

**Win-win negotiating is mandatory because
the other side survives the talks.**

THOMAS'S TRUISMS

Win-win negotiating isn't a matter of altruism, morality, or ethics. I practice and preach it for one simple, unsentimental reason: *it's the only thing that works*. It's the only way to pursue, conclude, and maintain rewarding agreements.

You've seen those ads for negotiating books and seminars that hype, "We'll teach you how to crush your adversaries—and have them ask for more!" Save your money. Any serious discussion of win-lose negotiating is ridiculous nonsense, for at least two reasons. First, the other side won't let it happen. They're not stupid, and they're not likely to sit still and play victim for you. Not for long, anyway. Second, even if you were somehow able to hose them, you wouldn't get away with it. Not for long, anyway. The other side wouldn't rest until they found a way to get even. In the end, both sides would lose.

You can shear a sheep again and again,
but you can only skin it once.

—Irish proverb

We're all trying to maximize our results. Win-lose negotiators are simply trying to maximize them immediately—in the present transaction—without regard to the consequences. Win-win negotiators are trying to maximize them over the long run by doing reasonably well in a whole boatload of transactions with counterparts who feel they did reasonably well, too.

These two approaches yield profoundly different results. In the very shortest of runs, win-lose negotiators sometimes *appear* to have outperformed win-win negotiators. However, in anything but the very shortest of runs, win-win negotiators consistently outperform win-lose negotiators. The results claimed by win-lose negotiators seem attractive only because they're incomplete. By the time vanquished counterparts finish settling accounts, the sad, lose-lose truth will be clear.

Win-win negotiating puts severe limits on a deal's allowable lopsidedness. While it's an extravagant oversimplification, if you could somehow dissolve all of a negotiation's issues into a single bucket of "net available benefit,"* a 51 to 55% share of that net available benefit would be a first-rate outcome. Larger disparities make it increasingly difficult for the other side to view the deal as a success. Eventually, the imbalance becomes so great that notwithstanding your best efforts to "Hollywood" their performance, the other side can no longer deny the obvious: They got whipped.

Win-win negotiating means *no hosing*. Even if you can, for some reason, hose them, it means *no hosing*. Even if they are, for some reason, *willing* to be hosed, it *still* means no hosing. The fact that your counterpart is a dolt doesn't mean that his boss is, too—and when his boss sees your exorbitant deal, you can count on some serious fallout. You have a vested interest in *protecting* dolts, not hosing them. If you hose them, they'll be replaced, and by the *worst* kind of person: somebody who equates employment security with beat-

---

* We'll look at some ways to expand a deal's "net available benefit" in Rule 7, Keep looking for creative concessions to trade.

ing *you*. You won't run into many dolts, but take care of them when you do.

Win-win negotiating means no trickery, lying, foul play, or misbehavior of any sort. It means diplomatically pointing out—not taking advantage of—the other side's mistakes. Win-win negotiating requires you to keep outcomes within reasonable limits, but it *doesn't* make you the guarantor of the other side's success. And it *certainly* doesn't require even-steven deals (this isn't *Negotiate to Tie*, after all.) I want you to win, consistently but *modestly*.

A few years ago one of my clients, the world's largest producer of a commodity metal used heavily in construction, electronics, and transportation, found itself in a situation many companies would envy. A series of events, including skyrocketing demand, strikes, political turmoil, mine accidents, and plant closures, had sharply reduced the metal's global availability, turning a buyer's market into a seller's market almost overnight. My client had the only stockpiles. They were the only source of this metal. If you wanted it, you had to buy it from them and pay their price.

Hosing opportunities like this don't come along every day. The shareholders and senior management rejoiced at their good fortune, and licked their lips at the coming slaughter. But the sales force rebelled. "Sure, we can hose 'em," they said. "And we'll make lots of money for a quarter or two. *Then* what? What'll we do when the market returns to normal? Our customers will never buy another thing from us. We'll be dead. We'll be bagging groceries at the Wawa. In exchange for a couple of kick-ass quarters, we'll be kissing off customer relationships we spent years cultivating.

"Here's our idea. What if we hosed them a *little* on price—we aren't philanthropists, after all—but instead of getting every last cent, we used the rest of our leverage to strengthen and broaden the relationship? We could have them sign longer-term contracts, make us their exclusive supplier, buy things from us that they've been buying from our competitors, that sort of thing. Instead of a blowout, we'd have an annuity."

Despite some initial skepticism on management's part, the sales-people ultimately prevailed, the customers saved face, and the company has never been more profitable.

There's only one situation where win-win negotiating isn't required: a one-shot deal. If you'll never be dealing with the other side again, they can't retaliate. In such a case (from a purely economic perspective, anyway), win-win negotiating isn't just unnecessary, it's positively wasteful. Bargain as aggressively as your conscience allows. Car deals? Hose 'em. House deals? Hose 'em. Buying or selling something through a private-party classified ad? Hose 'em.

If you were hoping for more examples, I'm sorry to disappoint you. Only the smallest fraction of our negotiations are one-shot deals. Cars, houses, and the odd classified ad deal are pretty much it.* You'll never encounter one-shot deals in the workplace, and only rarely elsewhere. One-shot deals get a hugely disproportionate amount of attention because cars and houses are such important personal financial transactions. Win-lose negotiating is fine in the isolated one-shot deal, but in the *other* 99.9% of our negotiations—the everyday ones where real or potential relationships are at stake—it's out of the question.

How Win-Win Happens

How do you do win-win? It'll take most of this book to fully answer that question, but here's the abridged answer: You give the other side concessions. You already know that concessions are the way we "buy" agreement when persuasion fails. Those same concessions do something else, something equally vital: They let us save face.

We feel good when we get concessions. They give us bragging rights. They're unmistakable proof of a successful hunt. We drag

---

* You can find negotiating tips on a variety of familiar topics—including cars and houses—in Chapter 12, Quickies.

them back to our corporate den and celebrate them with the negotiating equivalent of an end-zone dance: "Yeah, baby! Look what we got! We hammered 'em! Check it out!"

Getting concessions is also one of the best ways to relieve the pain of *making* concessions. They're a sort of cognitive tranquilizer that calms us with the drug of equivalence. They let us tell ourselves that we didn't just *give*, we *traded*. "Sure," we can say, "I gave a little, but look at what I got in return!"

Concessions may be the *sine qua non* of haggling, but how can we make them without giving away the ranch in the process? How can we be flexible without being lunch? By doing the two most important things negotiators do. First, by getting something in return—*trading* our concessions, not just giving them away; and second, by doing the 'ol negotiating two-step: opening with an assertive offer, and then, as the talks progress, deliberately dropping back to our real target.

That little maneuver—*start high, then drop back*—is a central feature of win-win negotiating. But what a bloody inefficient way to come to terms! What's the point of starting high only to drop back to a "fairer" position? Why not just tell it like it is—with a firm, fair initial offer—and skip all the rest? Wouldn't we all get home sooner? The answer, explored in detail in Rule 2, Start high, is profoundly simple: because the other side needs to save face.

From your viewpoint, a firm, fair, reasonable initial offer—seeking only what you truly need, no fluff added—is a logical and honest thing to propose. From your counterpart's viewpoint, your offer doesn't look "firm, fair, and reasonable" at all. Instead, it looks inflexible, self-righteous, and pigheaded—because it *never changes*. You know that it won't change because you pared it to the bone before you made it. The other side knows only that they're getting absolutely nowhere with you, and that nothing they say or do is having even the slightest influence on what they *thought* was an offer but with each passing second looks more like . . . yes, an ultimatum!

Who woulda' thunk it? That fair, prudent, uninflated offer you made in good faith and without pretense—an ultimatum? Yep, and I have more bad news. Thanks to your "firm, fair" gambit, your discussions now have only two possible outcomes, and they both stink: unconditional acceptance of your offer (and loss of face) by the other side, or deadlock. So much for telling it like it is.

Another difficulty in concession-making is overcoming our deep-rooted notion that equates concessions with weakness, capitulation, and failure. Making concessions is just plain uncomfortable for us. We admire those who "stand their ground" and "stick to their guns." If we're right, why should we move? The answer, of course, is to let the other side save face; moreover, many of the concessions we're making aren't substantive at all. They're padding, made up of items and issues we cobbled onto our real needs so that we could make face-saving concessions to the other side at little cost to ourselves. They were supposed to be given away. That was the plan from the beginning. But even when we know this, concession-making often involves an intellect-over-emotion struggle for us.

In the next chapter you'll begin exploring the 21 Rules of Negotiating. As you become more comfortable with the Rules—and particularly as they merge into something approximating a working instrument for you—don't be surprised if that start-high drop-back routine starts to feel a bit theatrical. Theater *permeates* negotiation! Bargaining is like a kabuki play in which the negotiators are both actors and audience. Negotiation has many of the elements of classical drama, including the same emotional payoff: *catharsis*.

Human relations would be so much easier without all the kabuki stuff—if we could just state our needs without embellishment and be answered with dispassioned logic. Negotiating is a frustratingly inefficient, roundabout, sometimes tortuous process. But it's *what humans do. It's us.* Nobody invented the elaborate *pas de deux* of bargaining. We do it because the process fulfills some deep human needs—to make a difference, to have some control, to be competent, to do well. Right or wrong, we're wired for the melodrama of negotiation.

PART TWO

THE 21 RULES OF SUCCESSFUL NEGOTIATING

Welcome to the crux of the matter. The next four chapters spell out the 21 Rules for successful negotiating. The Rules—and especially the seven Critical Rules in Chapter 6—are the focal point of *Negotiate to Win*. They explain how to bargain.

Every effective, reliable, ethical negotiating technique of any significance whatsoever is included in the Rules. That's why there are so many, *far* too many to remember. A 21-item list of *anything* is going to be impossible to remember. But you don't need to remember all of them, because only a handful are really important on a day-to-day basis.

So there won't be any doubt about where the real muscle in the Rules is, I've divided them into three categories: Critical, Important but Obvious, and Nice to Do. *Please* take these categories seriously. You've heard of the nine-level Richter Magnitude Scale for measuring earthquakes? Did you know that the Richter scale is logarithmic, not linear? Each one-point increase in the scale represents a *tenfold* increase in an earthquake's power. So a magnitude six earthquake is ten times more powerful than a magnitude five earthquake. The three categories of the Rules of Negotiating are on a Richter Scale of significance. The Critical Rules are an *order of magnitude* more important than anything else on the list, and the Important but Obvious Rules are vastly more important than the Nice to Do Rules. The numerical ranking of the individual Rules is a bit arbitrary, but the categories aren't.

The seven Critical Rules in Chapter 6 are the things you really need to know about negotiating. They drive the process, and they shape the resulting agreement. Eighty or ninety percent of everything important about negotiating—everything that significantly affects the outcome—is right here. If you learn nothing else, learn these seven Rules.

If you're not already doing the four Important but Obvious Rules in Chapter 7, you should be. Their guidance is basic for successful negotiating, but so straightforward that they usually don't warrant a lot of additional attention.

Each of the ten Nice to Do Rules in Chapter 8 can affect the outcome of a negotiation, but their influence is generally smaller and less consistent than the other Rules. In part this is because difficulties and exceptions seem to proliferate near the bottom of the Rules list. Some of the Nice to Do Rules are eclipsed by custom (for example, sellers typically make opening offers, not buyers). Others are limited by circumstances (for example, most sole practitioners don't do a lot of team negotiating) or image constraints (bankers and financial planners probably don't have many occasions to use good guy–bad guy). Many of the Nice to Do Rules have one or more exceptions (such as, it's *not* always best to have the other side make the first offer). You should have a basic understanding of these Rules because you'll use most of them at one time or another, but you needn't immerse yourself in them or memorize them.

6

The Critical Rules

**NO FREE GIFTS! SEEK A TRADE-OFF
("O.K., IF . . .")
FOR EACH CONCESSION YOU MAKE.**

NEGOTIATOR: [at the mountaintop, kneeling at the feet of the guru] Oh, ancient and all-knowing master, I have traveled a thousand days and nights to partake of your wisdom. Tell me, *what is the true meaning of negotiation?*

GURU: Trade.

NEGOTIATOR: That's *it?*

GURU: Trade *everything!*

Our Journey to Negotiating Enlightenment must begin with trading. Trading is what negotiating is all about. The principle is elegantly simple: Don't make a concession without seeking something in exchange for it. "I'll do A for you if you do B for me" is the classic *quid pro quo*,* the bread and butter of negotiating. A concession made without something received in return is called (yes, redundantly) a "free gift." Free gifts are the most common mistake in negotiating, and Americans are the worst offenders by far.

<hr>

THOMAS'S TRUISMS

**Don't make a concession without
seeking something in exchange.**

THOMAS'S TRUISMS

<hr>

The Right Way

Let's use our hypothetical Japanese negotiator for a demonstration. We've already described how he would never say "no" to a requested concession. Such a direct refusal—crude and undiplomatic, in the Japanese view—would cause the other side to lose face.

On the other hand, he would never simply say "yes," either. That would be a free gift, a waste of the valuable buying power of his concession. Instead, he would propose a trade. He would smile and say something like, "Yes! I'd be delighted to give that to you, if you'll give me X, Y, and Z in return. O.K.?"

Alternatively, if he wanted to reject the other side's request, he could do so by simply cranking up his "if" to Japanese No levels: "Yes! We'll be delighted to give that to you, if you'll give us your Korean subsidiary in return. O.K.?"

For negotiators, these are fundamental, must-have habits.

---

* "Something for something" in Latin. A trade or exchange, or something given or received in trade.

The American Way

Freedom is the spirit of America, and if you want to see that spirit at work, check out the way Americans handle concessions:

OTHER SIDE: I need X.
AMERICAN: Sure! Take it. Take two. Whatever you need.

We're the Free Gift People of Planet Earth. We happily grant concessions to the other side and then we wait—patiently, smiling, hands outstretched—for them to reciprocate.

They used to reciprocate. A generation or two ago, everybody reciprocated. Back then, "being in someone's debt" was a deeply felt obligation. We all shared the need to "settle up" on an obligation or a favor, to clear the ledger.

US: Here, take this free gift.
THEM: Gee, thanks. Here, you take this one.
US: All right! And I've got another one for you!

Even today, a few people (family and friends, mostly) can still be counted on to reciprocate. But only a few, and fewer every day. These days, free gifts are accepted. And that's the end of it.

US: Here, take this free gift.
THEM: Gee, thanks. Now, let's move on to the next point.

Where concessions are concerned, reciprocity is little more than a fond memory. Maybe it's the increased economic and interpersonal pressure we're all under. Maybe it's because people are less socially connected than they used to be. Maybe we've just gotten more cynical. Whatever the reason, if you give an American-style, unconditional concession today, the other side will accept it. Period. They might say "thank you." They *won't* reciprocate.

We need to face up to the fact that our cherished gift-giving-as-negotiation tradition is dead. This is sad, but true. From here on, to get what you want, you're going to have to trade for it.

Trading Tips

1. The big "if." Negotiation isn't about *giving*, it's about *trading*. When the other side asks you for something, get in the habit saying "yes, if" instead of "yes" or "no." Try to tie every concession you make to a specific *quid pro quo* from the other side. Spell out exactly what you want in return.

At the risk of overcomplicating things, there are actually four variations of the basic trade. To the other side's "I want X," you could respond:

Give   **Get**
1. I'll agree to X . . . . if I get Y in return.
2. I'll agree to X . . . . but then I won't be able to do Z.
3. I'll agree to [something
   other than X] . . . . if I get Y in return.
4. I'll agree to [something
   other than X] . . . . but then I won't be able to do Z.

As you can see, there are two alternatives on each side of the "give-get" equation. On the "give" side, you can offer the other side 1) exactly what they asked for, or 2) something *other* than what they asked for. On the "get" side, in exchange for whatever you're offering the other side, you can 1) require them to give you something in exchange, or 2) *take away* something you had tentatively conceded earlier. As Rule 5 will explain, concessions are always tentative until final agreement is reached.

Please note options 3 and 4 on the "give" side of the equation. Negotiators often take the other side's proposal—"I want X"—as a given, and direct all of their attention to the "get" side of the negotiation. This is a bad habit, and can be very costly. You certainly don't *have* to negotiate the other side's offer, but it's just as negotiable as anything else. Don't let yourself be hypnotized into thinking otherwise.

2. Wait for it. Never waste a concession. If the other side wants something but you can't immediately think of an appropriate "if" to request in exchange, just skip it for the moment and move on to something else. Simply say, "Let's set that aside for now and come back to it later." Never force a bad trade—or worse, give a freebie—because you can't think of the right thing to ask in exchange. Before the negotiation is over, you'll almost certainly think of something else you wanted from the other side—and when you do, you've got your "if." If absolutely nothing interesting turns up before the end of the negotiation, you can always use the orphaned item as a deal-closer: "O.K., I'll give you X if we have a deal."

3. "You owe me one" doesn't count. "You owe me one" (or "I owe you one") is a sorry excuse for a real "if." It's only slightly better than a complete freebie. "You owe me one" is a throwback to the old days of reciprocity. Try collecting on it.

Concessions are like new cars—as soon as you drive them off the lot, they start losing value. The instant your counterpart puts your concession in her pocket, it loses all of its bargaining value.

4. Don't say "no." Try to avoid saying "no"—literally—to the other side. An unvarnished "no" instantly turns the dialogue into a monologue. It makes the other side lose face. Instead, use a Japanese No whenever possible. It helps avoid hostility and keeps the negotiation moving forward.

THOMAS'S TRUISMS

Try to avoid saying "no" to
the other side. "Yes, if" is better.

For example, instead of saying "no" to a piece of business you really don't want (too risky, too small, not profitable enough, etc.,) say "yes" to it, but at an unacceptably high price. The other side will surely reject your proposal, but (because it was their choice, not yours) without loss of face.

I guarantee that if you negotiate long enough, somebody will eventually accept one of your Japanese Nos. Be sure to set the bar high enough to make rejection likely, and since the other side could, theoretically, agree to your offer, be certain it's something you could live with.

5. Every request is an opportunity. When the other side requests something from you, it's not a problem; it's an opportunity to get a concession in return. In time, you'll be thrilled when your counterparts utter those delightful words: "I need something from you."

6. Even-steven isn't necessary. There's nothing that requires negotiators to make equivalent concessions. Always try to get an "if" that's equal to or greater than the value of the concession you're offering. If necessary, ask for multiple items in order to get the value high enough. If the concession you receive is larger than the one you gave, you've done well. For face-saving purposes, of course, try to portray every exchange as a victory for the other side.

7. Logic isn't necessary. There needn't be any logical relationship between the concession the other side wants and the one you ask for in exchange. In your search for *quid pro quos*, don't limit yourself to items that directly relate to your counterpart's request:

THEM: I need a price of $10.00 per widget.

YOU: $9.00 if you give us half of your blivet business.

8. I'll try. An equivocal commitment from you may sometimes be enough to win a concession from the other side. "I'll try," "I'll look into it," "I'll do the best I can," and similar expressions can generate concessions without seeming to obligate you. However, don't be lulled into thinking that such assurances are meaningless. If you've said you'll try, you have an obligation to try—genuinely. If you can't obtain the requested concession, you have a responsibility to explain to your counterpart what actions you took and why they weren't successful.

Be skeptical of an "I'll try" from the other side. Try to get a real *quid pro quo* instead. If that's not possible, ask for a firm commitment that kicks in if their "try" fails: "I'll do my best, but if I can't, I'll do X, Y, and Z instead."

9. That "if" isn't just decoration. Don't forget that if the other side rejects your "if," she also rejects the concession you were offering. When you say "I'll lower my price from $2.25 to $2.13 if you increase your order by 5,000 units," and she says "No," or "I can only increase my order by 2,000 units," your price—technically, at least—stayed at $2.25.

As a practical matter, no matter what "if" you put on it, "$2.13" will be permanently imprinted on the other side's frontal lobes the instant it leaves your mouth. She'll never forget that number. She *will* forget—conveniently—the 5,000-unit condition on which you offered it. When you remind her that the lower price required a larger order, she'll waffle: "Yeah, yeah, I know, but that's way more than I need. So, $2.13's the number."

Once a concession is proposed—regardless of attached "ifs"—expectations begin to shift. The other side smells blood in the water. It can't be helped. Always remind your counterparts of any "ifs" they might try to forget, but don't belabor the matter. You may not have given them a concession, but you've definitely whetted their appetite. We'll get back to this later, in Rule 3.

10. You can use the same "if" again and again. If the other side rejects your proposed "if," you can use it again:

> **BOSS:** I need that Boingo report on Wednesday.
> **YOU:** You've got it, if I can have those two vacation weeks in July that we discussed.
> **BOSS:** It's out of the question. And I need the Frammis contract by Tuesday.
> **YOU:** I can do Frammis by Wednesday if I can have those two weeks in July.
> **BOSS:** What about the Boingo report?
> **YOU:** Boingo and Frammis on Thursday for the two weeks in July.
> **BOSS:** Wednesday.
> **YOU:** Wednesday afternoon.
> **BOSS:** Deal.

11. Gimmies. Notwithstanding what I've said about trading everything, some things are simply unworthy of trading. They're "gimmies." Trivia, good manners, and common courtesies are not the stuff of trades. "I'll tell you where the bathroom is if you give me X, Y, and Z" *won't do.*

12. Expand the deal. You may not be limited to the issues currently in play. Get your nose off the negotiating table and look around. Could the relationship between the parties be expanded? What else do you have that they might want, and vice versa? Always be on the lookout for more stuff to trade.

Let's say I'm a chemical company selling futyl butyl isomer (FBI) to my customer, Acme Company. Acme wants a better price on FBI, but I'd rather not go lower unless I can get an offsetting *quid pro quo*. Acme uses large amounts of another product I sell, chemically inert acetone (CIA) but they buy it from my competitor. I could offer Acme a price concession on FBI in exchange for half (or all!) of their CIA business.

The key question is "What else?" What else does the other side have? What else might it need (now and in the future)? What else do you have? What else might you need? There may be nothing more than the current issues, but anything you find represents valuable trading material.

13. Nonmonetary concessions. Nondollar concessions can be very rewarding additions to your deals. Every bit as interesting as monetary ones (such as price, item, quantity, feature, contract term, minimum, penalty), nonmonetary (also known as "soft") concessions are often far easier to obtain. Here are a few examples:

- Referrals to other divisions or interested third parties
- Warranty, service, quality, and delivery guarantees
- Intellectual property rights (software, data, derivative products, copyrights, patents)
- Training and documentation
- Assistance in testing new products
- Non-hire and non-compete provisions
- "Last look" opportunities on future bids
- Financial performance hurdles and options
- External triggering events (e.g., "if the Dow drops below X," "if the Consumer Price Index exceeds Y," etc.)
- Options to do—or prohibitions on doing—things at future dates or under defined circumstances

Concessions like these are the hallmarks of a smart, well-negotiated deal. They turn a simple, static agreement into a dynamic, self-adjusting, long-term relationship.

START HIGH.

Midway through his presidency, Ronald Reagan was confronted with a serious dilemma. His massive defense buildup and simultaneous tax cuts had pushed the federal budget deep into the red. To make matters worse, in the previous two years he had denied raises to all 3.5 million federal employees—who were, to say the least, unhappy about it. They wanted a raise, and they wanted it now.

It was time for Reagan to announce federal salaries for the upcoming year. He knew that the appalling budget deficit precluded a pay increase for federal employees. He also knew that, thanks in part to his two-year salary freeze, most of them were none too fond of him. His fear was that if he stiffed them for a third straight year, they'd hate him so much that they might try to sabotage his political agenda. His presidential legacy could be at risk.

Reagan's dilemma, in a nutshell, was how to stiff 3.5 million federal employees on a pay increase for the third consecutive year. *And have them like it.*

If he had tackled it like an American, Reagan would have called a press conference and announced, "Let me give it to you straight. Times are tough. The budget's out of whack. All of us have to do our part. That pay increase the federal employees were expecting? We just can't afford it. I'm sorry. Have a nice day." Direct and logical.

He didn't do it that way. He did it like a negotiator; like a Japanese or a Russian. He called a press conference and, with just one critical difference, made the same announcement. After saying, "We just can't afford it," he added, "In fact, we're going to have to cut their pay by 5%."

I'm not making this up.

Instant pandemonium in Washington. Three-and-a-half-million

federal employees, in unison, screamed, "What? Cut my pay? I can't pay my bills *now!*" There was a 24-hour picket line around the White House with marchers carrying "Reagan unfair!" signs.

Reagan let the mayhem continue for two weeks. In the negotiating trade, this period, deliberately set aside to allow the other side to act out its unhappiness with—and maybe get a little more reconciled to—your offer, is known as a "decent interval."

After a decent interval, he called another press conference. This time, Ron the Good showed up. He wore a sweater. There was a fire in the fireplace. The camera did a tight shot of his face. He tilted his head—to look extra sincere—and said, "I care about our federal workers. They're my kind of people. I've agonized over that pay cut. I've lost sleep over it. I've talked to Nancy about it. And we've decided that we're not going to cut their pay by 5%. In fact, we're not going to cut it at all. We're going to keep their salaries exactly where they are. We'll find another way to cut the budget." End of press conference.

Millions of federal workers, in unison, said, "Whew! That was close! We really dodged a bullet on that one! What a nice man he is!"

We're talking vaudeville, here, or maybe pro wrestling. But it worked. Reagan took something that was fundamentally unpalatable—no pay raise for the third consecutive year—and, by using the classic *start-high drop-back* negotiating two-step, made it palatable. He started high (at minus 5%), and then—ostensibly touched by the suffering of millions of federal employees—he dropped back (to no change at all).

The Most Important Moment

In negotiating, there's a direct, statistically predictable relationship between where you open and where you wind up. Those negotiators who start with more assertive ("high") opening offers—within reason—come out better. Those who start by putting more conservative opening offers on the table don't do as well. The inescapable conclusion: If you want better negotiating results, start higher.

THOMAS'S TRUISMS

If you ask for more (within reason), you'll get more.

THOMAS'S TRUISMS

The opening offer is the most important single moment in any negotiation. Nothing else even comes close. What's voiced at that instant will profoundly affect everything that follows. It will echo through every concession the parties exchange and any agreement they reach.

Shooting Straight at Ourselves

Americans are straight shooters. We ask for exactly what we want. If X is our goal, we walk right up to the other side and say, "Hi. Let's do X. Let me explain why." If the other side has some cheeky rejoinder about how "X is a little steep," or "There must be something we can do," we calmly explain again—more slowly, this time—why X is the deal.

We start fair, then *sell hard*.

And why not? We've already considered all the pros and cons. We've already cut here and trimmed there. X has already been negotiated. We did it ourselves, in our own heads, before we even *offered* it to them! All we need is for the other side to stop fooling around and accept it.

Unfortunately, all of that in-our-own-head negotiating stuff is completely lost on the other side. It does nothing for her ego. It gives her no bragging rights. It counts for *nada*. She wants concessions. But we've already given all the concessions we can—to ourselves! If we give any more, there won't be enough left in the deal for us. But if we refuse to budge, she'll either refuse to agree (and we'll deadlock) or she'll agree but lose face (because she didn't get any concessions) and retaliate later. Any way you look at it, we're both hosed.

All because we didn't start high.

"Start High" Is Shorthand

A couple of years ago a student walked up to me after a two-day Negotiate to Win class and said, completely seriously, "Loved the class. Got a question about 'start high,' though. If I was *buying* something, would I start high?"

Let's make sure we're all on the same page here. "Start high" is shorthand for "start with an assertive offer." When you're buying, you don't start high, you start *low*. I don't want to be getting any letters saying "Dear Jim: I just bought a new car, and just like you said, I started high. I walked up to the car salesman and said, 'A million.' And just like that, he said, 'Done.' So, tell me, did I do O.K.?"

How High Is Too High?

As the job interview drew to a close, the prospective employer asked the applicant, "What salary are you looking for?" "I'm hoping to at least double my current salary—depending on the benefits package, of course," answered the applicant. The employer replied, "What would you say to a package of five weeks of vacation, fourteen paid holidays per year, full medical and dental coverage, retirement at 100% of your highest salary, and a new company car every year?" Impressed, the applicant responded, "Wow! Are you kidding?" "Yes," said the employer, "but you started it."

More's Law ("If some's good, more's better") applies to opening of-fers. Starting high is good, and starting higher is better. But only up to a point. At some level, higher becomes too high, and too-high of-fers are destructive. The other side doesn't view them as assertive, but as insulting, frivolous, or ignorant.

THOMAS'S TRUISMS

**Your opening offer should be assertive,
but never ridiculous.**

THOMAS'S TRUISMS

Open assertively, not ridiculously. The exact boundary between as-sertive and ridiculous changes with every negotiation and negotia-tor, but as a general rule it's at the *very edge* of what's arguably realistic under the circumstances. The Japanese have a whimsical (but still quite valid) formula for determining this point, called the "Straight Face Rule": A proper opening offer is one that you can make with a straight face, but only with considerable difficulty.

Stress and Starting High

Opening assertively is so dramatically, reliably effective that you'd think we'd do it every time we bargain. We don't. Rule 2 is violated constantly. That's because the moment of the opening offer isn't just the most important moment in the negotiation, it's also the most stressful. We *know* what's going to happen next: The other side will be—or appear to be—unhappy with our proposal.

THOMAS'S TRUISMS

**The moment of the opening offer is the most important,
and most stressful, in the entire negotiation.**

THOMAS'S TRUISMS

Your counterpart's seeming unhappiness with your opening offer will be much easier to handle if you keep two things in mind. First, it's called flinching, and it's standard negotiating technique. Accomplished negotiators react with varying degrees of distress to *all* first offers, regardless of content. Second, your opening offer is *supposed* to be rejected. It's for positioning purposes only. The last thing you want is for your opening offer to be accepted.

> **JOE THE HOUSE PAINTER:** [Carefully looking you over]: I'll do it for five thousand dollars.
>
> **YOU.:** O.K.!
>
> **JOE:** [Now suspicious]: For the closets. Just the closets.

One of the most distressing moments you'll ever experience in negotiating is when you make what you thought was a good, assertive opening offer, and the other side says, "Done!" You may have just gotten the best deal in history, but your only thought will be about how you didn't ask for enough.

How much of what you don't ask for are you likely to get? And after concessions, how much of what you asked for will be left? Your opening offer freezes your negotiating upside; it's only downhill from there. You make it or break it with your opening offer, so if you're going to mess up one way or the other, better a too-assertive opening than a too-wimpy one. You can always come down (apologizing for having misunderstood the situation and begging the other side's forgiveness). You can *never* go up.

Don't get overly excited about the magnitude of the other side's opening offer, or panic at the seemingly insurmountable gulf between your initial positions. These are just the earliest preliminaries. On the other hand, never dignify a genuinely ridiculous offer with a concession. An unreasonable offer has no negotiating value, and if you make a concession in response, you've given the other side something for nothing. Insist on a legitimate offer before responding.

Never dignify an unreasonable offer with a concession.

Is "High" a Lie?

Asking for more than we need smacks of dishonesty to some people. If we're willing to take 50, the reasoning goes, "We want 70" is a lie. Subsequently conceding from 70 to 50 only serves to expose the lie to the other side.

Please don't struggle with this. "We want 70" is a totally truthful statement. You really *do* want 70! Sure, you probably won't get 70, and sure, you're willing to take less than 70, but 70 would be terrific. Honesty certainly doesn't require you to tell the other side that you're willing to take less, just as it doesn't require you to refer to your opening as your "first offer" or your "opening position."

As you drop to 50, your "ifs" will preserve the integrity of your 70 opening. You didn't just *give* those 20 points away, you traded (or tried to trade) for them. Each time you conceded something, you asked for an "if."

Finally, the exact language of the offer is important. Flexible phrases like "X makes sense," "X is reasonable," "We'd like X" (not "We *need* X"), "We're proposing X," and, "We have X in mind," will help keep you on a truthful footing. Avoid imperatives like "We've got to have X," or "X and that's it," if you're actually willing to take less, because any concessions will reveal that you were lying and damage your credibility.

Limitations on Starting High

1. **The commodity marketplace.** The "marketplace"—the circumstances in which you make your opening offer—always limits how

high you can realistically start. The closer you get to "commodity" conditions (where everybody's widgets are exactly the same), the smaller the gap between realistic and unrealistic offers. In an honest-to-goodness totally efficient commodity marketplace, you couldn't start high at all. Since price would be the only distinguishing factor between sellers, anyone opening so much as a farthing above the lowest price wouldn't get a single piece of business, ever. Fortunately, there's never been such a market. Instead, inefficiencies abound.

First, price is very important, but it isn't everything. Even today, people still buy from people. Most buyers won't go to a complete stranger to save half of a percent.

Second, products aren't the same. Your widget is better, and it's worth more. Astute buyers will work hard to convince you that it's exactly like (or worse than) everybody else's. The more you can differentiate your widget, the more justification you'll have to start high and negotiate from there.

Third, in a price-driven, commodity-style market, price may have to be an exception to the "start high" rule. Prudence may require you to start at the marketprice. Start high on other issues. With the buyer's attention focused on price, major concessions can be had on less sensitive things like quantity, length of contract, warranties, payment terms, shipping, schedules, monthly minimums, advertising, future rights, and other nonprice issues.

Fourth, in a commodity-style market where price is the *only* issue, you can't start high. However, you can still negotiate. Trading becomes all-important when you can't start high, because any free gifts will put you dangerously below your goal.

2. The extremely tight or sole source marketplace. After a tough day of negotiating with God, a tired Moses descended from Mt. Sinai. "I've got some good news and some bad news," he announced to the anxiously waiting Israelites. "The good news is, I got Him down to just ten Commandments. The bad news is, He wouldn't budge on adultery."

Unlike a commodity marketplace where lots of sellers are offering virtually the same thing, in a sole-source marketplace there's only one seller. In a tight market, there's not enough product to meet demand, so sellers have most of the bargaining power.

When you're lost in the desert, dying of thirst, and you stumble upon the only water-seller for a thousand miles, there's only one possible negotiated outcome: You're going to lose. The only question is, how badly. Anybody who tells you otherwise is just not being truthful. If the water-seller likes you, or feels sorry for you, or has her eye on the future (when there may be a competing water-seller), she may cut you some slack. That's your only chance. And it's not negotiating, it's charity.

THOMAS'S TRUISMS

**The swiftest negotiator can never
outrun supply and demand.**

THOMAS'S TRUISMS

In tight and sole-source markets, supply and demand trump negotiation. Sellers hold the cards, and sellers aren't stupid. With excellent bargaining and abundant luck, you may get a handful of concessions. And under the circumstances, that's outstanding. Console yourself with the knowledge that sellers who attempt to exploit these situations too aggressively eventually learn that what supply and demand giveth, it also taketh away—in the form of new sellers.

3. Especially sensitive situations. In high-sensitivity negotiations (involving potentially volatile personal issues like the sale of a home, divorce, inheritance, or a family business), there's an increased risk of starting too high. The subject matter makes the other side much more likely to see your offer, not as the curtain-raiser that you intended, but as a discussion-ending personal insult. Be more conservative when opening in these "close to the heart" situations. We'll look at how to handle some everyday personal negotiations in Chapter 12, Quickies.

4. Long-term relationships. The longer and closer your relationship with somebody, the less appropriate it is to start high (especially on routine matters). With time comes trust, and trust displaces negotiating. In recurring negotiations between the same players on the same issues, opening positions will, in time, converge almost to the point of unity. Trust has made negotiating unnecessary.

THOMAS'S TRUISMS

With enough trust, negotiating becomes unnecessary.

THOMAS'S TRUISMS

RULE
3

FOLLOW A DRAMATIC INITIAL CONCESSION
WITH SHARPLY DIMINISHING CONCESSIONS.

O.K., you've started high. You've got yourself a credible initial "bank account" of bargaining assets from which, without compromising your desired outcome, you're ready to make the face-saving concessions your counterpart needs. And you're not going to just give away those concessions this time, either; you're going to *trade* them. So far, so good.

Now what? When do you make those concessions? How big should they be? Should you make lots of little ones or a few big ones? Should you give more at the beginning or toward the end? And what about the middle? Why not make equal concessions throughout the negotiation? Or in a smaller-bigger-smaller bell curve? Or bigger-smaller-bigger? Or randomly? Does it even matter?

It matters a great deal. Concession management powerfully influences a negotiation's outcome.

The Envelope of Negotiation

It's time to introduce one of the most important concepts in this book, the Envelope of Negotiation. Over the years, literally thousands of my Negotiate to Win students have volunteered that the one thing they always remembered from the workshop—the single concept that was most responsible for improving their bargaining—was the Envelope of Negotiation. That many people can't be wrong.

Among its various meanings, the word "envelope" refers to a set of limitations within which a system can perform effectively. The Envelope of Negotiation is the set of limitations within which you believe a given issue can be negotiated effectively. It consists of the opening, target, and bottom line positions* that you've selected for that issue:

Envelope of Negotiation

Opening   Target   Bottom line

Setting an Envelope for each anticipated issue is the one thing you *must* do before you negotiate. At the left edge is the issue's opening position. You consider offers more assertive than this to be excessive. At the opposite edge is the bottom line, the *absolute minimum* you can accept on that issue. If the other side is unwilling or unable to agree to this, you must deadlock on the issue (and, necessarily, on the entire negotiation). In between the opening and the bottom line is your target for the issue, the result you'd like to achieve. The target is

---

* There's actually a fourth component to every issue's Envelope: its weight, or importance, relative to all the other issues. We'll take a more detailed look at Envelope-setting in Rule 8, Do your homework.

what you consider to be a realistic, reasonable outcome on that point. Although an issue's target must be between its opening and its bottom line, it needn't be (and usually isn't) equidistant from them. All points within your Envelope represent outcomes that are acceptable to you on that issue.

Your counterpart probably has her own Envelope (or something like it) for the issue. If the two Envelopes don't overlap, agreement isn't possible. If they do, your goal is to work out an advantageous deal.

You begin by offering the opening position set by the Envelope for the issue. You then moderate your stance on the issue with a series of concessions that move you toward your target. You hope to have the other side agree to a resolution of the issue at or around your target (something that won't be possible unless their bottom line on the issue equals or exceeds your target). If not, you continue making concessions, moving below your target toward your bottom line. If necessary, you'll go all the way to your bottom line on the issue (but not actually reaching it until the deadline). If the other side's bottom line on the issue doesn't equal or exceed yours, only deadlock—on the issue and the whole negotiation—is possible. If their bottom line on the issue equals or exceeds yours, you *must* resolve the issue (although deadlocks on other issues may still torpedo the larger negotiation).

The relative bargaining strength or weakness of the parties determines the size of their respective Envelopes. When you hear that somebody is "bargaining from a position of strength" (or weakness), what's really being discussed is the size of their Envelope(s). As a general rule, the stronger party has the smaller Envelope on an issue. The stronger party has more (and more attractive) alternatives than the weaker party, and will resort to those alternatives (deadlock) sooner, instead of making generous concessions. The weaker party has fewer (or no) alternatives, is more desperate, and is willing to make relatively greater concessions, if necessary, to reach agreement.

The Message in the Concession

The other side will stop negotiating and take the deal you're offering when two things occur simultaneously: (1) She's attained an acceptable result, according to her Envelope (or what passes for it); and (2) she figures she's pretty much gotten everything she's going to get out of you. You have very little influence on (1). You have *lots* of influence on (2).

As long as your counterpart thinks you have more concessions in your bag, she'll keep beating on you to get them. She may eventually drive you all the way to your bottom line. Since she probably won't stop until she thinks your concession bag's empty, it would be great if you could somehow make her *think* it's empty—that you're at your bottom line—when you're really at your target. By making your concessions in a very special way, you can do this.

Assume the following Envelope:

Opening	Target	Bottom line
3,000	2,000	1,000

For simplicity's sake, I've made the opening, target, and bottom line big, round, meaningless numbers. I've put the target exactly halfway between the opening and the bottom line (rare in reality). So that you can better see what's going on, I've stretched the Envelope horizontally. You'd almost never see such huge gaps between the opening, target, and bottom line. In the real world, something like 2,005–2,000–1,995 would be more likely.

I want to get a deal on this issue at around 2,000, if I can. The 1,000 points between my target and opening is pretty much fluff. I've added that for the other side. I *plan* to drop from 3,000 to 2,000 so they can save face. I'd rather not go below my target, 2,000, but I will if I have to. In the worst case, I'll go all the way down to 1,000, but let's not even think about that for now.

Here's the pivotal question: How can I make those concessions from 3,000 down to 2,000 in such a way that—assuming such an outcome is acceptable to them—makes it as likely as possible that the other side will agree to a deal at or near 2,000? Knowing the answer to that question is what separates the amateurs from the professionals in the negotiating business.

We're going to answer that question together. I'm going to show you a number of different ways to concede the 1,000 points from 3,000 down to 2,000. Each of the patterns will have a different sequence of concessions, but they'll add up to 1,000. The only difference between the patterns will be the sizes of the concessions.

This works best if you visualize yourself as a negotiator "receiving" each pattern's concessions from me. And forget that you know my target and bottom line. All you know is that I opened at 3,000, and you're trying to get me to the lowest number you can. After examining each pattern, ask yourself two questions:

- Are you inclined to accept 2,000, or to press on for further concessions?
- What do you think my next move, if any, might be?

O.K., let's begin.

Pattern 1:   3,000, 3,000, 3,000, 3,000, 3,000, 2,000

Description: After stonewalling for a while at 3,000, I suddenly drop to 2,000.

Accept 2,000 or press on? There's no way that 2,000 is the best I can do. You've got to press on. You're thinking, "Finally! Now we're moving!" You've just learned a very valuable negotiating lesson: patience. After a long drought of inflexibility, you were rewarded with a huge, 1,000-point concession. Your expectations are now sky-high.

My next move, if any? Hard to say exactly when, but I'll almost certainly be making more big concessions before it's over. Even if I hold at 2,000 for a while, you won't be worried. I did the same thing before, at 3,000. Then I dropped to 2,000. You'll just wait for another big move.

Conclusion: Pattern 1—a large concession after a prolonged period of inflexibility—is a disaster. Negotiators using it are likely to be hammered below their targets like tent pegs.

Pattern 2:   3,000, 2,800, 2,600, 2,400, 2,200, 2,000

Description: I make a series of substantial, similar-sized (in this case, identical) concessions.

Accept 2,000 or press on? Of course you'll press on! You're thinking, "Why stop now? I like the way you negotiate. You're on a roll! I'm going to clear my calendar for the rest of the day!" There's nothing even slightly special about 2,000 in this pattern—certainly nothing that would incline you to stop there rather than continue. It's simply 200 less than 2,200, which was 200 less than 2,400, and so on.

My next move, if any? Let's go way out on a limb and say 1,800. You've got this one solved.

Conclusion: Pattern 2—ongoing healthy-sized concessions—is another disaster. Its sole message is "Carry on! You'll get more!" Users of this pattern will quickly find themselves near their bottom line, or worse, deadlocked.

Pattern 3:   3,000, 2,980, 2,940, 2,850, 2,650, 2,000

Description: Each successive concession is radically larger than the one preceding it.

Accept 2,000 or press on? Stop negotiating? After a 650-point concession? You'd be crazy to stop, and you won't. The next concession ought to be a real doozie!

My next move, if any? Whatever it is, it's going to be exciting. It'll probably put me into negative numbers. Maybe *big* negative numbers! Your expectations are stratospheric.

Conclusion: Pattern 3, with its geometrically increasing concessions (and expectations!) is the worst of all. It may be the worst pattern possible. Negotiators using it will be fortunate to close at their bottom lines; deadlock is more probable.

If Pattern 3 seems a bit ludicrous, don't laugh too hard. It's a very common concession pattern for Americans. We hate to make concessions so we frequently stonewall at the beginning, hoping the other side will cave in. They don't, of course, and while we wait in vain for them to capitulate, the clock runs down. Suddenly facing an imminent deadline, we panic, making bigger and bigger concessions in a desperate bid to snatch a deal from the jaws of deadlock.

If you were sitting across the negotiating table from somebody who, with each tick of the clock, made larger and larger concessions, what would you do? Of course: *You'd keep negotiating!*

Pattern 4: 3,000, 2,950, 2,550, 2,450, 2,150, 2,000

Description: I make a series of randomly sized concessions.

Accept 2,000 or press on? You've got no idea what's going on. There's no trend whatsoever in my concessions. All you can do is keep negotiating in the hope that a pattern of some kind will eventually show up.

My next move, if any? Who knows? More concessions seem pretty certain, however.

Conclusion: Random concessions confuse the other side and encourage them to keep negotiating. The longer the talks, the more concessions anyone using this pattern will probably have to make.

Pattern 5: 3,000, 2,000, 2,000, 2,000, 2,000, 2,000

Description: My large initial concession is followed by complete inflexibility.

Accept 2,000 or press on? You can't help but think that if you wait a little longer you might get another biggie.

My next move, if any? Probably nothing, but maybe a beast.

Conclusion: A big concession at the beginning lets the other side save face, but also whets their appetite. Abundant repetitions of "2,000. Read my lips. 2,000. I'm serious. 2,000," may eventually convince them that 2,000 is the end. More plausibly, the slim prospect of a repeat of that first big concession will keep them negotiating.

Pattern 6: 3,000, 2,500, 2,200, 2,080, 2,010, 2,000

Description: a striking initial concession is followed by sharply declining moves that culminate in a final, reluctant, tiny drop.

Accept 2,000 or press on? I'm almost certainly maxed at 2,000. If 2,000 is inside your Envelope, you'll probably take it.

My next move, if any? A couple of points, at best. Nothing worth prolonging the negotiation for.

Conclusion: We've got our answer.

The Steeply Tapered Concession Pattern

Pattern 6 is an example of a steeply tapered concession pattern. This kind of pattern will consistently give you the best chance of closing at or near your target. The dramatic early moves set a constructive mood. They generate enthusiasm and momentum. You're obviously not fooling around. You're trying to work out a deal. You're being flexible. The small ending moves (especially the last, tiniest one) are powerful confidence-builders for the other side. They say, in effect, "You've done a good job. You've cleaned me out. There isn't anything more. You can stop now."

Your first concession should always be your largest. Each succeeding move should be sharply smaller than the one before it. Your last concession should be your smallest, and made with some reluctance. Any concession larger than its predecessor sends a dangerously confusing, expectation-raising message.

THOMAS'S TRUISMS

**Never make a concession that's larger
than the one preceding it.**

THOMAS'S TRUISMS

The Rule of Halves

A simple tool for figuring out a good, steeply tapered concession pattern is the Rule of Halves. This crude but very useful formula says that each successive concession you make should move you roughly halfway from your present position to your target.* Pattern 6 is an almost perfect Rule of Halves progression. On a graph, it looks like this:

* Please note: The *target* not the bottom line, is the referent for Rule of Halves calculations!

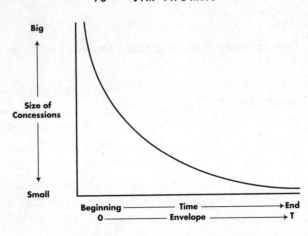

Figure 1. The steeply tapered Rule of Halves concession pattern

Rule of Halves concession patterns should *never* be used verbatim. There are two big problems with such patterns. First, they're too obvious. It doesn't take a genius to see that each new move is half the size of the previous one. If the other side is paying attention, they'll be able to extrapolate your target after the first few concessions. Second, because day-to-day bargainings with busy counterparts are often just minutes in length and may involve only three or four moves, the leisurely pace of anything close to a literal Rule of Halves concession progression would be ruinously slow.

The solution? *Always massage the moves.* Calculate a nominal Rule of Halves progression, then condense and skew. Mush the numbers around. Combine concessions. Stay near the nominal curve, but not right on top of it. Here's an example:

3,000, 2,375, 2,100, 2,040, 2,005, 2,000

That's a five-move, steeply tapered, skewed Rule of Halves concession pattern. More specifically, that's *my* five-move, steeply tapered, skewed Rule of Halves concession pattern. Thousands of potential variants would be equally suitable.

The absolute minimum number of concessions you can make and still have a "readable" pattern (that is, one that sends a message to the other side) is three. Here's an example (again, *my* example—yours might well differ) of a three-move, steeply tapered, skewed Rule of Halves pattern:

$$3,000, 2,215, 2,005, 2,000$$

Let's change examples. Here's a concession pattern for the completion date of a project:

Your Envelope

Opening:	Project complete immediately
Target:	Project complete within 6 months
Bottom line:	Project complete within 12 months

A Three-Move Steeply Tapered Skewed, Rule of Halves Pattern

Opening:	Now
First concession:	$3^1/2$ months
Second concession:	5 months
Third concession:	6 months (target)

Even if you obscure a Rule of Halves pattern somewhat, a professional negotiator may still be able to guesstimate your target. Don't worry about it. First, there aren't many professional negotiators out there. You can do a lot of negotiating without encountering anybody who has a clue about concession patterns. Second, while you may potentially reveal your approximate target to a true expert, you'd be revealing it to somebody you can probably trust to use that information constructively. A pro knows that you need to be successful, too. She'll help you meet your target if she can. As long as she gets what she needs, it's no skin off her nose.

Stinginess Vanquished

I've always harangued my Negotiate to Win students about concessions: Concessions are good, concessions are your friends, concessions aren't a sign of weakness or failure, concessions let the other
side save face.

Until a few years ago, they'd smile and nod their heads at these
entreaties and then, in the next negotiation exercise, at least a third
of them would deadlock. Not just deadlock, but deadlock horren-
dously. They'd be almost as far apart at the deadline as they were at
the beginning. After everything they'd been taught—Envelopes, concession patterns, the Rule of Halves, you name it—for a significant
number of my students, "negotiating" meant stubborn inflexibility.

The standard post-debacle debrief went like this:

ME: Help me understand what happened, here. Your Envelope set your opening at 10, your target at 15, and your
bottom line at 20. You opened at 10, then conceded to 13.
Perfect! But after that, you dug your heels in. You refused to
go any further than 13. You never even got to your *target*.
You didn't know it, but the other side's bottom line was 14.
Even a one-point concession would probably have closed
the deal. You deadlocked with seven potential concession
points still in your pocket. Unused. And by definition, any
deal up to and including 20 would have been better than
the deadlock you got. What happened?

STUDENT: You didn't want me to give everything away, did
you? Besides, the other side was a jerk. He wasn't being
flexible, so why should I?

I was mystified. How could so many intelligent, well-educated people listen to my little sermon on concession-making but then negotiate as if they hadn't heard a word I said? They weren't just failing to

come to terms, they were acting directly contrary to their own interests. It takes something big to make so many people do that, and eventually I figured out what it was: Humans are just plain *stingy*. We don't *like* to give our stuff away. It's against our nature to make concessions. Even when we build surplus concessions into our positions with every intention of discarding them, we need little or no encouragement to choke when it's time to write the check. A counterpart who we view as anything less than scrupulously polite and deserving is more than sufficient.

If I didn't figure out some way to reliably overcome their built-in distaste for concessions, a significant percentage of my students would never negotiate successfully. And many of those who bargained well under normal circumstances would deadlock whenever the fates decided to pony up less-than-admirable counterparts, foul moods, personal crises, crushing workloads, or bad hair days. Even if their interests were otherwise!

There was only one solution, however patronizing. Discretion in concession-making couldn't be permitted. Otherwise, stinginess would regularly trump common sense. The Rule of Halves would have to be more than just a guideline; it would have to be mandatory. Aside from some limited position-twisting for camouflage purposes, from here on my students would have to make their concessions in Rule of Halves progression whether they liked it or not.

The deadlocks stopped immediately. The Rule of Halves obliged even the stingiest to behave themselves. Miserly instincts notwithstanding, their only choice was to do the right thing.

I want you to manage your concessions by two simple rules:

1. *Use the Rule of Halves (with enough doctoring so that your target doesn't look like a big "X" on a treasure map).*
2. *When in doubt, see Rule 1.*

It's perfectly normal to be uptight about making concessions, and having to use a steeply tapered pattern only aggravates the problem.

The big initial moves are especially challenging. The Rule of Halves will insulate you from the passions that so often plague the concession-making process. It won't matter in the slightest whether you're feeling flexible or greedy, whether you're having a good day or a bad one, whether the other side is polite or rude, or whether you like them or hate them. You'll have a script, and if you rely on it, tight-fistedness will never derail another one of your negotiations.

The exact number of individual moves, and the precise size of any given move, will always be up to your judgment under the circumstances. Whatever you decide, don't deviate far from the basic Rule of Halves curve. Never forget that you're trying to tell a story, and you've only got a few scenes in which to tell it. Keep it simple and unsubtle: You were quite flexible, then less and less flexible, and now you've run out of flexibility. A big concession, a few medium-sized ones, and—after a lot of resistance—a little teeny one at the end. That's it. Anything more complicated is *too* complicated.

THOMAS'S TRUISMS

**Make your concessions in a skewed
Rule of Halves progression.**

THOMAS'S TRUISMS

You may find concession-making more palatable with a prefatory warm-up line like "We've given it considerable thought, and . . . ," "We've reflected on our position, and . . . ," "In the spirit of compromise . . . ," or "In the interest of settlement . . ."

Escalation

Escalation is a net worsening of a bargaining position *during* a negotiation. The concession curve is going the wrong way; after the escalation the two sides are farther apart than they were before.

SELLER OF LONDON CONDO,

TO PROSPECTIVE BUYER:	£500,000.
BUYER:	£440,000.
SELLER:	£480,000.
BUYER:	£430,000.

The buyer's £10,000 drop was an escalation. Why might a negotiator be tempted to do this? Perhaps she felt that she didn't start assertively enough. Or she wanted to send a message that she's not going to negotiate. Or she felt that she'd already made too many concessions and needed to pull back a little. Sometimes negotiators *counter-escalate*—escalate in retaliation to the other side's escalation.

THOMAS'S TRUISMS

Never escalate unless you have no alternative.

THOMAS'S TRUISMS

Escalate only as a last resort. And only in the very limited circumstances listed below. It's one of the most inflammatory things a negotiator can do. It makes the other side absolutely crazy. Deadlock is the usual result.

Repackaging your position—withdrawing some concessions but adding others of equal or greater value—isn't escalating. If you repackage, however, never assume that your counterpart will, without assistance, recognize your new offer's equal or greater value. Instead, she may see it as a step backward and you as an escalator. Before she gets the wrong idea, take some time to clearly explain your new offer's real value.

Sometimes you have no choice but to escalate—when circumstances change radically during the negotiation, or you get new instructions from the boss, or you've truly forgotten an important issue. Don't delay; tell the other party as soon as you know. Be as apologetic and informative as possible. Be prepared to take a verbal beating, and count on some damage to the bargaining climate.

If the other side escalates, take a deep breath. Resist the urge to get angry and tell them off, resist the urge to give in, and resist the urge to counterescalate. Instead, hold your current position and politely insist that the other side return to the *status quo ante* (their pre-escalation position). Stay at your current position until they do, then continue your planned concession pattern.

If the escalator refuses to return to the *status quo ante*, and the circumstances of your negotiation permit a counterescalation as a solution, you can, with a modicum of delicacy, suggest it: "We could certainly accommodate your [escalation], but in that case, in addition to A, B, and C, we'd also need X, Y, and Z [or we wouldn't be able to do U, V, or W"]. This will allow the talks to go forward whether the escalator backs down or not. Otherwise, maintain your current position until the deadline and if the other side's offer—escalated though it may be—is more attractive to you than a deadlock, take it.

Shaving Your Concessions

Let's say that your Rule of Halves game plan calls for your side to drop approximately 20 points in your next move. But when the time comes to make that 20-point drop, there's dissention in the ranks. Some of your teammates are saying, "The other side doesn't deserve a concession that big. Let's not move 20 points right now. Why not do a couple of tens? Or two sevens and a six? Let's stretch it out a little. What's the hurry?"

It's a tempting argument, but if you succumb to it you'll sharply lower your chances of closing at or near your target. You'll obliterate whatever concession pattern you've already established, and you won't have time to demonstrate a new one. Instead of an easily understood, smoothly declining arc of concessions, you'll be showing the other side something that looks more like a noodle. The arc makes sense to them. The noodle doesn't. Its only message is confusion, and when they're confused, they'll continue.

THOMAS'S TRUISMS

Never shave a concession. Either make
the whole concession that you're supposed to make,
or don't make any concession at all.

THOMAS'S TRUISMS

Don't shave your concessions. If you're not prepared to make the whole concession that the Rule of Halves says you're supposed to make, don't concede anything. Anything in between is likely to be harmful.

Below Your Target

So far, all of our discussions about concession patterns have assumed you'll close at or above your target. What if you execute a beautifully tapered concession pattern, but upon arriving at your target you're horrified to find that your counterpart is still miles away—perhaps near, or even below, your bottom line? What do you do now? Do you just sit at your target and wait for the other side to come all the way up to you? Sure, if you're prepared to wait until hell freezes over. As a matter of pride, they'll almost certainly refuse to close the entire gap themselves. They'll insist that you come part way.

Let's make it even simpler. What if the other side's bottom line is below your target? Now you're going to *have* to go below your target to have any chance of closing. Remember: Your bottom line, not your target, is your minimally acceptable deal. Going below your target is no box of chocolates, but it beats a deadlock any day. How do you move below your target, toward (or even *to*) your bottom line, without giving up any more than necessary to close the deal? What's the optimal pattern for concessions below your target?

The answer, for a change, is simple: kicking and screaming. Gone is the elegantly tapered arc that brought you to your target. The Rule of Halves doesn't apply down here. Below the target, your concession pattern is nothing more than small moves, made reluctantly and resistantly. Shave off one small slice, then another, resisting and trading all the way. Think of it as keeping just enough of a trickle of water flowing through a pipe to keep it from freezing. Do this all the way to your bottom line, if necessary. With luck, your counterpart's impatience will have motivated them to settle well before you get there.

This isn't pretty negotiating. You've long since abandoned any hope of hitting your target. The deal is getting less attractive with every slice. The further you move below your target, the more costly each concession becomes. Now you're just trying to hang on and close a deal—any deal—within your Envelope. Keep your composure, follow the Rules, and you'll maximize your outcome.

At the Deadline

Some days the magic just doesn't work. You're well below your target, making tiny concessions and praying that the other side will agree to something before you're driven all the way to your bottom line. And now you have a new problem: Time is running out. This negotiation has a deadline, and it's fast approaching. Deadlock is imminent.

Before proceeding, let me explain a few things about deadlines. There are two kinds of deadline: technical and practical. The technical deadline is an actual drop-dead, that's-all-folks cutoff (such as midnight on December 31). For negotiators, the practical deadline is the one that really matters. At some point, there will be only enough time remaining for the other side to receive one last offer from you, consider it, and give you a decision. That's the practical deadline. If the other side's necessary decision-makers are scattered all over the world, your practical deadline could be hours or even days before your technical deadline. If they're all at the table with you, the technical and practical deadlines could be almost the same.

At the practical deadline, negotiating must stop. Take a deep breath, then call the hand. If the other side's last offer is at or above your bottom line, nibble on it* and then close. If it's not, declare your bottom line. Yes, your real, honest-to-goodness bottom line. This should be the very first time the other side has heard those words from you.†

If you closed with a bottom-line deal, go easy on yourself. It's still an acceptable outcome—not overly attractive, certainly, but better than deadlock. You were wise enough not to let your pride stand in the way of an agreement.

If you deadlocked, you can at least comfort yourself (cold as that comfort may be) that you played your cards as well as they could have been played. No one can ask more of you than that. Fact is, the parties' Envelopes probably never overlapped in the first place; deadlock was inevitable.

Don't get to your bottom line a moment too soon. Delay your final move until as close to the practical deadline as possible. A great deal of concession-making often occurs at or near the deadline. If you wait until the last second, the other side may present an acceptable deal before you have to drop to your bottom line.

Your Incredible Shrinking Position

From the moment you make your opening offer, your bargaining position will melt away like an ice cream cone on a hot summer day. Freebies and less-than-equal trades will relentlessly erode it. They're supposed to. There's an unspoken, tacit agreement among negotiators that positions will eventually bend toward some central point of agreement. Otherwise, win-win negotiating would be impossible. The exact details of how much and when you move—the unique

---

* Get a small additional concession; see Rule 6, Conclude with a nibble.

† Rule 10 looks at the many lies and rare truths associated with the term "bottom line."

decisions that take you from point to point down your concession curve—are up to you, the negotiator. Staying near the theoretical Rule of Halves curve is very important. Beyond that, it's your call.

KRUNCH EARLY AND OFTEN.

THEM: $300,000 over two years.

That's an offer. Negotiation gives you just two tools (other than "yes" or "no," of course) with which to respond to an offer: You can counteroffer, or you can krunch.

YOU: $210,000 over three years.

That's a *counteroffer.* In reply to your counteroffer, the other side might counteroffer with $285,000, then you might counteroffer with $225,000, and so on. The exchange of offers and counteroffers is also known as *haggling,* and it's a fundamental and time-honored method of negotiating.

But there's an alternative—a very, very good alternative—to a counteroffer. Instead of responding to the other side's "$300,000 over two years" offer with a counteroffer, you could respond with a statement like this:

YOU: That's way too rich for me. I need a better number.

That's a *krunch.** It's nothing more than an indication (which needn't even be verbal) to the other side that you've heard their offer and you want a better one. Some people call them flinches or winces.

---

* *Krunch* is both a noun and a verb. The etymology of the word is unknown.

Whatever you call them, there are literally thousands, from gentle ("That doesn't give me a warm feeling") to ferocious ("Are you on drugs?"). Boiled down, they all say the same thing: "Do better. Give me more."

If krunching strikes you as childishly easy, you've got it. It's the dumbest, crudest, most lowbrow technique in all of negotiating. It's also very effective. I'm continually amazed at how even seasoned negotiators—people who should know better—will routinely respond with a concession to the most barefaced, juvenile krunch. Krunching is easy, it's ethical, and it's even been known to add a bit of fun to the occasionally disagreeable process of bargaining.

THOMAS'S TRUISMS

**The krunch is the simplest and most
frequently used tool in negotiating.**

THOMAS'S TRUISMS

The Many Virtues of Krunching

1. It's simple. Krunching isn't rocket science. Anybody can do it. None of negotiation's complicated stuff—offers, Envelopes, trades, concession patterns—is involved. You could record a bunch of them in advance and just press the button at the appropriate moment: PLAY. "Work with me on this." PAUSE. PLAY. "Which end of the horse do you think you're talking to?" PAUSE. PLAY. "That's not ringin' my bell."

2. It's tailored. With literally thousands of options, you can always find the perfect krunch for any occasion. Never use a more aggressive krunch than necessary. The more colorful krunches (such as "I usually get at least a kiss before this happens") should be reserved for counterparts with whom you're on extremely good terms, and delivered with a big smile. That, or avoided entirely.

3. It's a great beginning. A krunch, rather than a counteroffer, is the ideal way to respond to the other side's initial offer. The textbook kickoff to a negotiation is to get the other side to open,* krunch their opening, keep krunching until your krunches no longer produce concessions—usually when the other side insists that you declare a firm position—and *only then* make your opening offer.

One of the reasons Americans recoil from negotiating is the undeniable stress of the opening offer. The notion of offering $50 for an item with a $100 price tag is just too contentious for many of us to contemplate. The whole offer-counteroffer-counteroffer business is vaguely reminiscent of cartoon cavemen whacking each other over the head with clubs. Here's a much more civilized, painless approach: Don't offer anything. Instead, ease into things with a nice, gentle krunch: "I love it, but $100 is more than I wanted to spend. What can we do on the price?" There. Wasn't that easy?

4. It's good in sensitive situations. Krunches avoid the potentially destructive effects of too-aggressive counteroffers (particularly important when negotiating with very sensitive counterparts or in ticklish situations). Some circumstances are so delicate that virtually *any* counteroffer would be offensive to the other side. A gentle krunch ("Let's put our heads together on this," or "Where do we go from here on this?") is a safe, sound response.

5. It works even when you're ignorant. When you just don't have enough information to come up with an intelligent opening, you can avoid significant mistakes, conceal your cluelessness, and gain valuable information by krunching.

Say you're at an art show, and one of the exhibitors is offering an attractive piece of sculpture for $1,000. It's carved from a block of soapstone that couldn't have cost the guy more than maybe ten dollars, so you know that anything above that represents "added artistic

---

* See Rule 19: Try to have the other side make the first offer.

value," which is, of course, inherently negotiable. You could offer him $100, but who knows how he'll react? He may accept your offer. But then again, he may throw you out of his stall. You could offer him full price, but then you'd wallow in self-loathing for weeks— and what if he's willing to take less? Maybe the guy's desperate. Maybe the IRS is after him, or his bookie, or he has an alimony payment to make tomorrow. How do you move the negotiation forward without the risk of underoffering or overoffering? You krunch.

> **YOU:** That's a beautiful piece. You do incredible work. It would be perfect in my living room. But $1,000 is more than I want to spend. There must be some flexibility in your price.
>
> **HIM:** Thank you. You have a good eye for sculpture. I can let you have it for . . .

The number he mentions isn't important, because whatever it is, you're going to do the same thing: *krunch again*.

> **YOU:** I really appreciate that. We're definitely moving in the right direction. But even at that price, it's still too much for me. What more can we do?

You get the idea: As long as it's working, *keep krunching*. At some point—and probably pretty soon—he'll tire of being your krunch dummy and he'll ask, "What price did you have in mind?" You can avoid it no longer—you've got to give him a number. But what? Take a look at his responses to your krunches. If he's moved from $1,000 to $700, a $500 opening might be appropriate. If he's only moved to $980—or hasn't moved at all—then maybe a $900 offer would be more sensible.

When you krunch in an ambiguous situation, you gain information with which you can open more intelligently. The other side's flexibility, or lack of it, in response to your early krunches will give you vital clues about where you should open. Your krunches have become part of the homework process.

6. It's the perfect day-to-day negotiating technique. Krunching is the ideal way to handle those 30-second personal negotiations that come up all the time—with the fruit stand vendor, the firewood-seller, the auto mechanic, the plumber. You want to bargain a little, but you just don't have the time, the energy, or—and yes, it's O.K.—the chutzpah to figure out an Envelope and toss offers back and forth. And the other side may not want to play, anyway. Krunch a few times, then go with the result.

7. It's not just for buyers. Some salespeople flatly declare that krunching is only for buyers; that their customers would be offended by such statements. I think they're missing out on a fine bargaining technique. About the more aggressive krunches, they're certainly right. "Did you drink your lunch?" isn't likely to endear many customers. But almost nobody would be offended by a krunch like "That doesn't work for us," or "What are we really talking about here?" Salespeople can krunch. They just have to do it gently.

8. It's a great set of training wheels. Has your spouse always drawn back in horror at the suggestion that the "fixed" prices at Sears or Nordstrom's might actually be negotiable? "Negotiate? At *Sears?* You're not serious! You aren't actually going to do that, are you? That's disgusting! If you do that stuff around me, I'm leaving!"

Krunching is the perfect way to get determined nonbargainers hooked on the thrill of successful negotiating. Wait until the non-negotiating spouse needs to buy a relatively big-ticket item (like a dishwasher, a lawn mower, or a television set). Challenge him to a simple experiment: He *must* krunch the salesperson before he buys. Give him a list of a few nice, easy krunches, like "How can we cut that number?" and "It's still way over my budget" and "We're moving in the right direction, but we're not there yet." Point out that it may require two, three, or more krunches to get the salesperson to move. Bribe him: Tell him you'll take him out to dinner with whatever he saves. See what happens.

I'll bet he gets a concession or two. And when he does, he'll be in hog heaven. You'll hear of nothing else for a week. He'll think he invented krunching ("Honey, lemme tell you about this. I was great!"). He may go on from there to become a master bargainer. Even if he fails, you're no worse off than you were before.

9. It's the only way to respond to an unreasonable offer. A clearly unreasonable offer should always be responded to with a krunch, never a counteroffer. Any counteroffer to a ridiculous offer is a free gift.

THOMAS'S TRUISMS

**A krunch is the only way to respond to
an unreasonable offer.**

THOMAS'S TRUISMS

Stay on the Krunch Train

If the other side makes a concession in response to your krunch, krunch again. Keep krunching as long as your krunches are working: "We appreciate that. We're definitely getting warmer. What else can we do on this?" At some point (sometimes pretty quickly) the other side will realize that she's negotiating against herself ("I seem to be the only one making concessions! What are you willing to do?"). It's time for you to open (or, if you've already opened, make a concession). Then immediately return to krunching. You'll always be working back and forth between krunches and concessions, but krunching should be the ongoing background noise in your negotiations. Krunches are free. Concessions aren't.

**Every concession has a price,
but krunches cost nothing.**

Responding to a Krunch

You'll inevitably be krunched by the other side. The proper response to any krunch is always the same: some variation of the phrase "Make me an offer." For example, you'd respond to "That's just not satisfactory" (a krunch) with "What are you looking for?" or "What do you need?" or "What would it take?"

The Limits of the Krunch

Alas, there are limits to the effectiveness of this wonderful technique. The truth is, it doesn't work especially well on veteran negotiators. They know what you're doing. If they want your krunch to work—having decided, for example, that it's time for them to make a concession—they'll let it work. If they don't, they'll shut it down by insisting that you give them an offer.

Also, krunches don't work very well in writing. Real estate negotiations, for example, require the exchange of written offers and counteroffers. How can you krunch in such a situation? Mark a big "X" across the other side's offer and send it back? Return it with a note that says "No way, José"? Krunches work better in conversations.

Krunchlist

What follows is a pretty good, but by no means exhaustive, list of familiar, reasonably clean krunches. To most people they're everyday expressions. To negotiators, they're tools of the trade. They're arranged from the gentlest to the most aggressive. The gentler ones tend to explicitly or implicitly invite a concession ("Can you sharpen your pencil a little?") while the more contentious ones come very close to a face-losing "no" ("Get real!"). The more forceful krunches often contain a dangerous suggestion of ridicule toward the other side's offer ("Is your calculator working properly?") or their character ("Are you on drugs?"). The really pugnacious ones are principally for the sake of humor or tension relief with negotiating counterparts you know well.

Don't try to memorize this list. Your best bet is to get comfortable with the concept of krunching, then let the circumstances and your own personality determine the right krunch for the occassion.

SWEET, GENTLE KRUNCHES

- Where do we go from here?
- Let's put our heads together on this.
- What are we really talking about here?
- What can we do on this?
- That's not in the box.
- You know our situation.
- That doesn't pencil out for us.
- That doesn't work for us.
- That doesn't give me a warm feeling.
- You need to look at your figures again.
- We need your help on this.
- Can you cut us slack on this?
- Where can we cut this?
- I've got a problem with that.
- That really isn't what I expected.
- Let's talk flexibility.
- That's not *close* to my estimate.
- That's more than I want to spend.
- I *know* you can do better than that.
- I was looking for some more/a better number.
- Take another swing at that number.
- I'd like you to rethink your numbers and get back to us.
- Budgets are tight, you know.

- What if I paid cash/bought two?
- What's the sale price?
- That would be tough for us. *Real* tough.
- There must be *something* we can do.
- I hope you have room to negotiate.
- Can we talk?/We've gotta' talk.
- *Work* with me on this.
- That's not real attractive/exciting to us.
- That's certainly an optimistic proposal.

MIDDLE-OF-THE-ROAD KRUNCHES

- You've *got* to do better than that.
- You're going to have to sweeten that deal.
- There's no way we can accept that.
- I'm disappointed in that offer.
- I don't think you understand.
- You're too expensive.
- You and I have a problem.
- I just couldn't bring that back to my boss.
- [Name of higher-up] isn't going to like that.
- That's too skinny for me.
- My board won't go with that.
- What kind of a deal can you give me on this?
- What's my frequent-buyer/Thursday discount?
- You're not giving me anything on this.
- We'd be out in the cold/under water at that price.
- We can't live with that.
- [Repeat the other side's offer with a questioning and/or negative tone.]
- I can't do that/afford that.
- That doesn't turn me on.
- That won't do/That'll never do.
- That's not good enough/That just isn't enough.
- That's not commercially equitable.
- That's a little high/thin.
- That's not ringin' my bell.
- That's a pretty big bite.
- We could be here all night.
- There's got to be another way/an alternative.

- Be *reasonable.*
- I don't think we're *communicating.*
- Perhaps we have a misunderstanding here.
- Gimme a price on this . . . [After offer is received] Gimme another price.
- Sharpen your pencil . . . [After offer is received] Sharpen it some more.
- That's not in the ballpark.
- We're not in the same ballpark/city/universe.
- That's out of my league.
- They'll never buy it.
- It'll never fly.
- I need a *special* deal.
- I just can't get there.
- No can do.
- I just can't see it.
- That just won't wash/float.
- You're not speaking my language.
- You're just not competitive.
- Help me out, here.
- You need to reconsider your position.
- *How* much?
- . . . *and???*
- *What?*
- *Huh?*
- I *beg* your pardon!

REGIONAL/ETHNIC KRUNCHES

- *Talk* to me [New York].
- You're bustin' my *chops* [New York].
- Fuhgeddaboudit [New York].
- I can't *hear* you [New York].
- You're *killin'* me! I'm dyin'! [New York].
- So—*trumpets* should blow? [New York]
- Do you want my children to starve? [New York]
- Say *what*? [Southern]
- There's not enough juice in that for us [Southern].
- That's not a big enough worm [Southern].
- That bug [*mudbug,* crawfish] won't boil [Southern].
- That dog won't hunt/pig won't fly [Southern].
- You're in the right church but the wrong pew [Southern].
- We're within hugging distance, but we're not ready to kiss yet [Southern].
- Is it my singin', or you just don't like the song? [Southern]

- Which end of the horse do you think you're talkin' to? [Southern]

MORE AGGRESSIVE KRUNCHES

- Ouch!
- Yeah. Right.
- That's below my *cost*.
- Do you want my business, or *what*?
- That's not the right answer.
- Do you want me to lose my job?
- At that price, I'll sell it to/buy it from *you*.
- That doesn't cut it.
- I thought we were *friends*.
- That's *tribute!*
- Come *on*.
- That's not satisfactory.
- I'm not a tourist. I *live* here.
- How can you say that with a straight face?
- We were hoping to make a *profit* this year.
- We're not a charitable organization/the United Way/the Salvation Army.
- Charity begins at home, and I'm at work.
- We're not a bank.
- You must think I'm *made* of money.
- Would you run that by me again? My ears won't believe it.
- We must have a bad connection.
- My copy must be wrong.
- How important is this deal to you?
- We do *lots* of business with you.
- I think someone at corporate screwed up.
- What's your *real* offer?
- We're not on the same page/sheet of music.
- I'm floored/astounded/ stunned/flabbergasted.
- Gimme a *break*.
- Is that *it*?
- I don't want the gold plating.
- You're being silly.
- Would you like my arm/leg/first-born child also?
- Friendship only goes so far.
- You're not even *close*.
- We're *miles* apart.
- I thought you came here to *negotiate*.
- That's not where I live.
- I've got a *family* to feed.
- I've gotta' make a *little* profit.

- That's way over my budget.
- You're out in left field.
- The decimal point must be in the wrong place.
- Are we talking about the same thing?
- There must be a typo in your offer.
- Are you sure about your math?
- Does your calculator need a new battery?
- I think you've got the wrong file.
- Surely you jest.
- Is this a joke?
- I love your humor.
- All kidding aside, now.
- You've *got* to be kidding.
- You can't be serious.
- Maybe you need to switch to decaf.
- Be serious/Be realistic.
- So, realistically . . .
- That's funny! Now, let's get serious.
- Be still, my heart!
- You must think I was born yesterday.
- That'll kill/That's a death sentence for the deal.
- Does the phrase "deal breaker" mean anything to you?
- At that price, we can't even *talk*.
- If I go back with that offer, I'm *dead*.
- I can't walk through walls.
- You can't *mean* that!
- Come on, I have to *eat*.
- You're taking me for a ride.
- You need to stop by the concession stand
- Do I look like a concession stand?
- That doesn't make my socks go up and down.
- Don't you like our business?
- What are you gonna do for me? [Typically follows "Acme has offered me $___."]
- So, where's the fat?
- *That's* your offer?
- This isn't my first rodeo.

INFLAMMATORY KRUNCHES (SAY THESE WITH A BIG SMILE)

- Are you for real?
- My mama drowned all the dumb ones.
- My mama didn't raise no fool.
- Come back when you're serious.

- You're insulting my intelligence.
- I was born at night, but not *last* night!
- It's still ___ months until Christmas.
- I thought you guys only landed in wheat fields.
- Over my dead body.
- Do you also have a bridge you'd like to sell me?
- Is that in dollars or pesos/rubles/yen?
- Is this the new math?
- [In response to a written offer] We got your joke in the mail.
- 50,000 comedians are out of work, and you're trying to be funny.
- Leave a message at the tone.
- I accepted a proposal that bad once, but now I'm divorced.
- Is it on loan from a *museum?*
- [Holding chest] Call 911! This is the big one!
- I should have brought a paramedic.
- I was 6'4" when we started. Now I'm 4'6"!
- [Pulling up pants leg] It's getting pretty deep in here.
- Get outta' here!
- Go rub a lamp.
- You're dreaming.
- I've got to lie down for a minute.
- Is this a negotiation or a burial?
- [In response to a salary offer] Oh—I didn't know it was a part-time job!
- [In response to an offer from a house seller] Oh—I didn't know it had a pool!
- When hell freezes over.
- When donkeys fly.
- What are you, crazy?
- What do you want, blood?
- What planet are you from?
- Do I look like Santa Claus/Mother Theresa/Rockefeller?
- Is there an idiot sign on my back?
- Try again.
- Do I look like I just fell off the turnip truck?
- Do I look like the tooth fairy?
- You need a rendezvous with reality.
- At least Jesse James wore a mask.
- At that price, you should be wearing a mask.

- Go pound sand.
- I'm offended.
- You're wasting my time.
- You're outta your mind/gourd.
- Did I offend you in another life?
- Not in my lifetime.
- If I gave you my whole company, how much would I still owe you?
- You call that an offer?
- What part of "no" don't you understand?
- [Laughter.]
- Don't make me laugh.
- That's laughable/ridiculous/absurd.
- Who sent you, Thieves 'R Us?
- I hope your résumé is current.
- Did you fall out of a tree on your head?
- Have you lost touch with the mother ship?
- What are you smoking?
- Would you send in the next salesperson?
- [Pointing at offer] Oh—that must be your competition's phone number!
- Have a nice flight home.

NONVERBAL KRUNCHES

- [Feigned heart attack, choking, or pulling-knife-out-of-chest gestures.]
- [Silence.]
- [Rolling eyes.]
- [Looking at the ceiling.]
- [Not responding to their letter.]
- [A caucus—especially a long one.]
- [Pulling the ends of necktie over the head, like a noose.]
- [A walkout—not recommended.]
- [Shaking head back and forth, slowly.]

ENSUING KRUNCHES (FOR USE FOLLOWING A SUCCESSFUL KRUNCH)

- That's a step in the right direction.
- We're making progress.
- That's an improvement, but we're still not nearly where we need to be.
- We appreciate that. What more can we do?
- You're getting warmer.
- That's still not real attractive to us.
- You're still too expensive.
- That's a start.

- We're still not there.
- That's still not in the ballpark.
- You're not hearing me.
- That doesn't change the landscape.

RESPONSES TO KRUNCHES
- Make me an offer.
- Give me a number you'd be happy with.
- What are you looking for?
- What's your hot button?
- What would it take?
- What could you live with?
- What do we have to do?
- What do you need?
- Do you have a figure in mind?

- What's it worth to you?
- Give me some guidance, here.
- What's your budget?
- What's equitable/fair?
- Where do we need to be?
- What were you thinking about?
- Does it help if I [change a parameter, e.g., "increase the term?"]
- If you were in my shoes, what would you do?
- I can't sharpen my pencil any more—it's gone!
- There's nothing more in the cookie jar.

NEVER SETTLE ISSUES INDIVIDUALLY.
SETTLE ALL ISSUES AS A PACKAGE–
ONLY **AS A PACKAGE–AT THE END.**

Leverage Is the Name of the Game

Let's say I'm a prospective tenant, negotiating an office lease with a landlord. The issues are rent, lease term, parking, and tenant improvements. Early in our discussions, the landlord says, "I'll give you three extra parking spaces if you'll agree to a rental rate of $20 per square foot right now." It seems like an O.K. deal, so I agree. Later, he makes a surprisingly paltry offer on tenant improvements. Then he insists on a too-long lease term. How do I respond? Can I ask for more parking spaces? No. Can I ask for lower rent? No. Those issues are off the table—their leverage value lost—because I've already agreed to them.

It's simply impossible to know how flexible or frugal to be on early issues when you don't know how later issues will be handled. That's why you can't safely settle any individual issue until you settle them all, simultaneously, at the end. You agree to one deal, not a bunch of mini-deals. Everything must be kept in play until the end of the negotiation, then packaged into one comprehensive, negotiation-settling understanding.

This goes strongly contrary to instinct. It's actually hard to keep everything unresolved until the end. Humans are natural-born serial processors. We like to settle one task before moving on to the next. When we negotiate, we like to discuss an issue, resolve it, nail it to the table, then move on to the next issue. The problem with this piecemeal approach is that the instant an issue is resolved, its bargaining power drops to zero. It had leverage against other issues only while it stayed unresolved. Settled, it's worthless, a "done deal." The other side can stop worrying about it. But when you deliberately keep all the balls in the air until the final handshake, you maintain 100% of your leverage until the end. If you're pummeled on one issue, you can compensate by being less flexible on other issues.

The procedure is painless. Negotiate an issue to near resolution, then move on to another item. The other side will ask, "So, do we have a deal on [the prior Issue]?" Answer truthfully: "I don't see any problem with it. It looks great. But I can't settle it by itself. It's part of a larger agreement. Assuming the other issues play out like I'm sure they will, it'll be just fine. Let's set it aside for now, work on the other issues, then wrap everything up as a package."

You can give the other side a great deal of comfort on an issue—

that is, confidence that your interim understanding is unlikely to be changed—without firmly committing yourself. Remember, though, that the more comfort you provide, the more animosity you'll encounter if you must later reopen the issue.

No matter how hard your counterpart pushes, never settle an individual issue "early." In fact, the harder he pushes to resolve a particular issue independently, the more important it is to keep that issue unresolved. It's obviously a high-value item for him, and as long as it's in doubt, he'll behave himself in the negotiation.

THOMAS'S TRUISMS

**Only the final handshake seals the deal.
Until then, all issues remain open.**

THOMAS'S TRUISMS

Be a Shark: Keep Moving

Sharks never rest. They need to keep swimming to force oxygenated water over their gills. If they stop swimming, they drown.

Attack the issues like a shark: Keep moving. If you're not making progress on one issue, skip it and move on to another one. Don't keep working an issue that's not going anywhere. All you'll do is frustrate yourself and your counterpart. Promptly abandon the issue and proceed to another point. Work on some other items, then revisit the earlier issue. If you're still stuck, defer it yet again.

THOMAS'S TRUISMS

**Never stick with an issue that's not working.
Skip it and move on to something else.**

THOMAS'S TRUISMS

At some point the handful of "stuck" issues will be the only things standing in the way of a deal. With the accumulated leverage of all the tentatively settled issues bearing down on them, the other side may start to find those last few points less important than before, and suddenly "discover" some newfound flexibility on them.

Ethics and Rule 5

The "it's not over 'till it's all over" approach can cause some unhappiness on the other side of the table. Even when you've scrupulously avoided a firm commitment on an issue, your counterpart may think it's settled. Don't be surprised if you're the recipient of an occasional "bargaining in bad faith" accusation. Relax. You're on the sturdiest ethical ground. Since all of your concessions are tentative, you have every right to revisit any of them—repeatedly, if necessary—until everything is satisfactory and you give your final handshake. Until that moment, you haven't agreed to anything.

CONCLUDE WITH A NIBBLE.

THEM: How about this: six units at $375,000 plus shipping, net 60 terms, the first unit ships in four months, the rest ship every two months after that. Deal?

YOU: [fingertips to forehead, eyes cast downward, shaking head slightly] I don't know. I still don't think the boss is gonna like it. But we're close. We're *very* close. [long pause] I'll tell you what. If you'll pay the shipping, you've got yourself a deal.

The Nibble, Defined

That last little item in the example above—the business about shipping? That's a nibble. A nibble is a small concession obtained at the very end of a negotiation, immediately before (and, most compellingly, *in exchange for*) closure.

Let's clarify our terminology. Small concessions happen all the time in negotiating, but only the ones at the very end are technically nibbles. All the rest are just "small concessions."

Nibbles are negotiating's equivalent of a layup.* They're extremely low risk and dependably successful. They're just too small to be controversial. They're not worth deadlocking over. But they add up: Habitual nibblers (and that should include you) gain an extra percentage point or two almost every time they negotiate. That could mean a 25% or greater boost in the profit of a typical negotiated transaction today. Not a bad return for a few moments' work!

THOMAS'S TRUISMS

The nibble is negotiating's equivalent of a layup.

THOMAS'S TRUISMS

The Stupid Period

The final minutes of a negotiation are a very special time. An air of generosity—previously unfelt—now infuses the discussions, revealing itself in statements like "We'll throw that in," "Don't worry about that," and "We'll take care of it."

It's the stupid period. The deal's not over, but everybody's acting like it is. The stupid period is when you nibble.

---

* **layup** (n.) A high-probability basketball shot made from a position under or beside the basket.

I am constantly astounded by how much stuff gets conceded in the final minutes of a deal. Hours of work are routinely compromised in a last-minute flurry of wanton benevolence. Have you ever wondered why car dealers wait until the final fifteen minutes of a three-hour hoseathon to introduce the extended warranty, paint protection, rustproofing, credit life insurance, door guards, tinted glass, anti-theft system, and a host of other "must-have" options? Because it's 8:45 P.M. and it's the stupid period. It would have been hard to sell you this stuff before, but during the stupid period it's easy. Car dealers are a lot of things; dumb isn't one of them.

What causes the stupid period? Probably a combination of relief and investment. With the deal virtually done, the players begin to experience a bit of relief from the stress of the encounter. They can relax and kick back a little. And, having expended the effort to bring it to the verge of closure, their investment in the deal—and potential loss if it doesn't close—is at its peak. Now, giving up a little "extra" to close the deal seems like a singularly sensible thing to do.

Imagine walking into a clothing store and telling the salesperson, "I want to buy a suit, but I also want a free tie." It won't work. The salesperson hasn't invested any time in you. If you walk, he's lost nothing. But after 45 minutes spent showing you suits, his investment in you is considerable. Now, when you say, "I'll take it if you throw in a free tie," the stakes are different. The salesperson has almost an hour of his life riding on you. He may resist your first attempted nibble, and perhaps even your second, but when he's convinced that you're serious (and his investment could be lost) he'll usually relent.

The stupid period—when the players are particularly susceptible to nibbling—doesn't last long. Focus on two things: nibbling, and defending against being nibbled upon. You can kick back after the final handshake, when it's really over.

Nibbling is part of doing a complete job as a negotiator.

It Ain't Pretty, but It Sure Can Cook

Going for a few extra crumbs at the last minute is not, and never will be, a glamorous negotiating technique. For many Americans, nibbling falls somewhere between unsporting and sleazy. But in a business where success is often measured in crumbs, nibbling is important. It's part of doing a complete job as a negotiator.

Have you ever seen a rich person negotiate? If you need help getting over the notion that nibbling is undignified, watch somebody wealthy. You'll never see a more energetic nibbler. Rich people aren't too proud to pick up a couple of crumbs; the rest of us shouldn't be either. If it's worth it for them, you *know* it's worth it for us.

Sellers Can Nibble, Too

Salespeople are often reluctant to nibble because they're afraid the customer will be offended—and a deal that was ready to close will deadlock. This fear, while understandable, is groundless. Nibbling works just as well for sellers as it does for buyers. There's almost no risk, and considerable reward. Buyers are so distracted by closure that they'll scarcely even notice the nibble they gave up for it. Even if they completely freak out you can always quickly withdraw your nibble and accept their prior offer. Personally, I can't think of a single deal I've ever killed by nibbling.

Nibbling Technique

Nibbling is easy. Here's the basic storyline: You're a little unhappy with the deal, but your happiness will be restored if you get the nibble you're requesting.

First, select a couple of candidate nibbles (see Sources of Nibbles, below). Next, as you near the end of the negotiation, set up the nibble by establishing your misgivings about the deal that's taking shape. Frown, grimace, put your fingertips to your eyebrows or forehead. Whine a little: "If I bring this deal back, I probably won't have a job tomorrow." "You're one heck of a negotiator. You've gotten everything but my shorts."

Finally, pause for effect, then ask for your nibble in exchange for closure: "Tell you what. Let's settle this. Give me [*insert nibble here*] and we've got a deal." That's all there is to it. Your little nibble is now the only thing standing in the way of a deal.

What if the other side steadfastly refuses? Should you deadlock? Of course not! You've invested just as much time and effort as they have, and you're not about to kiss it goodbye just because you didn't get a little "sweetener" at the end. Don't give up easily, but if necessary, settle without the nibble.

Don't be a nibble pig. Nibbles should never be more than a small percentage of the total deal. The larger the nibble, the smaller the chance of success and the greater the risk of backlash.

Sources of Nibbles

Don't limit your nibbles to small, stand-alone items (such as free shipping, early delivery, more time to pay). While such issues make excellent nibbles, it's also perfectly O.K. to nibble on a main issue: "If you can get the price down another 2%, I'll take it." It's also O.K. to reintroduce, as a deal-closing nibble, an issue that the other side rejected earlier: "I know you said no to shrink-wrapping, but if you could do it we could settle this right now."

Defending Against the Nibble

Rule 1 is the only defense to nibbling that you'll ever need. Just say "Yes, if . . ."

> **THEM:** I'll take the suit if you throw in a free tie.
> **YOU:** I'll throw in a free tie if you buy a shirt.

That would be a yes. This would be a Japanese No:

> **THEM:** I'll take the suit if you throw in a free tie.
> **YOU:** I'll throw in a free tie if you buy a second suit.

Nibbling and Win-Win Negotiating

Nibbling truly is a win-win negotiating technique. Besides gaining you an extra slice, it has another, frequently overlooked benefit: it helps relieve the other side's PNR (Post-Negotiation Remorse).

We all want to do well, and when the negotiation's over we all worry about how well we did. Did we leave things on the table? Did we made mistakes? Are they laughing as they drive away? Will we still have a job when our boss hears about this deal? That's Post-Negotiation Remorse.

Since the other side won't tell us how we did (and we wouldn't believe them anyway), and we're not telepathic, we must sift through the available clues to find answers. One of the biggest clues is the other side's behavior, and that's where nibbling comes in. When you nibble in exchange for closure, you tell the other side that the nibble was just enough—but no more—to make the deal minimally acceptable to you. The nibble tipped the balance. That's wonderfully comforting news to your counterpart. Add a bit of sniveling and it's an even more effective PNR-reliever. It reassures her (rightly or wrongly) that she left little or nothing on the table.

Finishing Up

The following bit of dialogue completes the brief exchange at the beginning of this section. It illustrates a fairly typical negotiation endgame, with a determined negotiator successfully nibbling against considerable resistance.

YOU: I'll tell you what. If you'll pay the shipping, you've got yourself a deal.

THEM: No can do.

YOU: How about terms?

THEM: I've already given you sixty days!

YOU: Ninety days would be a big help.

THEM: I can give you ninety on the first invoice.

YOU: What can you do on shipping?

THEM: Nothing! The money's not there.

YOU: Will you ship the first three? That's only half the order.

THEM: We can't afford it.

YOU: I'll tell you what. I'll agree to your ninety days on the first invoice if you ship the first three units. That's fair. I'll sign it right now.

THEM: We'll ship the first two.

YOU: [Reluctantly] O.K. Let's do it.

Oh, there's just one more thing, sir.

—Columbo, nibbling

KEEP LOOKING FOR CREATIVE (HIGH VALUE–LOW COST) CONCESSIONS TO TRADE.

The Million-Dollar Ranch

The following story may or may not be apocryphal. Either way, it's a good story.

Many years ago, Ronald Reagan was living in Pacific Palisades, California, an affluent suburb of Los Angeles. At the time, Reagan was a veteran "B movie" actor and television regular. He was starting to dabble in politics. He was successful, but by no means wealthy. His neighbors, on the other hand, were loaded. Most of them were in the entertainment industry, and all of them were millionaires. In fact, Reagan scarcely knew anyone who wasn't a millionaire. Everyone at his country club was a millionaire. Everyone at his grocery store was a millionaire. His gardener was a millionaire. He had recently married Nancy Davis; she was a millionaire. Ron was the only nonmillionaire in the whole crowd.

Ron was a proud man, and didn't like this situation at all. He was sure everyone was laughing behind his back. Nancy was constantly on his case. Every day she'd ask, "Ron, are you a millionaire yet? I've been very patient with you, Ron. Don't tell me I married the wrong guy. Was Jane Wyman right about you?"

Eventually, Ron could stand it no longer. He went to his accountant and said, "I've got to become a millionaire, as fast as possible. What should I do?" The accountant replied, "Ron, I've got two words for you: real estate." Ron went right out and bought a number of small, adjacent parcels of land overlooking the ocean at Malibu. Over the next few years he paid off the mortgages, then merged the parcels into a single property known, in the local vernacular, as a ranch. Shortly thereafter, he put his ranch on the market. Asking price: one million dollars.

Within a week, Ron got two offers for his ranch. The first, from an individual who didn't know the Reagans, was for $950,000 cash. Ron rejected it. He'd gone through this whole drill to be a millionaire, and nothing less would do. Being a $950,000-aire just wouldn't cut it.

The second offer was from a friend of the Reagan family who was acquainted with Ron's, shall we say, millionaire issue. His offer was for a million dollars; $900,000 in cash, and $100,000 in 30-year government bonds. Ron accepted it.

The net present value of $100,000 in 30-year government bonds is about $10,000. Reagan had accepted a $910,000 offer in lieu of a $950,000 offer. Did he know what he was doing? Sure he knew. He'd gotten exactly what he wanted: a contract that said "Ronald W. Reagan" and "one million bucks." Reagan couldn't care less that he was maturing faster than those bonds. He could now walk up to his fat-cat friends at the country club and say, "See this contract? See my name there? See all those zeros? I'm as good as you are." Even better, he could finally tell Nancy to shut up.

And let's not forget about the buyer. He knew Reagan's hot button, and got a great price on the ranch as a result. The story's two morals: (1) make no assumptions about the other side's motivations; and (2) tailor your incentives.

THOMAS'S TRUISMS

Sometimes people find satisfactions in strange places.

THOMAS'S TRUISMS

Going Beyond Win-Win, Zero-Sum Negotiating

Win-win negotiating imposes some strict limits on us. It prohibits extreme deals. Neither side should "clean the table." Each side should feel they did as well as reasonably possible. No trickery, dishonesty, or deceit should be employed. Nobody should lose face. Under such constraints, the "play" in our negotiations is often so limited, you almost need a microscope to see it. Most of the time we're just gaining and giving small advantages.

Let's diagram it:

100/0——80/20——60/40	55/45–50/50–45/55	40/60——80/20——0/100
WIN-LOSE	**WIN-WIN**	**WIN-LOSE**

This is a representation (hugely oversimplified and one-dimensional) of all the possible allocations of the "net available benefit" (the sum of everything in contention) between two players in a given negotiation, from 100/0 (all for you, nothing for the other side) to 0/100 (all for the other side, nothing for you). Win-win negotiations mostly fall within the 50/50 to 55/45 range. Outside of this, deals become so extreme that, no matter how much praise they receive, one player or the other will almost surely feel beaten.

We want you to win, so only outcomes of 51/49 or better are acceptable. Does this mean that as a win-win negotiator you have to spend your entire career working that 4% band between 51/49 and 55/45? That's *it*? Can you ever get 60%? Or 70%? Or 80%? Isn't there some way to get outside of these limits and still have the other side feel it was a win-win deal? There is. It's the most fickle and capricious tool in negotiating, often more a matter of luck than skill. But when it works, it's dynamite. It's creativity.

THOMAS'S TRUISMS

Creativity is the most fickle and capricious tool in negotiating.

THOMAS'S TRUISMS

As logical American negotiators, we naturally assume that the values the other side assigns to the various issues—what's important and what's not—are roughly the same as ours. Usually, we're right. In most cases there is surprisingly good agreement among the players as to the "worth"—both relative and absolute—of the issues being negotiated. In such cases, negotiations amount to dividing up a finite "pie." More for me means less for you, and vice versa. This is called zero-sum or "positional" negotiating. The vast majority of the billions of negotiations taking place every day are zero-sum.

But sometimes we're very, very wrong: Two equally intelligent, fully rational adults may place very different values on the same item. When they do, a potential creative concession is born. And the bigger the spread between the perceived values, the more creatively exciting the issue becomes.

Finding and exploiting these special, "anomalous" issues is what creative negotiating is all about. Creativity is the way—the *only* way—that you can climb out of the trenches of zero-sum negotiating. If you can work one or more of these special issues into your negotiation, you can make a new kind of pie, one that looks radically different to you than it does to your counterpart. You can get 60, 70, 80% or more of this pie and simultaneously have the other side feel it's gotten a fair share.

Creative negotiating is really nothing more than a high-powered kind of trading. It's just like ordinary negotiating, but with plutonium—that is, creative—concessions. We trade a creative concession just like we'd trade any other concession, but with one big distinction: From the other side's perspective, the trade is a fair one. From your perspective, it's exceptional.

Of the seven Critical Rules, creativity is by far the most problematical. It's very difficult to teach. It's notoriously unquantifiable and unreliable. Some people never seem to get it. But for all of its problems, creativity can produce the sweetest, most heartwarming, most spectacular deals you'll ever close.

Hot Buttons: The Wellspring of Creativity

A couple of years ago I negotiated the lease of a new office building located just outside of Washington, D.C. I represented the building's owner. The prospective tenant was a major consulting firm, run by a well-known, very successful local entrepreneur. They were looking at a ten-year lease for 80% of the building. In commercial leasing, a ten year lease for 80% of a property is a very big deal; it carries a lot of bargaining clout.

The entrepreneur and I sat down in his office to negotiate the lease. He was doing his own negotiating—a mistake, since he had full authority.* This gentleman was the consummate American-style negotiator. After about one second of small talk ("Jim, hawaya?"), he announced, "If we're going to do this deal, I've gotta have my name on the roof." He wanted his company's name and logo at the top of the building, in place of the current sign (which happened to be my client's name and logo). He wasn't talking about rent, or parking, or tenant improvements. He was talking about signage.

The signage clause in a commercial lease—specifying what signs are permitted—is usually right up there in importance with the Acts of God ("What if the building's hit by a meteor? Do I still have to pay rent?") and Termination of Lease in the Event of Civil Insurrection clauses. It's just not a big deal. In a case like this, where the tenant is taking essentially the whole building, it's virtually a given that he can put up a sign.

I may not be the smartest person in the world, but even I can detect a potential hot button when it falls into my lap. Signage is a genuinely strange issue to lead off with. It must really mean a lot to this guy. Fifteen years earlier, I would have said something like "Sign?

---

* See Rule 17: Negotiate against higher-authority people whenever possible. Keep your authority limited.

Done. What's the next issue? We're rolling now!" But as I've matured, I've come to realize that in negotiation, the values I attach to things often don't matter. The fact that I think the sign's virtually irrelevant doesn't matter. What matters is that the other side thinks it's very important. And what really, *really* matters is that since it's so important to him, he should be willing to pay appropriately for it.

"I'll talk to my client about it, but I wouldn't be optimistic," I replied.

He was crestfallen. We negotiated for the next two hours, with me periodically making calls back to my client. These calls were not about the sign. Every fifteen minutes or so the entrepreneur would say something like, "What about the sign?" And I would respond, "I'm working on it. This is a very important issue to my client."

After a couple of hours we had tentative agreements on everything but the rental rate and the sign. The entrepreneur said, "Well, it all comes down to the name on the roof. Yes or no?" I responded, "I've talked to my client about it, and I think I can get him to agree to your sign. But in exchange, we'd need to get our asking price for the rent." He instantly responded, "Done."

Perhaps I hadn't asked enough for the sign.

Every time that entrepreneur sees his name in big letters on that building, he thinks about all the times his dad said, "Son, you're a jerk and you'll never amount to anything." And he says to himself, "Dad was wrong, and this proves it." It also proves that people sometimes find satisfactions in strange places.

The sign was a hot button. Hot buttons—things one side ardently desires, or can't stand, out of all proportion to their "objective" value—are the primary source of creative concessions. When you find one, you trade it for a *quid pro quo* equal to or greater than the full value the other side puts on it. Presto! You've turned lemons into lemonade. You've given up a little and gotten back a lot.

Hot buttons can be emotional, or frivolous, or even silly. I've had the purchase of a commercial passenger aircraft close, at a very attractive nine-figure price, when the seller agreed to throw in a model of the plane painted with the buyer's colors. I've had a client set the selling price of his business not on the value of the business's assets, cash flow, and goodwill, but at a figure greater than what his brother—the object of a lifelong sibling rivalry—got for *his* business. I've had more than a few deals settle—and one deadlock—over a handful of words in a suggested postnegotiation press release. In employment negotiations, I've found that the right job title—or the right office, or even the right parking space—can be as important as money. I've had business clients who, while willing to fight a federally imposed penalty all the way to the Supreme Court, agreed to pay the same amount to a "National Workplace Safety Training Fund" instead.

Lenders know that corporate bigwigs will haggle endlessly for the lowest interest rate on their business credit line because it gives them bragging rights among fellow bigwigs. The low rate is more than offset by the hefty loan fees they pay, but that's beside the point. When the bigwigs match rates, they never mention the fees.

Compensation and performance-appraisal issues are a potential hot button cornucopia. If the other side gets a bonus, or makes quota, or wins a trip, or if a deal comes in sooner, or later, or with or without certain features, you may be able to offer—at little cost to you—a package they find irresistibly attractive.

Options are a rich source of would-be hot buttons. An option to do something—for example, to renew a contract for an additional period, or to have the "right of first refusal" or "last look" over some future opportunity—can be exceedingly attractive to one side or the other. On paper at least, options can be very impressive. But most options are never used. Either the conditions of their exercise never occur, or they're left in a file and forgotten until after they've expired.

Referrals—personal introductions to potential new sources of business—can be big-time hot buttons. Referrals cost the giver next to nothing, but can be extremely valuable to the receiver. The same is true of offering the chance to become a demo site for a new model or process. Or providing a high-visibility opportunity to address an industry group. Or arranging an article featuring your counterpart in the company or trade association newsletter.

Tax issues are a fountainhead of hot buttons. Slight changes in how a transaction is handled can generate major tax advantages (or liabilities) for one player, often at little or no cost to the other. For example, the wording of a settlement agreement in a personal injury matter may determine whether the compensation paid to the injured party is taxable or not.

All of these illustrations share the same distinctive feature: high value to the getter and low cost to the giver. If there's a potential hot button in your negotiation, you must try to determine its value to your counterpart without revealing how significant (or insignificant) it is to you. The value the other side puts on the item is what counts. Introduce it with some "what if" statements: "What if we were willing to do so-and-so? Would you be interested? What would you offer in return?"

Limitations on Creativity in Negotiation

1. Luck. Creative negotiating is very sexy. It exerts a powerful attraction. The deals that result from creative concessions are often spectacular. Everybody wants to hit a home run, but home runs are pretty rare in this business. The actual payoff from all the time and energy devoted to creativity is surprisingly limited. An awful lot of dominoes must fall the right way for it to work. The bottom line: Creativity in negotiation depends to a great extent on luck.

Far more often than not, there aren't any creative concessions to be had (or, at least, none that are relevant). Our value system and our counterpart's usually knit together seamlessly. We have a basic, one-dimensional negotiating problem on our hands. Even when creative concessions are available, in the simple day-to-day, split-second kinds of negotiations we all do constantly, nobody has the time or energy—or is willing to take the risk—to pursue them.

I have substantial control over the operation of the other six Critical Rules. I decide what to trade for (Rule 1), how high to start (Rule 2), how big or small a concession to make, and when to make it (Rule 3). I decide when to krunch and when to counteroffer (Rule 4), when to give or withhold final agreement (Rule 5), and what to nibble for (Rule 6). But creativity I really can't control. I just have to be in the right place when lightning strikes. Sometimes I can encourage it a little (see Fostering Creativity, below). And I can certainly be ready to vigorously trade whatever creative opportunities the Bargaining Gods might toss my way. But mostly, I have to be lucky.

The sign-on-the-building case is an excellent example. I can't take credit for that. It fell into my lap. I reacted appropriately when it occurred: I was patient, I tested its value to my counterpart, I didn't reveal its insignificance to me, and I traded assertively for it. But I didn't make it happen. I was lucky, pure and simple. And that's always going to be the big problem with creativity.

The ongoing search for creative concessions should be viewed as a sideline in day-to-day negotiations. Occasionally it will turn up an extraordinary item. But make no mistake: It's icing on the cake, not the cake itself. I've seen too many potentially outstanding negotiators chase after the Holy Grail of creativity only to come up empty-handed and bitter. Distracted by their endless search for creative solutions, they fail to conscientiously attend to the mundane but very real issues already on the table.

2. Guilt. Most Americans have a strong sense of fairness. It's very difficult for us to ask a lot for something we don't personally think is worth much. We feel guilty. When we put a low value on a concession, we naturally tend to trade it away cheaply, regardless of how highly the other side prizes it and how much they might be willing to pay for it.

When trading creative concessions, it's important to remember that what matters is the value of the concession to the other side, not the value to you. The fact that a concession might benefit you hugely or cost you virtually nothing is irrelevant when figuring a sufficient *quid pro quo* from your counterpart. If she thinks the concession is momentous, she will expect to pay handsomely for it. If she thinks it's insignificant, she will expect to pay little for it. That's all that matters.

THOMAS'S TRUISMS

The value of the concession to the other side is what matters.

THOMAS'S TRUISMS

---

3. Risk. The field of creativity is littered with the bones of unwary negotiators. Any time you do something a little different, you increase the risk of things going wrong. Creative negotiating naturally consists of doing the unusual. Complex, creative deals will occasionally fail spectacularly, when a simple give-and-take would have succeeded. Before you commit, do your best to think through all the possible scenarios for problems. Consult with experts. Be careful.

Lawyers, in my experience, are rather uncreative negotiators. Risk is the reason. Lawyers are trained to avoid risk. We do things in the predictable, tried and true way. Our clients don't pay us to be creative, they pay us to be monotonously right. In the law, repetitive is usually right.

Fostering Creativity in Negotiation

A well-known West Coast zoo has an exhibit called Monkey Island. It's the zoo's main monkey display. Monkey Island is basically a mound of cement and dirt, surrounded by a water moat. There are no fences. It's supposed to look like the monkeys' natural habitat. The monkeys don't escape because monkeys can't swim.

The inside story on Monkey Island is that the contractor who built it didn't excavate a deep, expensive moat. He simply scraped off the top six inches of dirt in a big circle all the way around Monkey Island, poured a three-inch layer of concrete into the circle, painted it black, and filled it with three inches of water.

That three-inch deep moat has been there 30 years, and to this very day not a single monkey has ever escaped from Monkey Island. They all look at that moat and say to themselves, "If I put a paw out there, I'm gonna die." Perhaps some day a brave, visionary monkey will stick his paw in and test that assumption. Can you imagine that moment? "Three inches? Damn! We've been fooled! Yo, monkeys, let's go!" There'd be monkeys all over town.

I'm convinced that when it comes to negotiating creatively, most of us are stuck on our own little Monkey Island. We limit our thinking with a host of assumptions—what the other side wants, what it might find interesting, what it can and can't do. We use old ideas in old ways, over and over.

How do we get off Monkey Island? There are a number of well-known devices for unlocking creativity. Put yourself in the other side's shoes. Remind yourself that everyone has multiple interests. There are undoubtedly many more things to take into account than you or the other side have considered.

Good prenegotiation homework facilitates creative negotiating. Brainstorming with a group—listing everything that comes to mind, no matter how unconventional or extreme, without any evaluations, corrections, or criticisms—always generates new ideas. In fact, just talking things over with a group can be helpful. Role playing—imagining that you're looking at the issues through someone else's eyes—can also stimulate new thinking. How would a lawyer view it? An accountant? An engineer?

Once the negotiation begins, the other side will be your best source of creative ideas. A negotiating partnership that features mutual trust, respect, and confidentiality will help break down the barriers that inhibit creativity. Invest lots of time in small talk and climate-building. Seek to create an inquisitive, problem-solving environment in which your counterpart feels he can open up to you without danger. Stimulate new solutions with open-ended questions: "You know our situation. What will work? I'm out of ideas. Help me on this. What's the hot button for you?" Avoid narrow-mindedness ("Let's just stick to the issues") and criticism ("That's completely crazy"). Use lots of hypotheticals: "What if we tried X? How about Y? How about X and Y? How about X on Thursday and Y on Friday? Would it help if I did A and B?" Even if creative lightning doesn't strike, you'll have a good foundation on which to build a win-win agreement.

7

The Important but Obvious Rules

DO YOUR HOMEWORK.

Introduction

I get a lot of flak for not making homework a Critical Rule. I have two reasons for this. First, there's nothing particularly unique about homework for negotiating. With the exception of Envelope-setting, it's just like any other sort of homework. You do the same things that you'd do to get ready for any important meeting. Second, it's not a deficit area for Americans. We actually do a pretty good job at homework. Our negotiating technique stinks, but we know the facts.

Any experienced negotiator will tell you that you make it or break it when you do your homework. Your investment in prenegotiation homework will usually be paid back multifold in better negotiating results. Obviously, homework takes time and costs money, and the smaller the deal, the less homework can be justified. But within the limits of your time and your budget, do as much home-work as you can. And don't wait until the last minute. The earlier you start, the easier it will be.

Veteran negotiators need to take special care regarding home-work. At one time or another, all of us have been tempted to "wing it" with less than adequate homework, figuring that we'll get by on our experience and skill. This is a very bad idea. The side with the most information usually has the upper hand in negotiation, no matter how brilliant the negotiators might be. There simply is no substitute for doing your homework.

A Homework Checklist

Here's a simple nine-item homework checklist I've used for years and found satisfactory. It's entirely too comprehensive for most ne-gotiations, but it will help focus your thinking about homework: (1) subject matter; (2) your organization; (3) your counterpart's organi-zation; (4) your counterpart, individually; (5) your Envelopes; (6) authority issues; (7) team preparation; (8) nibbles; and (9) creative concessions. The fifth item, your Envelopes, is unquestionably the most important of the lot.

1. Subject matter. Obviously, you've got to be thoroughly knowl-edgeable about the subject of the negotiation. In many cases you'll already be an expert on the topic. If not, you must quickly learn as much as you reasonably can, and fill in the gaps with subject-matter experts.

2. Your organization. The fully prepared negotiator searches her whole organization for carrots and sticks. The more carrots and sticks, the more leverage. Go on a leverage hunt. Who else in your or-ganization has something the other side might want—or needs something the other side might have? Purchasing, credit, sales, and other departments should be polled to insure that no potential trade-offs are being overlooked or wasted. Any handy requirements to fulfill, adjustments to make, or disputes to resolve can become trading ammunition. If you don't know about it, you can't offer it or ask for it.

Many things that an organization ordinarily gives away can be turned into trading fodder. Let's say that Able Corporation's Sales Department wants customers to try a new product. Let's also say that Able Corp's Customer Service Department has decided to give client Baker Corporation a $10,000 credit due to late deliveries. If Customer Service simply gives the $10,000 credit to Baker Corp, Baker Corp will be happy—and Able Corp will have lost an opportunity. What if Able's Customer Service Department—full of well-trained negotiators who know a valuable concession when they see one—alerts the other Able Corp departments about the pending credit? The Sales Department could use it as negotiating leverage. Sales could say to Baker, "I think I can get that $10,000 credit approved, if you'll try our new product." Bingo! Sales is a hero, Baker is happy, and the product gets tested. Able Corp has transformed a routine customer adjustment into a negotiation asset.

Even a simple multidepartment joint purchase can boost negotiating leverage. Thus, if Department A (trying to get a good price on some new PCs) and Department B (also interested in getting some PCs) can pool their requirements, the added leverage of purchasing more units from the same vendor will help both departments get a better price.

3. Your counterpart's organization. What's their history, financial situation, political situation, culture, reputation? What are their short- and long-term goals? How can you assist? What does their organization chart look like? Who reports to whom? What's their deadline? Are there potential cross-cultural negotiating issues?

4. Your counterpart, individually. What's your counterpart like? What's her reputation? Has she told you her position? Her secondary interests? If not, what are they likely to be? What concessions—obvious and obscure—might appeal to her? Is she known to use specific negotiating techniques (such as starting high, limited authority, good guy–bad guy)? If so, she's almost certain to use them again. Does she tell the truth? Does she keep her word? Has she written anything that might give you some information? What personal interests might she have that you could use as small-talk material? Is she from a different culture and/or country?

5. Your Envelopes. More than anything else, homework is about Envelope-setting. It's by far your most important homework task. Everything you learn while doing your homework will ultimately be reflected in your Envelopes. If you have multiple issues, you must set an Envelope for each issue and also give it a relative value.

THOMAS'S TRUISMS

Setting your Envelopes is your most important homework task.

THOMAS'S TRUISMS

If you take the time to determine your Envelopes with care, you're almost automatically going to do most of the important things right. You'll start high. You'll trade your concessions. You'll make each concession smaller than the one before. You'll nibble at the end. You'll know when to deadlock, if necessary. If you don't have your Envelopes, I just don't see how you can negotiate successfully.

Start with the key issue to be negotiated. Set your target on that issue—what you'd be reasonably comfortable with, considering all the circumstances. Next, set your opening. Finally, set your bottom line—the absolute minimum you would accept, the point below which it would be better to deadlock. Your bottom line on an issue can be zero—that is, the issue is totally expendable, if necessary.

Go through this procedure with each issue to be negotiated. Multiple issues will require you to calculate a fourth variable, in addition to opening, target, and bottom line: the variable of weight. To do this, simply pick an issue (it doesn't matter which one) and assign it a weight of one. Then, cross-weight all of the other issues against that issue. For example, if an issue is ten times as significant, it would be given a weight of ten. If it were one-quarter as important, it would be given a weight of .25.

When the arduous task of setting Envelopes and weights is finished, you'll have established a "common currency" linking all of your issues, allowing you to readily calculate the true cost of a given potential concession. In more complex negotiations, these values can easily be plugged into a spreadsheet program, giving you the ability to make reasonably accurate cost calculations in real time.

Please don't make the mistake of spending a lot of energy trying to figure out the other side's Envelope(s). It's natural to be curious, but this is usually a waste of time. It's a distraction from other more productive homework tasks; also, you're almost certain to get it wrong, and it really shouldn't affect your negotiating behavior anyway. Your *own* Envelope is what matters.

6. **Authority issues.*** The homework period is the time to get your authority straightened out with your boss and organization. Detailed approvals at this stage will help avoid misunderstandings later. Beware of overly broad grants of authority. Get the higher-ups on your side to agree to stay out of the bargaining. Prepare them for patient negotiations with long stretches devoid of apparent progress.

7. **Team preparation.**† Will you be part of a negotiating team? If so, have you minimized the team's size? Have you briefed everybody on the overall game plan? Have you assigned roles (note-taking, num-

---

* See Rule 17: Negotiate against higher-authority people whenever possible. Keep your authority limited.

† See Rule 20: Keep your team small and under control, for a detailed look at team negotiating.

bers)? Most importantly, have you and your team discussed and agreed upon your communication rules: There will be a single spokesperson, there will be no note-passing or whispering, and team members can call a caucus whenever they wish?

8. Nibbles. What are some worthwhile things to nibble for? What nibbles might the other side seek? If they did, what would you ask for in return? Having a list of candidate nibbles in advance will significantly improve the overall quality of your nibbling. At the end of a negotiation you're often tired and not especially imaginative; it's not a good time to have to think of quality nibbles.

9. Creative concessions. Can you identify any concessions that, while not particularly costly to you, might be especially appealing to your counterpart? To her boss? To her Chairman of the Board? Can the relationship between the sides be expanded so as to provide more potential trade-offs? Are you making any unwarranted assumptions about what she needs, wants, knows, can do, will find acceptable, will pay?

KEEP THE CLIMATE POSITIVE.

Climates Are Precious

Negotiating inevitably involves conflict between the interests—and sometimes the personalities—of the parties. Keeping an agreeable climate in the midst of that conflict can challenge anyone. No matter who or what you're negotiating, a positive climate will help you reach agreement. A negative one, on the other hand, can make it impossible to reach a deal notwithstanding everyone's genuine desire to settle. The climate of your negotiation determines your ability to communicate with the other side. If it breaks down, you might as well go home.

Separate the people from the problem.
Be hard on the problem but soft on the people.

Let's cover a few general points about negotiating climates. First, the more we can separate the people from the problem, the easier it will be to achieve a cooperative atmosphere. Try to remember that the other side, in most cases, is just a representative. Your conflict isn't with her personally, but with the ideas she is representing. She may be part of a larger organization. She may only be following—perhaps reluctantly—her instructions. Her organization may have a simplistic and adversarial view of the negotiation. Her very career may be at stake. You can be hard on the problem and still be soft on the people.

Next, keep in mind that comfortable players make more concessions. The wise negotiator does everything he can to put his counterpart at ease. This immediately rules out the many negative negotiating routines we've heard so much about—intimidation, walkouts, threats, sarcasm, emotional outbursts—and suggests nice things like praise, apologies, and comfortable physical arrangements.

We make more concessions to friends.

If your counterparts like you, they're generally going to give you more concessions. It makes sense, then, to act like a friend—if for no other reason than to attract more concessions. In Rule 12, Start slowly, we recommend that you invest in some cozy prenegotiation chitchat. By personalizing yourself to the other side, you become more influential. You gain their empathy. You give them a reason to treat you preferentially.

No matter how the other side behaves, be diplomatic and positive. Resolve to remain cool and courteous under all circumstances. Paste a smile on your face and keep it there throughout the discussions. If you disagree, do so on a positive note. Even a single critical comment can ruin a negotiating climate. Be constructive when discussing the other side's position and problems. Agree with them whenever possible. Don't debate. If you argue, they'll defend. The luxury of telling the other side what you really think of them is something that you, as a negotiator, simply cannot afford. Adopt an investigative attitude rather than a judgmental one. Solicit your counterpart's help in solving your joint problem. Be unyieldingly positive. Infuse your negotiations with the attitude that "We can make this work."

THOMAS'S TRUISMS

Climates tend to persist.

THOMAS'S TRUISMS

A positive climate, once established, will easily outlast brief periods of unpleasantness (and even the closest counterparts scrap a little, sometimes). A negative climate will often resist your best efforts to turn it around.

Humor

If you're inclined toward humor, use it freely when you negotiate. Everybody will appreciate your efforts. A little laughter is a welcome respite from the tension of negotiating. I can't imagine a negotiation so dignified that it couldn't benefit from a little levity. Laughter clears the air. It helps us think better, gives us a brighter outlook, makes us more creative and less defensive. However, don't go overboard. Choose your topics with care, and always avoid humor with ethnic or sexual overtones.

Emotional Episodes

A host of melodramatic events—some deliberate, some not—may drastically affect your negotiating climate.

1. Threats. Threats serve no worthwhile purpose in negotiating. Almost never do they provide the other side with information it didn't already have, or motivate it to act in a desired way. On the contrary, threats have the almost magical ability to turn otherwise rational negotiators into enraged dimwits so incensed by the threat that they no longer care how the negotiation turns out.

Never threaten the other side under any circumstances. If you truly believe that your counterpart may not fully appreciate the situation, you can attempt to educate her in a patient, respectful way. Unfortunately, the line between educating and threatening is an incredibly fine one—and its location is determined by the other side! Depending on the hearer, the same statement can be taken as an explanation or a threat.

If you're the recipient of a threat, don't reply. This isn't a debate; you lose no points by not responding. Listen quietly and don't interrupt. Remain calm; take a deep breath; don't lose your self-control. The other side may be threatening you specifically to impair your judgment.

2. Outbursts. Negotiators have very different reactions to anger, raised voices, tears, and table-thumping. Some question what they might have done to cause it. They figure a rational person wouldn't act that way unless provoked, so it must be their own fault. Feeling guilty, they give in. Others react the same way to such outbursts as they do to threats: They become indignant. Either way, most of us find it difficult to effectively deal with emotional displays during a negotiation. As a result, in the very short term, the "when in doubt, scream and shout" approach will sometimes score a few concessions.

Respond to an emotional outburst the same way you would to a threat: Relax and don't reply. Don't interrupt, disagree, or debate. When he's finished, thank your counterpart for expressing his position so vigorously. If the emotions are genuine, the outburst will be a good way for him to let off steam. If they're not, you're going to have to sit through the show anyway. Cheer yourself with the knowledge that an emotional outburst often indicates a weak position.

3. Walkouts. A walkout is really nothing more than a dramatic, physical krunch. When you slam your briefcase and stalk out the door you're saying, in effect, "You've got to do better than that." But a walkout is also an emotional ploy. When the other side walks out, it can shock and embarrass us into doubting the propriety of our conduct. This doubt can translate into concessions. Remember: The goal of the walker is to have the other side coax him to return—with a concession.

I cannot recommend walkout as a useful negotiating technique under anything but the most extraordinary circumstances. It's undignified and unprofessional. It shatters any illusion of partnership between problem-solving colleagues. It brings the negotiation to a screeching halt. If the negotiator on the other side's a pro, the walkout won't influence him in the slightest. If the walkout doesn't work and the walker really needs to close the deal, he's going to have to contact the other side and attempt to reopen the talks—a veritable banquet of crow-eating. Even if the walkout prompts an interim concession, it may be taken back once the emotion of the moment has dissipated. If you're going to krunch, do it the normal way. Don't leave.

If you're the victim of a walkout, first calm down. Coolly and without comment, let the other side leave. Allow a bit of time to pass, then try to resume the negotiations. Don't stand on ceremony about who should call whom. If you don't hear from the other side, go ahead and call them. Show concern. Apologize for anything you might have said that they found offensive. Express your strong desire to continue the talks. Then, respond to the walkout just as you would to any other krunch: Ask the other side to make you an offer. Find out what it would take to move the negotiations forward.

4. Impasses and deadlocks. Everyone who negotiates will encounter impasses and deadlocks from time to time. They are a natural and healthy part of the bargaining process. While the terms are often used synonymously, "impasse" usually suggests a more temporary cessation of the discussions; "deadlock" implies a more permanent stalemate. In reality, there's no clear distinction; as long as the negotiators are still breathing, nothing's irrevocably deadlocked.

The declaration of an impasse or a deadlock can be a very emotional moment. A great deal of hard work may be on the line. You'll probably wonder if you shouldn't have been more flexible. If the deadline has not yet arrived, assume that the other side is bluffing and continue negotiating. If time has run out, you're at your bottom line, and there's no deal, you've got a genuine deadlock. Resist the very natural temptation to end the talks with an angry speech. Yes, you're frustrated and you've wasted a lot of valuable time, but think long-term. You and your counterpart will almost certainly meet again. Regardless of the outcome, always end on a positive note.

Over the years I've observed that Americans are very quick to bolt from a negotiation: "We're deadlocked! I'm out of here!" We seem to be willing to seize almost any opportunity to declare failure and get out. I suspect more than a few of us are secretly happy for the stalemate so that we can move on to something more comfortable. But throwing in the towel should be your very last alternative. There must be other things you haven't tried yet. If there's still time, there's still hope.

5. Anger. Angry negotiators are usually foolish negotiators. It's very rare for a negotiator who gets really angry not to do something he regrets later. If your counterpart can make you angry, she can beat you. Your anger interferes with your ability to process information. Some negotiators will deliberately try to anger the other side, hoping to take advantage of their mistakes. Keeping your cool gives you a great advantage over the other side. Self control is power, and it's something people respect.

Try to avoid provocative language. Never have "demands"—instead, have "proposals," "suggestions," "ideas," "thoughts," "positions," and the like. Rather than telling the other side what you "insist on," tell them what you're "looking for" or what "makes sense."

As soon as you become angry you're disqualified as a negotiator, and you remain disqualified for as long as you remain angry. Take a time-out. Refocus on your long-term interests. Don't resume negotiations until you've cooled off. This will allow the other side to calm down, also.

Physical Arrangements

1. Seating and table shape. Seating is of very little significance in negotiation—as long as the seats are comfortable and you can hear and see; that's all that matters. Your power seat is the seat that feels good to you. If the other side wants a particular seat, by all means let them have it. The more comfortable they are, the better for you. Ditto table shape—it's just about irrelevant. Sitting side-by-side, or at right angles, might create a slightly greater feeling of collaboration than sitting opposite each other. Consider round tables instead of the traditional square or rectangular ones. They may give the parties a more unified, problem-solving orientation.

2. Meeting time and day. It makes very little difference. I personally favor breakfast meetings because everyone is fresh and the day is less impacted. Be careful of starting too late and then hurrying to settle by the end of the business day. Resist pressure to finish by an arbitrary time. If necessary, carry the discussions over to a subsequent day. Avoid marathon sessions and late-night deals. Never negotiate when fatigued—tired negotiators make foolish errors and are easily influenced by the other side.

Friday is the only day to watch out for. Beware of the "Friday factor," the headlong rush to settle before the weekend. Unless there's an excellent reason to close a deal late on Friday afternoon, why not wait until Monday?

3. Telephone and written negotiations. Negotiating in person is always best. Face-to-face, you're far more persuasive, more effective at personalizing, and harder to say "no" to. The telephone, by comparison, is the most dangerous medium for negotiating. Telephone deals are often quick deals. The callee is often not prepared for the call and is frequently disorganized and distracted. Important points may be overlooked or misunderstood. Your personal influence is diluted because the other side doesn't have to deal with that look on your face; you can't observe their reactions, either. There's also pressure to hurry up and close. If you must negotiate by phone, take your time. Be the caller whenever possible. If you're the callee and you're unprepared, call back. Take careful notes, and confirm agreements in writing as soon as possible.

While written negotiations have the advantage of a certain degree of built-in patience, they suffer from even greater isolation than telephone negotiations. It's extremely easy to say "no" in writing. Your personalizing efforts are substantially compromised by being reduced to black and white, and the other side's feelings can only be poorly deduced from their written words.

NEVER ASSUME THAT AN ISSUE IS NON-NEGOTIABLE JUST BECAUSE THE OTHER SIDE *SAYS* IT IS. IN REALITY, ALMOST EVERYTHING IS NEGOTIABLE.

Maniacs on the Loose

After a couple of days of intense Negotiate to Win training, some of my students can get a little overzealous. On the way home from the workshop, one of them will inevitably stop off at the grocery store. When they reach the checker, it happens. "Let's talk peas," they say. "Waddya mean, 99 cents? Come on, help me out with these peas. Cut me a little slack, here." The poor checker looks at the ceiling and mutters, "Why me, God? Why are you doing this to me?"

Yes, you might get a deal on the peas. Is it worth the humiliation of doing it? Leave the people at the grocery store alone. Leave the people at the restaurant alone. And the people at the fast food place, and the gas station. Have some dignity about this.

Don't Negotiate Everything

You have the power to change things by negotiating. And "everything's negotiable" is a wonderful attitude to bring to your negotiations. But it doesn't follow that everything should be negotiated. On the contrary, you shouldn't negotiate most things. If you try, you will surely fail. In the process you'll drive everybody crazy. You'll wear yourself out. You'll never accomplish anything. Your life will go on hold. You have neither the time nor the energy to pursue even a tiny fraction of the negotiating opportunities available to you.

Even if you could, it wouldn't work. People aren't stupid. If you always negotiated, they'd eventually figure it out. They'd know that you always started high, and you always made concessions, and you always nibbled. They'd simply adjust their position to compensate.

Let most things go. If you've got a genuinely close, long-term relationship with somebody—a lover, a friend, a colleague, even a customer—and you really know and trust each other, it may be best not to negotiate most of the time. The wise negotiator is content with the knowledge that while she could negotiate this thing or that, for a variety of reasons she'll regularly elect not to do so.

THOMAS'S TRUISMS

The wise negotiator frequently chooses not to negotiate.

THOMAS'S TRUISMS

The Biggest Lie in Negotiation

A negotiator from Tyson Chicken went to the Vatican and arranged an audience with the Pope. "Your Holiness," he said, "I know you're busy with your many papal duties, so I'll cut to the chase. I'll give you $500 million if you'll change the words of the Lord's Prayer from 'Give us this day our daily bread' to 'Give us this day our daily chicken.' " The Holy Father was aghast. "It's out of the question," he said. "I couldn't change those words for any amount of money. It would be heresy. The language is sacred." Undaunted, the Tyson Chicken negotiator responded, "All right, $700 million, then." The Pope replied with the same litany: "It's inconceivable. It's divine scripture. To change it would be blasphemy." Finally, the intrepid Tyson

Chicken negotiator declared, "O.K., your Holiness, you win. You drive a hard bargain. A billion." "Done," was the Pontiff's answer.

The next day, the Pope called together all of his Cardinals and announced to them, "Gentlemen, I have some good news and some bad news. The good news is that we have received a billion dollars from Tyson Chicken to change the words of the Lord's Prayer from 'daily bread' to 'daily chicken.' The bad news is, now we have to break our deal with Wonder Bread."

I'm not all that worried about you going out and negotiating everything. That problem tends to be self-correcting: You'll be a social pariah until you get over it. What I'm much more concerned about—and the real idea behind Rule 10—is how you deal with the Biggest Lie in Negotiation: "It's my bottom line," and all kindred expressions.

THOMAS'S TRUISMS

"It's my bottom line" is the biggest lie in negotiation.

THOMAS'S TRUISMS

There must be thousands of variations of this phrase: "That matter isn't up for discussion"; "We will not reveal our costs under any circumstances"; "That's the best I can possibly do"; "I insist on it"; "That's it"; "We're at the end of our rope"; "I'm tapped out"; "It's my doorknob price"; "It's the very least I can accept"; "My way or the highway"; "That's my final offer"; "These are non-negotiable demands."

Such declarations are so commonplace, and so consistently untrue, that successful negotiators can't take them seriously. Some negotiators seem to tack one onto virtually every offer they make. They're part of the background noise of negotiation. It is imperative that you train yourself to let such phrases go in one ear and out the other. They are to be afforded no value whatsoever.

THEM: It's my bottom line.

YOU: Uh-huh.

THEM: I'm tapped out. That's my final offer.

YOU: I understand.

THEM: These are non-negotiable demands.

YOU: I hear you, but there must be something we can do.

If the other side can stop you from further negotiating simply by declaring that they've reached their bottom line, they can beat you every time. In negotiation, as in so many other things, talk is cheap.

The Big Secret

I'll let you in on a big secret. How can you be sure the other side is truly at its bottom line? *They don't move anymore!* You krunch, they don't move. You counteroffer, they don't move. You nibble, they don't move. You're patient, they don't move. They just repeat the same position, again and again. If, over an extended period, in spite of considerable pressure from you, there's no more movement from the other side, perhaps they really are at their bottom line. But that's the very last conclusion you can reach. And you can *never* take their word for it.

THOMAS'S TRUISMS

Only when the other side doesn't move anymore can you be sure they're truly at their bottom line.

THOMAS'S TRUISMS

How can you get your counterpart to sit still while you repeatedly test their claimed bottom line? By keeping a positive climate. If the atmosphere becomes adversarial, they'll head for the door long before you can be sure they're genuinely at their bottom line. As long as the climate stays positive, you should have ample opportunity to verify this.

Never Lie About Your Bottom Line

While you must assume that every statement the other side makes about its bottom line is a lie, you must never lie about your own bottom line or how close you are to it. Say nothing about your bottom line. The only time the other side should hear the words "bottom line" or their equivalent from you is in the unfortunate circumstance that you're actually at your bottom line.

THOMAS'S TRUISMS

Never say you're at your bottom line unless you are.

THOMAS'S TRUISMS

If you've lied about your bottom line, what do you say if you actually get there? "This is my bottom line, and I really mean it this time. You have to believe me!" The other side's going to think, "You were obviously lying the other 300 times you said you were at your bottom line. I'll bet you're lying now, too. I'm going to wait and see." You must protect the integrity of that "bottom line" phrase against the unfortunate rainy day when you might actually have to use it.

The simple solution is to make nice, clean offers. Avoid adding imperatives, prefixes or suffixes. The best offers are not embellished at all; they're just "We want X" or "We're offering Y." Don't dress them up with phrases like "We can't take less than X" or "If you can't do Y, then I guess we're done." Otherwise, you back yourself into a corner. If your offer isn't accepted, your only choices are to stonewall, or to move and destroy your credibility. If you give a concession after making such an offer, it proves that you were lying about your bottom line.

Almost as damaging are offers indicating that you're *not* at your bottom line, such as "I'm just about at my bottom line," "We've gone almost as far as we can go," or "The best I can do at this point is X." Such statements merely tell the other side, "Keep negotiating with me. I have more to give." Make clean offers; don't dress them up.

Don't Ask the Other Side for Its Bottom Line

Even when their counterparts haven't falsely declared something their "final position," impatient negotiators will often actually encourage such pronouncements by asking questions like, "So, that's your bottom line?" or "Is that your final offer?" or "Is that your firm position?" What could possibly be gained by such questions? Regardless of the other side's answer, you're going to keep negotiating with them. The question is so confrontational, it almost cries out for a "yes" answer—out of spite. And if they say "yes," you'll have to get them to contradict themselves before the negotiation can go anywhere. Never encourage your counterpart to call anything her bottom line. Always assume her latest position is negotiable, and keep working on it.

When You're Asked for Your Bottom Line

If the other side is so bad-mannered as to actually ask you for your bottom line, or ask you if you're at your bottom line, you're confronted with one of the most dangerous moments in all of negotiation. Such a question must be answered in a very specific and unnatural way. This isn't a good time to ad lib.

The problem is that you can't say yes and you can't say no. If you say "Yes, it's my bottom line," and then you concede further, your credibility is shot. And you certainly can't say it's not your bottom line. Can you imagine that?

THEM: Is this your bottom line?

YOU: No, I've got more. I've got a lot more, in fact.

You must finesse—that is, not answer—the question. The correct response is a two-step process. If the first step works, you don't have to do the second. First, answer the question "Is this your bottom line?" or its equivalent, by calling your offer a good one. You can use whatever adjective you like in place of "good:"

- "It's an extremely competitive proposal."
- "We think our proposals have been very generous."
- "It's a very attractive offer."

If this doesn't suffice (that is, if the other side says something like, "I didn't ask you if it was a good offer. I asked you if it was your bottom line"), you've got to move on to the second step. Propose repackaging your offer: "If it's not to your liking, perhaps we can repackage it in a way you'll find more attractive." Notice the use of the word "repackage." You could also use "restructure." I didn't say "We can be flexible on this," or "We can help you with this." Such statements suggest that I'm prepared to make additional unilateral concessions. "Repackage" strongly implies that a *quid pro quo* will be expected for every further concession; that the shape of the deal can change a bit, but the overall weight must remain the same.

RULE 11

NEVER ACCEPT THE OTHER SIDE'S FIRST OFFER.

How to Make the Other Side Crazy

You list your house for sale with a real estate agent. After reviewing the selling prices of comparable homes, you and she agree on an offering price of $400,000. The next morning she shows up at your front door with a noncontingent $400,000 contract for your house from a qualified buyer, a deposit check, a bottle of champagne, and two glasses. She says, "Can you believe it? I sold your house for the full price in one day! Let's celebrate!"

Do you feel like celebrating? Are you overjoyed? I doubt it. The first thing you're going to think is, "You underlisted my house! We should have asked $425,000, or $450,000. All those years, scrimping and saving! All that equity! Gone! Wasted!"

And it gets even more bizarre. Do you know what would have made you happy? $397,500. That's right. At $397,500, you can still cling to the illusion that you maximized your position. At $400,000, you can't. You know you left money on the table. The only question is how much. And you'll *never* get an answer to that.

Do you want to make the other side crazy? Accept their first offer. Give them less than what they've asked for, and they're happier. What's going on here?

What Happens When You Take Their First Offer

Accepting the other side's opening offer results in a cascade of negotiating misfortunes:

1) **You will almost certainly have left concessions on the table.** Do you really think the other side would reveal its absolute minimum position at the start of the discussions? *Nobody* opens at their bottom line. Even if they try to, there are still concessions to be had: The other side simply hasn't thought of them yet! In sum: Your counterpart would surely have made concessions from her opening position if you had simply negotiated for them.

Nobody likes having their first offer accepted.

2) **Far from being delighted with the deal, the other side is likely to be very unhappy with it.** At the least, they'll have a severe case of PNR (Post-Negotiation Remorse, discussed earlier in Rule 6, Conclude with a nibble). They'll imagine that they could have gotten much more if they had asked for it. They'll think that there must be something wrong with what they got. They may try to renegotiate, or look for ways out, or chisel. They'll gripe and grumble and accuse you of taking advantage.

3) **They'll vow not to let this happen again.** The next time they negotiate with you they'll come to the table with much higher expectations. And they'll be looking to get even.

Let's review. One, you left money on the table. Two, you have a counterpart who's unhappy with you. Three, you've set yourself up as a target for revenge in the next negotiation. All because you accepted their opening offer!

The Hardest Case of All

One opening-offer situation will challenge even the most accomplished negotiator: When the other side opens by offering *exactly what you wanted*—or worse, when their opening is better than what you imagined you'd ever get. Every bone in your body is saying, "Take it! Take it before he changes his mind! Take it before he's hit by lightning and dies on you!"

Don't take it. The fact that their opening is so exceptional only means that your expectations were way too low. You misunderstood the situation. You didn't set your Envelope correctly.

Instead of accepting, krunch. I'll admit, believably krunching an offer that's already outstanding will test your acting skills. Put your hand over your mouth so the other side can't see you smile as you say, "There must be some more flexibility on that. What are we really talking about here?" At the very minimum, equivocate for a few seconds before accepting.

"Sold"

I collect antique telephones. A number of years ago I bought one at a place outside of Washington, D.C., called Thieve's Market. Thieve's Market was an old warehouse full of antiques dealers, all with their own plywood and chicken wire stalls. The place was dark and grungy, but lots of fun. And it was well known that you could negotiate there.

On a Saturday morning—I remember it like it was yesterday—I spotted this gorgeous telephone in one of the stalls. It was oak, from the early 1900s, in beautiful condition. Even the generator worked—the bell rang when you turned the crank. The price was $400, a red-tag "special sale price," supposedly marked down from $750. I wanted that phone. But I didn't want to pay $400 for it. I wanted to haggle. I walked up to the shopkeeper and said, "Sir, I'll give you $200 cash for that phone."

And he said, "Sold."

I was stupefied. What? Sold? What do you mean, sold? We're supposed to haggle first! I should have started lower. I should have offered $150, or $100. Is this thing a reproduction? What's wrong with it? Maybe it isn't even his shop! Maybe he's the cleaning person! If that guy had an ounce of consideration he would have insisted on not a penny less than $300 for the phone. I would have paid it, and I would have been much happier.

I had the phone hooked up and hung it in the kitchen. Every time it rings, it reminds me that I should have started lower.

"Never accept the other side's first offer" goes to the heart of why humans negotiate and what purpose these techniques serve. The dance of negotiation produces more than just a deal. It provides the players with a sense of confidence, accomplishment, and satisfaction. The patient give-and-take, with the slow convergence of positions culminating in an agreement, gives us comfort that we did our best under the circumstances. Don't deprive your counterpart of this comfort by taking her opening offer. You owe her the courtesy of a little haggle.

8

The Nice to Do Rules

START SLOWLY.

Small Talk Is a Big Deal

Americans are usually good for about five seconds of small talk before getting down to business. Our typical flying start is something like, "Hi. Howsit goin'? Well, enough small talk. Are we gonna do this deal, or what?" This John Wayne–style kickoff misses a marvelous opportunity with at least three major benefits:

1. Power. Rule 9, Keep the climate positive, describes how we make more concessions to people we regard as friends. The small-talk period is the time to personalize yourself to the other side. Personalizing is an easy and inexpensive way to improve your bargaining position. The weaker you are, the more important it is to personalize yourself to your counterpart. In fact, if you have essentially no bargaining power—nothing of importance to offer the other side—this may be your only source of influence. Your counterpart may still give you a concession because she likes you. When you're stopped by a police officer, you'd better be schmoozing your brains out. You'd better be schmoozing before the wheels stop turning. Engage that officer in conversation. Apologize, explain, cry, laugh; it's your only hope. If he sees you as just a routine traffic stop, you're going to get a ticket.

This is, shall we say, humble negotiating. Indeed, somewhere around here we leave the realm of bargaining and enter the realm of begging. But when you're desperate you take what you can get.

THOMAS'S TRUISMS

Schmoozing is the last refuge of the weak negotiator.

THOMAS'S TRUISMS

Moreover, this friendship business cuts both ways. If you really like your counterpart—and thus need her approval—it's much more difficult to say "yes, if" instead of just "yes" (or, in the appropriate case, "no"). That's one of the reasons why it's so hard to negotiate with the people close to you.

2. Climate. As described in Rule 9, Keep the climate positive, you start setting the climate during the small-talk period, and climates persist. A positive mood, solidly established early, will tend to linger through the remainder of the negotiation.

3. Homework. While homework (Rule 8) is a neverending process, the small-talk period offers some incomparable intelligence-collecting opportunities. Since these preliminary conversations often center on personal, as opposed to purely business matters, they're an excellent time to identify potential "hot button" issues that are at the heart of Rule 7, Keep looking for creative concessions to trade.

Tips for Getting Started

There is no special formula for kicking off the negotiation, but here are a few ideas:

- Even though it's tempting to get started quickly—particularly with a full agenda or a counterpart who's pressuring you to "get to the point"—try to spend the first few minutes of the meeting making nonsubstantive small talk.
- The best small talk is about the other side. Demonstrate your interest in your counterpart as an individual. Ask what she thinks about some not-too-controversial current event. If you're in her office, look around; ask about the picture on her desk, the award on the wall, where she went to school. Ask about her Optimist Club activities or her son's softball game. If you have a negotiating team, introduce the members. Be as casual, friendly, and relaxed as possible.
- A few people absolutely cannot tolerate small talk. Be sensitive to this possibility and don't force the issue.
- Meet face-to-face whenever possible. Telephone negotiations tend to curb small talk.
- Ask lots of questions, and remember to take turns. Interrupting the other side disrupts the conversational rhythm.
- Be careful that any personal questions are tactful. Avoid gossip, innuendo, and indiscreet opinions.
- Open-ended questions such as "What first brought you to Acme Company?" are a good way to get the chitchat rolling.

- Breaking bread together has important symbolic, emotional, and practical value. Sharing a meal draws the parties closer, encourages a collaborative relationship, and best of all can provide an hour or more of schmoozing time.
- Learn the name of everyone on the other side, and use it often.
- Beware of ethnic, sexual, and political humor. What, you may ask, is left? Lawyer jokes are always a hit. Ask the other side if she heard about the lawyer who walked across the barnyard, stepped in some cow dung, looked down at his shoes and thought he was melting.

RULE 13

SET A COMPLETE AGENDA.

We all want to negotiate smartly and completely, without giving away any more than necessary in order to achieve a win-win result. We don't want to be surprised, and we don't want to leave out anything important. This means we've got to put some borders around the problem before we start bargaining. Otherwise, the negotiation will keep spreading out.

The agenda is simply a list of the matters to be discussed during the negotiation. In most cases everybody already knows—in general terms, at least—what's going to be discussed. When anyone requests a meeting, the first question is "What's it about?" If a proposal has been submitted or there's been any premeeting correspondence, these almost certainly identify the key issues.

But the headline rarely tells the whole story. Both sides usually have additional issues. Whether or not your counterpart reveals her interests in advance, if she's thinking like a negotiator she'll see the meeting as an opportunity to use them as leverage. What's more, topics on either side may raise significant new matters that hadn't been considered. These concerns won't just go away. They must be confronted, understood, and negotiated.

Notice the word "complete" in Rule 13. We use this to remind you to actively solicit your counterpart's agenda before you begin negotiating. In so doing, you'll minimize the danger of issues lurking unseen in the shadows of the negotiation. Less experienced negotiators sometimes think that if they leave some tricky issue unmentioned, the other side may forget about it. Not likely. It's much more probable that they'll remember it just as you were about to propose a final deal, requiring you to renegotiate the entire agreement. Sure, everyone's afraid of what they don't know. But you can't hide from the issues; the other side will bring them up, if not in the current negotiation, then later, in a separate one. And you may not have as much leverage then as you do now.

THOMAS'S TRUISMS

It's better to bring things up now, when you've got some leverage, than later when you don't.

THOMAS'S TRUISMS

If your counterpart is determined to conceal an issue now and "spring" it on you later in the talks, no amount of probing is likely to stop him. Fortunately, there's a foolproof defense in Rule 5, Never settle issues individually. Settle all issues as a package—*only* as a package—at the end. Until the final handshake, you can easily offset any new issue simply by adjusting your stance on other issues.

Setting a complete agenda is usually an agreeable, unperilous task that should take no more than a few minutes.

- Following the small-talk period, move right into agenda-setting. Take out a piece of paper and say something like, "O.K., what have we got here? Let's make a list of the issues we need to consider. We should cover A, B, and C." Identify each issue to be negotiated. As you list each point, write it down.

- If you've only got one or two issues, you certainly don't need a written agenda.
- If the other side has taken the time to prepare an agenda in advance, go ahead and use it—but only as a starting point. Note carefully what they've placed near the top (it may indicate their major issues) and what they've left out.
- If you wish to prepare a draft agenda in advance, that's fine. Just be sure to include lots of white space for issues to be added by your counterpart. I personally find it somewhat presumptuous when I'm presented with a tight, printed agenda from the other side. My reaction is, "What is this, an ambush? Do I have any input on this?"
- The agenda should never contain actual offers or arguments, just the simplest identification of the issues.
- Rule 14, Discuss the small things first, explains why it's desirable—although certainly not mandatory—to put your minor matters toward the top of the list and your bigger issues toward the bottom. If the other side asks you to prioritize, tell them *all* the issues are important.
- Next, plug the other side's issues, if any, into the developing agenda. Probe energetically for their topics. Turn the paper around so that your counterpart can see it, and ask, "Have we left out any of your concerns?" Don't be shy about asking, "What else?" Try to follow the earlier pattern of listing the small issues toward the top, and pushing the bigger ones toward the bottom.
- Be sensitive about the word "agenda." Some people get very defensive when it's used, believing that the agenda discussion is a definitive, make-or-break proposition. "List of the issues," or "menu," or "checklist" may be more relaxing terms.
- Beware of broad preliminary "agreements on principal."

You may be confronted with a request to agree up front to some innocuous-sounding statement such as: "Let's agree in advance that whatever's caused by your actions is your responsibility, and whatever's caused by our actions is our responsibility."

Such statements are dangerous. In reality, they are empty platitudes that may close options for you later in the discussions. Don't be trapped. Be very suspicious of any general statement of principal. Tell the other side, "In general terms, we agree, but each case must be examined individually. We certainly want to be fair and reasonable. Now, what exactly are you proposing?'

Like any negotiated agreement, no agenda is written in stone. As the discussions unfold, new issues will sometimes arise—from inside and outside the negotiation—which must be added. Temper your desire to keep a boundary around the problem by the need to do a complete job. Claiming that something is "not on the agenda" is, at best, a stopgap measure. If the item is meaningful to your counterpart, then it's on the agenda. If you want to negotiate a durable, long-lasting agreement, you might as well face the music and deal with it.

DISCUSS THE SMALL THINGS FIRST.

Investment Equals Flexibility

Once both sides have agreed upon the agenda, it's time to start negotiating. Smaller items should generally be brought up earlier in the negotiation, and major issues deferred until later. Why? Investment. With each passing minute of the negotiation, investment grows.

More and more time, effort, and thought are poured into the talks. But until there's a final deal, all of this heightening investment remains at risk. If we deadlock, it's all lost.

If a big issue is brought up early in the negotiations, the other side can take a tough stance—even deadlock—with little cost. Because she has only a few minutes' investment, she has little to lose. But after an hour or two of negotiating, the situation is very different.

The other side can defeat Rule 14 simply by insisting that major issues be discussed first. If they declare, "I won't talk about anything else until we discuss Issue X"—and they mean it—what are you going to say? "No, I won't talk about it now"? I don't think so. If the other side is adamant, you're going to have to discuss Issue X now. I've seen too many novice negotiators come to the table with an elaborately drafted small-to-big agenda, only to have the whole thing come apart in the first five seconds because the other side refused to follow their script. From that moment on, they're totally thrown and they perform ineffectively.

And investment, of course, cuts both ways. As the negotiation continues, your investment (and, perhaps, your flexibility) goes up too. However, your awareness of the danger may help you resist the temptation to settle things by giving in.

The answer to all your agenda worries is Rule 5, Never settle issues individually. Settle all issues as a package—*only* as a package—at the end. By requiring that regardless of when it's discussed—early, late, or in between—no issue, major or minor, can be firmly agreed to until the end of the negotiation, Rule 5 provides a simple and complete solution to each of these headaches.

Don't confuse Rule 14 with Rule 3. I'll admit that there's a superficial resemblance, but they're vastly different in importance. Rule 3 says that whenever you negotiate a particular issue, your first concession on that issue should be your largest, and each one after it should be radically smaller. Rule 14 says that over the course of the entire negotiation, it would be best if lesser issues were discussed toward the beginning, and larger issues deferred until later. Rule 3 is imperative to successful negotiating and entirely within your control. Rule 14 is, at most, discretionary, and requires the compliance of the other side in order to work.

BE PATIENT.

A woman learned from her doctor that she had only six months to live. Distraught at the news, she asked him for advice. "Marry a lawyer," he said. "It'll be the longest six months of your life."

Patience is the ultimate testing technique in negotiation. It cuts through all the baloney. Patience reveals the soft points in the other side's position. Your counterpart may give you his best deal if you're patient. If you're not, he probably won't.

Why is patience important? Your counterpart needs some time to change her mind. She didn't arrive at her point of view lightly, and she's not going to surrender it lightly, either. Your proposals are different—perhaps greatly different—from what she was expecting. For the first time, she may be facing the idea of getting considerably less than she had planned. She needs some time to sort things out, to separate wishes from reality. She needs to go home, think about it, pound the wall, yell a little, weigh her alternatives, and—perhaps—lower her expectations.

The process is similar to grieving. She needs to "grieve" her way to a lower position. It can't be hurried; she must go through it at her own speed. If you pressure her, you're apt to get simple, blind resistance. Give her the courtesy of a little time to change her mind and come to a satisfying conclusion. The more important the item under discussion, or the greater the distance between the initial positions of the negotiators, the more "grieving" time will be required.

If you're anticipating a big stink from the other side, you may want to consider making a "five o'clock offer." A five o'clock offer is one you make at the end of the business day on the express condition that the other side not give you their response until the next morning. Tell them, "I'm going to make you an offer. I think it's a very fair proposal. But before I do I want you to promise me you won't give me your answer today. Just think about it for now. Sleep on it. I'll call you first thing tomorrow morning for your response." If they agree to this, make your offer and end the conversation promptly. If they don't, make your offer anyway and let the screaming begin.

If they gave you their answer at five o'clock, it would be "Hell, no!" or worse. But overnight, magical things can happen. What was totally objectionable the night before is often far more palatable in the light of the new day. By the next morning, the immediate post-offer rage has dissipated. The other side has had a chance to mull things over, to vent, to lower expectations. You may get a "maybe," a counteroffer, or even a "yes."

The quicker the deal, the more danger you're in. A quick deal may be a good deal or a bad deal—but a slower deal is much more likely to be a good deal. More leisurely negotiations provide the time to recognize and correct errors. Probing questions can be asked and comprehensive answers received. If somebody is going to be seriously ripped off, it's probably going to be in a quick deal. If the other side is pushing you to close quickly, beware. A potential slam-dunk may be afoot.

THOMAS'S TRUISMS

The quicker the deal, the greater the risk.

THOMAS'S TRUISMS

The easy solutions are usually unmistakable to all. Rarely are the most creative, mutually profitable options immediately obvious. It takes some time for them to bubble up to the surface. Slower negotiations allow the parties to relax and get to know each other better.

They can take a break from the discussions and do additional homework, if necessary. They can learn how to benefit each other in more subtle and original ways.

Hundreds of my students have said to me, at one time or another, "I can never be a good negotiator because I can't think quickly on my feet." But you usually don't have to think quickly on your feet when negotiating—and in most cases it would be unwise to do so. Never let the other side hurry you. Insist on enough time to come to a prudent conclusion. The more you're pressured to hurry, the more you should resist.

You have a brilliant mind (the powers of which most of us never use beyond a small fraction) and you have wonderful instincts. Give them time to work. Your mind continues to analyze problems—often in mysterious, nonlinear ways—while you do other tasks and even while you sleep. You'll be a better negotiator if you get into the habit of "sleeping on it"—letting things sit for a day or two—whenever possible.

Negotiation isn't a race. There are no extra points for being fast. If you're not prepared to discuss an issue, state a position, or make a concession, then don't. Give yourself time to think. If you're surprised, take a break. If the other side proposes a new alternative or, more challengingly, a bunch of new alternatives, take the time to patiently calculate the true, long-term cost and value of each. Never just respond "off the cuff."

If you feel you need an excuse to buy some time, call a restroom or a meal break. Make a telephone call for additional information. If you have a team, call a caucus. Better yet, don't use any excuse at all. I've always found it enormously classy for a negotiator to have the self-confidence and discipline to just sit there, in silence, and run the numbers or otherwise evaluate the proposal that was just made. "That's an interesting proposal. Give me a few minutes to cost it out. Let's see what we have." Remember, your silence is a krunch.

USE/BEWARE THE POWER OF LEGITIMACY.

The Three "Up There" Rules

Rules 16 (legitimacy), 17 (limited authority), and 18 (good guy–bad guy) could be called, collectively, the Up There Rules. Each is a variation on the same theme: Something "up there" is constraining my negotiating latitude "down here."

- Legitimacy: "Hey, I'd love to do it, but I can't—it's policy."
- Limited authority: "Hey, I'd love to do it, but I can't—the boss won't authorize it. However, I can do X, Y, and Z."
- Good guy–bad guy: "Hey, I'd love to do it, but I can't—the boss won't authorize it. And you don't want me to ask her about it again. I had to fight with her for two hours this morning just to get this. I've never heard such language!"

In each case, I, the negotiator, am merely an innocent pawn commanded by forces far greater than myself.

There's considerable overlap between these three Rules. Since they all work basically the same way, it's not usually necessary to distinguish between them. However, if you're curious about exactly which of the three applies in a particular situation, the important questions are: Is it alive, and is it upset? In legitimacy, the thing "up there" is neither—it's inanimate, like "policy" or "the official price." In limited authority, the thing "up there" is alive—a boss whose approval is required to deviate from the deal I'm offering. In good guy–bad guy, the thing "up there" is both alive *and* upset with the deal I'm offering.

The Cloak of Legitimacy

Legitimacy is the tendency of something that seems authoritative or official to be accepted unquestioningly by the other side. By cloaking your position in legitimacy you discourage your counterpart from negotiating it. The more official it looks, the less subject to being negotiated it appears to be. Put differently, the greater the perceived legitimacy of something, the lower its perceived negotiability. If I can better legitimize my position on an issue, I can make it appear less negotiable—and maybe not negotiable at all.

Legitimacy is a pretty minor principle in the larger world of negotiation. Still, in the right circumstances it can be a useful tool. And it must always be defended against. There are two broad categories of legitimacy: presentation and verbal. Verbal legitimacy is indisputably the more influential.

Presentation Legitimacy

The more formal and imposing the presentation, the less inclined people are to negotiate the content. Printed is more legitimate than handwritten. Handwritten is more legitimate than verbal. Glossy is more legitimate than flat. Color is more legitimate than black and white. Graphics are more legitimate than text. Online is more legitimate than offline. In general, the more official-looking the document, the less negotiable it seems to be. People look at all that tiny print and their eyes glaze over.

Prepare and use your own forms whenever possible. With the right people in the right circumstances, presentation legitimacy can work wonders. It's especially effective with less experienced negotiators. When you give a pro your printed form, she'll probably (and correctly) just take out her pen and start marking it up—or offer you *her* printed form. Beware of the subtly hypnotic effect of the other side's elegant, polished documents. Read closely and critically. Always be ready to pull out your pen and make changes.

Verbal Legitimacy

Certain phrases have tremendous legitimacy. We respond to them without thinking. By far the most compelling of these expressions—the granddaddy of them all—is "Let's split the difference." That phrase touches something in our DNA. Ever since we were kids, whenever somebody said, "Let's split the difference," we responded dumbly, "Well, O.K." It's the way we're programmed. "Let's split the difference" is the Universal Settlement Principle, a sort of Geneva Convention under which we can declare an honorable negotiating truce.

"Let's split the difference" is based on Western concepts of fairness. It assumes there's something appropriate about each party moving roughly the same amount to reach closure—regardless of the merits of their positions, where they opened, or what concessions they made thereafter. Only in the most special circumstances should you ever offer to split the difference. The party making that offer almost always gives more than half. Never accept any offer to split the difference, either, if a significant distance between the parties' positions remains. It's a cheesy shortcut for the real negotiating you still have to do. Respond with, "I can't afford to." *

If the negotiation's essentially finished but for a tiny gap separating the parties' positions and neither side appears willing to move, it's O.K. to use "split the difference" as a comfortable, deal-closing mechanism. Even then, you should try to get the other side to make

---

* Be sure to check out the look on the other side's face when you say this. They'll be stunned. They'll respond, "What's the matter with you? You're supposed to say, 'Well, O.K.' You're not from around here, are you?" You'll almost certainly wind up with more than half. If you really want to astonish them, after saying, "I can't afford to split the difference," add, "but I'll come halfway to where you are *now*."

the offer. Set it up for them: "Hey, I'm tired, you're tired, we've been working on this thing all day. I'm out of ideas. What would be a fair [we're suckers for anything "fair"] way to wrap this up?" They'll respond, "Well, we could split the difference." And you'll reply, "I can't afford to, but . . ."

Here are a few more phrases from our legitimacy scrapbook:

- Let's round it off to . . . [The more zeros a number ends in, the more legitimacy.]
- It's the standard form/customary wording.
- Everybody signs it.
- It's already in the computer/It won't go into the computer like that.
- It's industry standard.
- The Legal/Tax/Finance/Contracts people require it.
- It's already been approved.
- Fair's fair.
- It's only reasonable.
- It's always done this way.
- That's the procedure/policy.
- It's in the regulations.
- It's an insurance thing.
- All the kids are doing it.

You can use the legitimacy of these and thousands of similar phrases as a noncontroversial way to decline the other side's request that you change your position. As with presentation legitimacy, since veterans are likely to be more skeptical, the effectiveness of such phrases will be greater with less-accomplished negotiators. And, of course, you should always challenge such expressions when they're used against you.

KEEP YOUR AUTHORITY LIMITED.
TRY TO NEGOTIATE AGAINST PEOPLE WITH
HIGHER AUTHORITY.

Limited Authority Is Your Friend

Authority is the power to commit to an agreement. If your authority is limited, there are constraints on what you can agree to. The more severe the constraints, the more limited your authority. If you have full authority, you can agree to pretty much anything. Negotiators with more authority make more concessions than negotiators with less. Some of negotiation's most famous last words are: "Do your best, you have full authority." If you want to reduce your concessions, it's smart to limit your authority.

**The more authority you have,
the more concessions you'll make.**

Limited authority is a wonderful source of bargaining strength. It allows you to say "no" with warmth and grace: "I'd love to lower the price to X. I'd do it in a heartbeat if I could. But headquarters won't let me." Limited authority makes it much harder for the other side to get upset with you. It's not your fault, after all. Someone else is making the decision.

The ideal outcome is that your counterpart will drop his request because he's too impatient to wait for an exception to be approved, or because he thinks approval is unlikely. If that doesn't happen, you'll check with your higher authority and then tell your counterpart the answer is "yes, if" (or still "no"). Either way, limited authority will keep you from giving away more than you should.

You must have some authority—otherwise, you're not a negotiator, you're a messenger. When the other side asks, "Do you have the authority to make a deal?" you should be able to truthfully answer, "Yes." Unspoken, and also true, should be the observation, ". . . within very narrow limits that you haven't got a snowball's chance of hitting." That part you keep to yourself.

Authority and Americans

Americans don't like this limited-authority business one bit. It sticks in our craw. John Wayne never had to call back to the home office. "What's the matter," we say, "don't you trust me? Am I some kind of errand boy?" Individual freedom is one of our cornerstone values. We're self-reliant, strong-willed, and ruggedly independent. When we negotiate, we like to have *lots* of authority. That's one of the reasons why our negotiating counterparts like us so much.

Negotiating for Yourself

Of all the people you could have negotiating on your behalf, you're the absolute worst choice. You're emotionally involved. You care too much. But most importantly, *you have full authority*. It's just too easy for you to make quick, impulsive decisions. That's why agents almost always negotiate better deals than their principals. When you're out there by yourself, you're an accident waiting to happen.

If you must negotiate for yourself, be especially careful. Set and adhere strictly to an Envelope. Slow down. Sleep on it. A bachelor friend of mine insists that his "wife" approve all of his deals before he agrees to them. I can't support the ethics of his approach, but it keeps him out of trouble.

Try to Offer a Viable Alternative

Using limited authority simply to say "no" ("I can't approve that") will often just goad your counterpart into seeking someone who can say "yes": "Then let me talk with somebody who can." Sometimes this will be your competitor, but usually it will be your boss. Bypassing the other negotiator and bargaining instead with his boss is called an "end run." As we'll explain later in this chapter, if the other side makes a successful end run to your boss, you're in trouble.

To reduce the danger of an end run, when you claim limited authority it's smart to offer the other side an option that's within your authority: "I'd love to do W, but I can't. However, I can do X, Y, and Z." By presenting an alternative that can be accepted without higher approval, you give your counterpart three choices: (1) She can deadlock (and waste all of her invested effort); (2) she can try to go over your head (and who knows what will happen then); or (3) she can take the sure thing you've offered (not everything she wants, but a certainty). She'll tend to take the path of least resistance: the sure thing.

Try to Negotiate With the Big Kahuna

When the famous bank robber "Slick Willie" Sutton was asked why he robbed banks, he replied simply, "Because that's where the money is." Why do you always want to negotiate with the top dog? Because that's where the concessions are. Negotiate with the highest-authority person you can get access to. The higher you go, the more concessions the other side will make.

Of course, it's much more comfortable to bargain with a flunky than a higher-up. Everyone naturally feels a little timid about dealing with more senior people. "Who am I," we ask, "to be negotiating with somebody at that level?" The answer is, we're negotiators who want to be successful. The more senior our counterpart is, compared to us, the better.

The Japanese use a very effective limited-authority gambit. In Japan, your initial meeting is usually with a low-level functionary. Each successive meeting is with a higher-level person, until you finally meet with the senior person. Conventional wisdom says you should let the underlings save face by giving each of them a concession. But the problem with this strategy is, you don't know how long the flunky-procession is going to continue. By the time you finally get to the top person, your goodie bag may be empty. Worse, the big hitter will probably want more face-saving concessions than anyone else (to justify his big-hitter status, of course). Worse still, this "top person" may surprise you with an even-higher person!

The solution to this dilemma is to try to determine, early in the game, who the real decision-makers are. Inquire firmly, and seek an unequivocal answer. Try to work your way to the top as soon as possible. Above all, don't waste your precious concessions on minor functionaries who have nothing to give in return.

Unless you simply have no alternative, don't negotiate with anyone who lacks authority, or whose authority is ambiguous. A very useful question to ask your counterpart during the small-talk period is something along the lines of, "Will anyone else need to sign off on what we agree to?" If the answer is "yes," you may be negotiating with the wrong person. If the approval of a boss or a committee is required, try to meet with them yourself. If this isn't possible, inquire as to how much influence your counterpart has. Ask him, "Do they usually go with your recommendations?" Put together an agreement subject only to the missing approval, and get your counterpart's firm commitment to make a glowing recommendation of the deal.

Keep Your Bosses Out of It

If you don't control the other side's access to your higher-ups, and if your higher-ups won't stay out of the negotiation, limited authority won't work. Lock them up, cut the phone lines; don't let your bosses negotiate. Bosses give away the ranch. When there's negotiating going on, you want to be the rancher, not the ranchee. The ideal situation is to be a negotiator with limited authority, supported by a boss who refuses to get involved in the negotiation.

THOMAS'S TRUISMS

Bosses give away the ranch.

THOMAS'S TRUISMS

The head of an organization is the worst person to negotiate for it. Higher-ups can't possibly know the details of the issues and players as well as their subordinates do. They have 50 other things on their plate. They aren't going to hang in there and negotiate patiently and creatively, making smaller concessions, trading everything, krunching, and nibbling at the end. They're much more likely to say, "Oh, the heck with it. Let's just do it. Where do I sign? I've got a meeting in 15 minutes and I've gotta get out of here. Will you call me a cab?"

Your counterpart almost certainly wants to negotiate with your boss. She's no fool. It's exactly the right thing for her to do. He's got a bigger bucket than you. It doesn't mean that you should let her do it. Even inviting your boss to meet your counterpart can be a dangerous move. Once they've gotten to know each other, if you take a tough position on an issue or claim limited authority, she may just get on the phone and call her new friend—your boss. It's hard to keep 'em down on the farm after they've seen Paree!

Unfortunately, from a marketing and a selling perspective, it's very desirable to get the boss involved with the customer. It helps dramatize how much you value the customer, her company, and her business. But from a negotiating perspective, it's the kiss of death. It opens up a vein for the other side, and they'll drink you dry. Go ahead and use the boss for show-the-flag marketing and sales purposes. But when the negotiations start, pen him up. If the other side attempts an end run, have the boss claim some legitimacy excuse: "You know I'd like to get involved, but I can't. It's policy. I've got to stay out of it. Sally's our negotiator. She's updating me every ten minutes on how things are going. Maybe when it's over we can all get together for lunch."

Some bosses have a very difficult time letting go. If you have one of these, a little flattery may help. Explain to your boss about limited authority; explain how negotiating is really unsuited to high-power people and really should be left to lower-down folks. Remind him how important he is, and how much power he has. Maybe he'll get the idea: "You're right. I am powerful. I'm very powerful. I may be too powerful to negotiate. I should leave it to you." It could happen.

Managing Limited Authority

This section is especially for bosses. Send your underlings out into the negotiating fray. You stay out of it. Sure, the lower-downs will deadlock a little more, but they won't make serious mistakes. They can't: They haven't got the authority! Let them fight and scratch and claw and try their best to close the deal within the limits of their authority. If they succeed, wonderful. If they don't, they'll come back to you for another helping of authority. They'll stand in front of you with their little authority buckets outstretched and say, "More, please." If you decide to give them another little helping, they'll go back out and fight and scratch and claw some more. Meanwhile, the other side's expectations will continue to drop. This authority dol-ing-out process tends to insure that: (1) deals close near the mini-mum level the other side will accept; (2) creative options, if any, have a chance to reveal themselves; and (3) no serious, haste-provoked errors are made by either side. At the very least, it slows down the whole process a little, which is almost always a good idea.

There's nothing that says your negotiator must know your side's true bottom line. Never lie to your negotiator (or anyone else, for that matter) about your bottom line, but finesse the question along the lines we describe in Rule 10. Even when your negotiator knows your true bottom line, it may be wise to set sub-limits, thresholds she cannot exceed without further consultation.

One related point deserves a brief mention. If you step in and close the deal at the last minute, you rob your subordinate of the satisfaction of seeing the negotiation through to the end. Without realizing it, you're disparaging him in front of the other side. You lower his confidence and self-esteem. This can be a real heartbreaker, particularly if you give away concessions that you told him—and he worked hard—to keep. The next time you try to get the underling pumped up to go out there and negotiate conscientiously, he may say to himself, "Why? The boss is just going to jump in at the last second and give it away again. What's the point?" It's difficult enough to motivate people to negotiate without the added challenge of bosses' last-second involvement. Flatter your people, and make your life easier: Stay out of it.

Making an End Run

If the other side is smart and aggressive, they'll sometimes try to do an end run over your head to your boss. Should you use the same tactic with your counterparts? I wouldn't. End runs are extraordinarily risky. Your counterpart may take it as a personal insult. Her boss may see it as sleazy and desperate. Even if it succeeds once, the other side may be so outraged by the circumvention that the relationship will be irreparably harmed.

But if the other side simply won't move, or they're a complete pain the neck, an end run may be the only solution. If you're absolutely sure you have no alternative, attempt to do the end run with the other side's consent. Ask your counterpart to invite her boss to the next meeting. Or set up an "annual business review" with the other side, at which her boss is requested to present his views on the relationship. If your counterpart is clever, she either won't permit these sanctioned end runs or she'll insist that you also bring your boss. The old routine of waiting until your counterpart is out of town (during summer vacation is classic), and then having an "emergency" that requires an immediate meeting with a decision-maker may work—once—but it's sure to make the other side suspicious.

RULE 18

CONSIDER USING GOOD GUY–BAD GUY.

How Good Guy–Bad Guy Works

Good guy–bad guy, the last of the three "Up There" Rules, is simply a variation on the old shill routine. Two words make good guy–bad guy work: *by comparison*.

In the prototypical good guy–bad guy scenario, you face a team composed of a bad guy and one or more good guys. The bad guy (usually a higher-up) takes a much tougher stand than his associate (the good guy, usually the lead negotiator, your counterpart). The bad guy scares you with threats of disaster: reduced or lost business, legal disputes, contract cancellations, and the like. He may accuse you of being unreasonable, and speak glowingly of your competition. He is often abrasive, sometimes even rude. The good guy disagrees with him, and tries to placate him. Sometimes the good guy and bad guy stage a fight. Then the bad guy leaves.

You're now alone with the good guy, who apologizes for the bad guy's conduct and expresses regret at all the horrible things that the bad guy says are going to happen. You and the good guy commiserate. Suddenly, the good guy has an idea. He's going to help you out. He describes a possible compromise, adding that the bad guy "owes him one" and that, if you'll just be a little flexible, he'll "go to bat for you" and "just may be able to pull this one out." However, to make the deal work he "really needs your help" in the form of some hefty concessions.

The good guy's deal, while objectively not particularly attractive, is fabulous by comparison to the misfortune and catastrophe offered by the bad guy. You hurry to accept it before the bad guy comes back.

You've just taken part in a bit of amateur theater. The good guy and bad guy set the whole thing up in advance.

Pros and Cons

On the plus side, good guy–bad guy is clearly a win-win negotiating technique. By letting your boss play the heavy, you preserve your relationship with your counterpart. Good guy–bad guy can strengthen rapport with your counterpart; you're teammates, struggling against a common "enemy." The other side may even feel somewhat indebted after you have "done battle" for them. Good guy–bad guy also tends to quash end runs to your higher-ups. If the other side believes that your boss will offer a worse deal than you, they're not likely to head upstairs.

The principal drawback to good guy–bad guy is that it's, well, tacky. Many organizations rightly consider good guy–bad guy inappropriate. They feel that their negotiators should accept full ownership and responsibility for all of the organization's bargaining positions, and not try to distance themselves or shift the blame to someone else. They believe that from the other side's perspective, the organization should always appear totally unified. The implied disloyalty inherent in good guy–bad guy may actually worry the other side: "Who are you working for, anyway?" they may wonder. "Are you some kind of a free agent?"

Another drawback to good guy–bad guy is ethical: If the bad guy doesn't actually endorse the position you say he does, you're lying. If the other side finds out that your boss really loved the deal that you swore he hated, your credibility will take a major hit.

The Two Main Variations: "Live" or Absent Bad Guy

If you choose to use good guy–bad guy, you can have the bad guy physically present at the discussions, or, better, you can simply refer to an absent bad guy. Having a "live" bad guy is full of hazards, mostly those associated with teams and too much authority. A live bad guy automatically means a team, and as pointed out in Rule 20, Keep your team small and under control, teams are inherently risky. The bad guy may really get into the role, abusing your counterpart far more than you had planned. He may ruin the climate you worked so hard to establish. Once unleashed, a bad guy with a dramatic flair can be hard to rein in. Also, since the bad guy is often a higher-up, having him physically present violates the no-bosses provisions of Rule 17.

All of this can be avoided simply by referring to an absent bad guy. That way, you can turn the bad guy on and off when you wish and make him as fearsome or accommodating as circumstances require: "I understand how you feel about that, but I know Sam. He's borderline with the deal right now. He could go either way. If I suggest it to him, he might call the whole thing off. I'd rather not take that chance. Just between us, I'd drop it."

Countermeasures

The best countermeasure to good guy–bad guy is simply to recognize what's going on. Whenever you see a disagreement on the other side of the negotiation, suspect good guy–bad guy. Once you realize that the "antagonist" is merely playing a part, good guy–bad guy doesn't work anymore. Ask yourself: Is the other side's organization really so undisciplined that they'd have a fight and let me watch? In most cases the answer is going to be "no." If they're fighting in full view, it's almost certainly for you to see.

When you recognize good guy–bad guy, it's probably best not to confront the other side with it ("Will you please stop with the good guy–bad guy stuff?"). Instead, just smile and carry on.

TRY TO HAVE THE OTHER SIDE
MAKE THE FIRST OFFER.

NEGOTIATOR TO MAGICIAN: Make me an offer.
MAGICIAN TO NEGOTIATOR: Presto! [waves wand] You're an offer.

He Who Speaks First . . .

If you stopped somebody on the street and asked him to tell you the first negotiating principle that came to mind, chances are it would be: "Get the other person to offer first." This dictum has been passed from generation to generation with a knowing wink; it's how "real" bargaining is done. Through constant retelling, a minor principle has achieved undeservedly huge importance. A popular variation of

this concept is: "He who speak first, loses." If only it were true. Negotiating would be so much simpler if "victory" always went to
whichever player outwaited the other.

Speaking order doesn't determine the outcome of a negotiation.
How assertively you open is far, far more important than whether
you open first or not.

THOMAS'S TRUISMS

It's where you open, not when, that matters.

THOMAS'S TRUISMS

Long before most negotiations begin, it's eminently clear who's
supposed to make the first offer. The relationship between the
parties, or the nature of the issue, usually predetermine who's going to open. To go contrary to that expectation would be so pecu-
liar it could easily derail the discussions before they even begin.
Moms generally don't ask, "So, Tommy, what are your ideas about
tonight's bedtime?" Can you imagine a buyer's reaction if a salesperson asked, "What would you be willing to pay for an item like
this?"

It's Best If They Open

When it's not already clear who's expected to open, it's generally
desirable to have the other side make the first offer on an issue. Getting them to open first gives you two things: last peek, and first
krunch.

"Last peek" simply means that when the other side opens first,
you're given the advantage of hearing and evaluating their starting
position before you have to commit to yours. Last peek is helpful because you can never really know where the other side is going to

open. Homework is valuable in this regard, but it's not even close to foolproof. The other side will routinely amaze you with its openings, confounding your most informed predictions. They may open a lot closer to your target than you were expecting. They may open better than your target. They may even open better than your planned opening!

If the other side opens first, you can adjust. You can modify your opening offer—your whole Envelope, if necessary—to take into account what their opening has revealed to you of their expectations. If they open very assertively, you may wish to open somewhat more assertively yourself. This will allow you to concede as liberally as they do on your way to an agreement.

None of this is possible if you open first. Your opening may be at the other side's target, or worse, at their planned opening. If your counterpart is not much of a negotiator, she'll say, "You've got a deal" (and you'll know you've been hosed). If she's a pro, your opening will reveal to her that her expectations were way too low, and she'll quickly redraw her Envelope. Either way, you'll lose.

"First krunch" is even more important than last peek. As soon as their offer ("We want X") is on the table, you're perfectly teed up to do one thing: krunch ("That's not going to work for us. What else can you do?"). If they make a concession in response to your krunch, krunch again ("We appreciate that. We're making progress. What more can you do?"). Keep krunching until it stops working, and then—only then—make your first offer.

Give It Two Tries

The simplest technique for getting the other side to open first is to just keep probing: "What did you have in mind on this?" "Tell me what you were looking for here." "Before I explain our position, why don't you tell me what you're proposing to do?" "What's your number?" Sometimes a brief period of silence will trigger an offer. If they refuse to open, simply change the subject to another issue.

Here's the big problem with Rule 19. Your counterpart's read the same book. If she's leafed through even the simplest primer on negotiation, she knows she's supposed to try to get you to open first. So there you are, each scheming to maneuver the other into making the opening offer, like some sort of old Alphonse and Gaston— routine.* ("After you, Alphonse." "No, after *you,* Gaston"). Meanwhile, your climate is heading south. You're impressing each other only with how crafty you are.

My suggestion is to give it two tries. If they still refuse to open after two attempts by you to get them to do so, give up and put an offer on the table. *Somebody's* got to open. Remember, it's not that big a deal. Preserving your climate is much more important than who opens first.

Interestingly, it's not always desirable to get the other side to open first. If you have reason to believe that there's a huge disparity in the parties' expectations—you're thinking 10 and they're thinking 100, for example—it makes a lot of sense for you to open first. Your opening shifts the whole paradigm of the talks in your direction. This is called a "preemptive" opening. Your offer may moderate the other side's opening, and will act as a subtle "baseline" against which later offers are judged.

Similarly, if you have a standard contract or form with clauses that are particularly significant to you, it may be wise to go ahead and make the opening offer using your contract. By getting your form on the table first, you make it the latticework for the negotiated agreement. If the other side objects to any of its provisions, they have to negotiate them with you, one by one.

---

* Famous comic strip characters in the first half of the twentieth century, created by Frederick Burr Opper.

KEEP YOUR TEAM SMALL AND UNDER CONTROL.

Why Are You Kicking Me?

A couple of years ago I negotiated the lease of an aircraft to a Pacific Rim carrier. I represented the aircraft's owner. There were six of us in all, three on each side. I had a couple of technical specialists with me, as did the negotiator for the airline. We were very close to agreement, and I had just presented a deal-wrapping "package." My counterpart nibbled for a few minor items—extra tires, copies of the maintenance manuals, a few extra slots in the manufacturer's training program for mechanics, and some other items. Trivia, really (as nibbles rightly should be), and all quite acceptable. I could have comfortably just said "fine" to all of them and the deal would have been great. But that's not the way it's done. As you know by now, nibbles shouldn't just be given away; they should be traded for some *quid pro quo* nibbles.

One of the members of the airline's team was its director of maintenance operations. It was obvious that this man had had more than his fill of bargaining. He just wanted his airplane. As I got ready to start trading nibbles, he spoke for the first time in a full day of negotiating. And he wasn't talking to me; he was talking to his own team leader. "I don't know what we're gonna do with those extra wheels," he said. "We don't have any place to store 'em. And we can just copy the manuals as we need them. And we won't be hiring those mechanics for at least eighteen months. We can hire 'em already certified." He went on like this, ticking off each of his colleague's nibbles, one by one.

His team leader stared at the table, while I encouraged my newfound sidekick to continue. Suddenly he stopped, looked at his team leader, and said, "Why are you kicking me?"

I love teams—when they're on the other side.

Disadvantages

Whenever multiple players make up either side of a negotiation, there's a team. With each additional person added to a negotiating team, the risk of a screw-up increases. More players raise the overall level of confusion. People may talk out of turn. Differences of opinion among team members may be revealed to the other side (look for the person who says "I" more than "we"). Sensitive information may inadvertently be disclosed.

THOMAS'S TRUISMS

Teams are inherently dangerous, and the bigger the team, the greater the risk.

THOMAS'S TRUISMS

My general disapproval of negotiating teams does not apply to small, established negotiating teams that have worked together successfully for years. Through practice and experience such teams often speak with one voice, negotiating more as a single entity than as individuals. The teams to which this Rule is addressed are the short-lived *ad hoc* groups, large and small, which every organization cobbles together from time to time to negotiate on its behalf.

Advantages

Teams aren't all bad, and in some cases may be absolutely necessary. There's no way you can be an authority on everything; specialists on your team can provide the necessary technical expertise that you lack. Teams are often more creative than individual negotiators, as the different technical backgrounds of the members can mean a wealth of approaches. In difficult, protracted negotiations, it's nice to be able to delegate a few things. The first responsibility I like to pass off is note-taking; the second is number-crunching. Teams reduce the likelihood of mistakes and serious errors in judgment— there's somebody on your side to point out the stupidity of what you're about to do. If you're by yourself, you just do it (and hear about it later). In international negotiations, teams are almost a necessity.*

Selecting the Team

In general, *the smaller the team, the better.* Never include members who aren't needed. Also, beware the team member with the need to talk. Be especially careful in choosing your technical folks. The leading guru on a particular subject can be an especially dangerous team member. Such individuals are used to having their opinions solicited and respected, and they don't appreciate being managed—particularly being asked to be silent—by nonspecialists. They are especially prone to talking out of turn and taking stances at odds with the team position. Consider having purely technical people available for consultation but not included on the team. Remember, if you need additional information during the negotiation, you can always caucus and make some phone calls.

THOMAS'S TRUISMS

Being outnumbered means you're in a
target-rich environment.

THOMAS'S TRUISMS

* See Chapter 11, International Negotiating.

If the other side is foolish enough to bring a large, undisciplined team to negotiate, you're truly fortunate. Don't think of it as being outnumbered, think of it as being in a target-rich environment. Someone on the other side is the weakest link, and sooner or later he'll reveal himself by talking out of turn. Encourage him, "Jack, we haven't heard from you in a while. What do you think?" If he's in the room, he's fair game.

The Japanese are notorious for having huge negotiating teams. On a number of occasions I've had the honor of negotiating opposite one of these vast Japanese teams. More than once it's been me and a translator on one side and 20 Japanese on the other. The Japanese will be sitting three rows deep. They'll all be dressed alike—blue suit, white shirt, and penny loafers. They'll all be smoking cigarettes. And when the team leader says something, they'll all nod at the same time—all 20 of them. I don't care how good a negotiator you are, when you see 20 adults nodding simultaneously, you can't help but think, "Maybe they're right. That many people can't all be wrong at once. It's got to be me."

In spite of their size, Japanese teams are rigorously disciplined. The Japanese have a saying, "The nail that sticks its head up gets hammered down." It would be unthinkable for a member of a Japanese team to talk out of turn. In America, we're all free spirits. We say what we want, when we want to. If your negotiating team members are Japanese, make your team as large as you want. If they're Americans, I'd keep it *real* small.

Managing the Team

Having chosen the smallest possible team, your next job is to keep it under control. It is vital that the team speak with one voice. The best way to do this is to have a single spokesperson, with everybody else remaining quiet. This may seem a bit stilted and artificial at first, but it's the only safe way to conduct team negotiations. Once you try it, you'll never go back to the anybody-talks-whenever-they-want style. Having a single spokesperson avoids the problems of unauthorized or dissenting statements, too-talkative team members, and weaker members being victimized by the other side. The spokesperson usually is, but needn't be, the team leader.

Try to avoid changing spokespersons. Your spokesperson's rapport with his opposite number is quite valuable, and if you switch spokespersons you may have to develop this affinity all over again. However, don't hesitate to switch if there's a personality conflict between the two spokespersons.

Consider assigning roles to members, including note-taking and number-crunching. Continually emphasize the importance of security. Brief your team members on your overall game plan, but limit the team's access to information. Everyone on your team doesn't have to know everything.

Caucuses

If only the spokesperson can talk, how, you may ask, can anybody but the spokesperson contribute an idea? And what's the point of having a team? The answer is that anybody on the team can call a caucus, whenever they want. Calling a caucus is the sole exception to the one-spokesperson rule.

Caucuses—during which the negotiating teams separate and meet privately—are wonderful things. They allow both sides to speak freely with their people, to consider new ideas, new positions, and possible concessions. They clear the air. They let everybody relax. Much of the movement in team negotiations is generated in caucuses. Be sure to caucus often, for short periods. I don't think I've ever seen a team caucus too much.

The caucus is the solution to the dangers of negotiating teams.

A natural first reaction to the idea of caucusing is that it might look antagonistic to the other side. In practice, however, caucuses come across as extremely polished and professional. They demonstrate good team organization and discipline. Urge your team members to call a caucus whenever they think it appropriate. They'll hesitate to do so unless you specifically encourage them. The exact language of the call is unimportant. "We need to talk privately for a minute" or "Let's take a break" are fine.

When a team member calls a caucus, try to honor their request promptly. Don't keep them waiting while you go on negotiating. If you do, they may talk out of turn. Likewise, if somebody has called a caucus that you didn't feel was necessary, never criticize them for it. Such criticism will have a chilling effect on the team's willingness to call caucuses thereafter. And that means people talking out of turn.

Team members shouldn't signal between themselves. Signals are distracting, easily overlooked by your people, and easily intercepted by the other side. Notes and whispering are also too distracting. Plus, notes create a security problem. They can't just be tossed in the trash. If a message is important enough for you to signal it, whisper it, or write it, it's more than important enough to caucus about it.

When you call a caucus, pull all of your people out. Don't leave anyone behind. The reason is that as soon as your last person leaves, the other team will immediately caucus. In fact, it's perfectly O.K. to call a caucus not because you have anything to discuss with your team, but in order to make the other side caucus.

The calling of a caucus tends to underline whatever statement preceded it. It's normal to caucus upon receiving an offer. One side will say, "We propose X," and the other side will respond, "We appreciate your offer. We'll discuss it and get right back to you." At that point the team heads out to the hall. In fact, if you didn't caucus, it would signal that the offer wasn't worthy of consideration. More discretion may be called for in other circumstances. When one side is making a seemingly innocuous statement and someone on the other side suddenly says, "Oh! Caucus! Caucus!" they've just given away valuable information. Unless the reason is obvious to all (like an offer), it may be wise to let a minute or two pass before calling the caucus.

TRY TO HAVE THE OTHER SIDE TRAVEL TO YOU.

Rule 21 is another one of those minor negotiating principles (like Rule 19: Try to have the other side make the first offer) that, in the process of being passed down through the years, has gained significance it just doesn't deserve. The popular rendition of the concept—"Always negotiate on your own turf"—is wildly overstated.

Truth is, the locale of the negotiation just doesn't have much effect on the outcome. Rule 21 operates in very limited circumstances, and when it does, it is the most subtle of influences. In the same way that it often determines who makes the first offer, the relationship between the negotiators commonly decides the locale of the negotiation. Salespeople, for example, almost always travel to meet buyers.

Travel and Investment

If only one of two negotiators must travel to the negotiation, the traveling negotiator may tend to be slightly more flexible than the nontraveling one. The reason: investment. Because of the additional resources (time, effort, and expense) invested by the traveling negotiator in making the trip, he feels additional pressure to show a successful result. The amount of this additional pressure is a function of resources expended: time, distance, and difficulty.

When my counterpart travels in from Cleveland to negotiate with me in Washington, he (and his organization) make a significant investment. He's got to pack, say goodbye to his family, taxi to the airport, fly, taxi to the hotel, and unpack. After the meeting, he's got to do it all again, in reverse. The whole time he's gone, his regular work is piling up. It's two feet deep by the time he gets back.

Travel also brings discomfort, inefficiency, and loneliness. When he's on the road, all of my counterpart's personal routines are disrupted. He's sleeping in a strange bed, eating strange food, showering in a strange bathroom. He misses his wife and kids. If he needs anything typed or copied, he's got to ask a favor. All of his communications are by telephone or computer—when he can be reached. He's using somebody else's conference room. Most of his documents are elsewhere.

Is he going to go through all of this and end up back in Cleveland without a deal in his briefcase? Maybe. But I'd venture it's a lot less likely than if he hadn't come to Washington. Having expended the resources to get here (and having still more to expend getting back), he may find himself somewhat more pliable than he would have been otherwise. He took the trip to close a deal, not to impasse.

As long as you're aware that a long transit may incline you toward extra flexibility—and may even cause you to "chase" a deal that is no longer in your best interest—you're safe. Adhere strictly to your Envelope. Remember that exceptions are especially tempting when you're on the road. Resist the urge to depart from your Envelope (especially your bottom line) just because you happen to be in some colorful new locale.

The Japanese know about all this turf business. That's why they always want you to fly to Tokyo to negotiate with them. From where I live, Tokyo's seventeen hours by air. And seventeen hours back. That's almost a full work-week in the air. The prospect of going through all of that and coming back empty-handed is painful at best.

Without Travel, It's a Draw

Rule 21 really only works where long distance, city-to-city travel is involved. When both players are in the same vicinity it doesn't matter who goes where. The amount of time invested in getting across town is so small that it has no measurable influence on the negotiation. In fact, if you're in the same general area as your counterpart, it may be better to negotiate at her office. Remember, you want comfortable counterparts, because they make more concessions. At her office, she has all the stuff that makes her comfortable—her desk, her chair, her pictures, her administrative resources, her files. Plus, her boss is just down the hall so it's much harder for her to claim limited authority. While you can focus entirely on the discussions, she's distracted with her ongoing day-to-day responsibilities.

Your turf is O.K., too. At home, you can play host. Your generosity with resources—administrative, secretarial, travel, entertainment—can help establish and maintain a spirit of goodwill in the discussions. Your counterpart may even feel somewhat indebted to you, and may reciprocate with flexibility. On the other hand, you're more distracted by interruptions, it's more difficult for you to plead lack of authority, and worst of all, your boss may try to get into the act.

If turf becomes an issue between the negotiators, an alternative or neutral site may be more acceptable. Consider a branch office, an attorney's or banker's office, a neutral third party's office, or a hotel as a bargaining site. Offer to meet your Japanese friends halfway. Halfway's fair, isn't it? Hawaii's halfway to Tokyo. Meet them on Maui. They own everything there, anyway. They can get you a room.

9

Putting It All Together

From Beginning to End: A Model Negotiation

I'm going to walk you through a complete negotiation from start to finish, showing you where each of the 21 Rules fits as we go.

Start by doing your homework (Rule 8). By far your most important homework task is the establishing of an Envelope—an opening, target, and bottom line—for each issue. Don't even think about negotiating without Envelopes. Get your authority limits squared away, and arrange to keep your higher-ups in the background (Rule 17). If you must have a team, this is the time to select and coach it (Rule 20). Keep the team small and lay down good communication rules (a single spokesperson, everybody permitted to call a caucus whenever they want, and frequent caucuses). If you plan to use good guy–bad guy, roles and limits should be scripted in advance (Rule 18). If the parties are located in different cities and a face-to-face negotiation is planned, endeavor to arrange for the other side to come to you (Rule 21).

O.K., it's time to start. Begin the negotiation with some small talk (Rule 12). The weaker you are, the more schmoozing you should do (and the harder you should try to bargain face-to-face instead of on the phone). Remember that a positive negotiating climate facilitates agreement and, if established early, tends to continue throughout the discussions (Rule 9). Next, try to sketch out an agenda that includes everybody's issues (Rule 13).

Now you're ready to bargain. Scan the agenda and identify a small issue to begin with (Rule 14). If appropriate, try to have the other side make the first offer on the issue (Rule 19). Tell your counterpart, "Why don't we start with issue X [a smaller issue]. What did you have in mind here? What are you looking for?"

If he opens with a very aggressive offer, don't overreact. Remember, the opening offer is just for positioning purposes. No matter how bleak things look or how far apart you are at this stage, keep going. Often the real movement in the other side's position won't occur until the last few moments. Remember also that "It's my bottom line" and similar expressions are the Biggest Lies in Negotiation (Rule 10). As long as you've got concessions in your Envelope and time on the clock, you've got a chance at an agreement. Press on.

Conversely, no matter how attractive your counterpart's opening offer is, never simply accept it (Rule 11). Try not to just say "no" to it, either, unless it's completely nonnegotiable (that is, ethically, legally, or administratively prohibited). Instead, krunch (Rule 4). At the very minimum, equivocate for a few seconds before accepting.

Whether the other side's opening offer is good, bad, or indifferent, krunching should be your standard response: "I appreciate your proposal, but it's outside the box for us. Let's put our heads together on this. What can we do to change your position?" Keep krunching until he stops making concessions on the issue: "We're definitely getting warmer. What else can we do on this?"

If circumstances make it inappropriate for the other side to open first, or if, after a couple of attempts, you just can't get them to make an opening offer on the issue, then you're going to have to make the first offer. Even if the other side does open first, eventually they'll stop making concessions in response to your krunches and will insist that you state a position on the issue: "I seem to be the only one making concessions here. Where do you stand on issue X?" Either way, a critical, unique moment has arrived: It's the moment of your opening offer. When the time comes, start high (Rule 2): "That's a fair question. What we had in mind on issue X is . . ." This is likely to be the moment of maximum stress in the entire negotiation. Prepare yourself for a negative—perhaps a *very* negative—response to your opening.

If you should be so lucky as to have a counterpart actually accept your opening offer on the issue, it's conditionally (but only conditionally, per Rule 5) settled. Move on to the next issue and repeat the above procedure: Try to get the other side to open, krunch their opening, keep krunching until they stop moving, then you open.

A krunch (or a simple "no") or a counteroffer is a much more likely response to your initial offer. If it's a krunch or a "no," attempt to elicit a counteroffer by asking your counterpart to make you an offer. If it's a counteroffer, krunch, and continue krunching until he stops making further concessions.

Neither approach will delay the inevitable for very long: You're going to have to make your first concession, that first big move down your steeply tapered concession curve. Don't wait too long before making this initial move. I try to make my major drop on an issue during the first quarter of the anticipated time available, and I try to be at my target no later than the third quarter. That way, I've still got some time to move below my target if it becomes necessary.

Don't be stingy with this initial move, as it sets the tone for the balance of the session. Move at least halfway to your target on the issue (Rule 3) requesting a healthy *quid pro quo* in exchange (Rule 1): "We'd be willing to move to A, in exchange for C, D, and E." Expect a krunch or a counteroffer from the other side in response, and reply accordingly. When your counterpart again stops moving, make your next concession—again, at least half the (remaining) distance to your target. Alternate between krunches and counteroffers (always favoring krunches), narrowing the distance between the parties' positions on the issue. Remember that each concession you make is more than just a concession; it's a message signaling how close you are to your limit. Each should be radically smaller than the one before.

There are so many variables in any negotiation that it's impossible to say how much one side should give relative to the other, or precisely when a krunch or a counteroffer should be used. Decisions about concession-making are subjective and situational; you must feel your way along. Under no circumstances should the other side's claims that they have been "much more flexible than you" spur you to greater generosity on an issue. Nor should their tightfistedness keep you from moving down your planned concession curve. Remember, one party may have started far more assertively (or have a much larger Envelope) than the other, and so will have more room to move.

Still, you don't want to empty your pockets on an issue while your counterpart sits on her hands, not making concessions. Don't let the concessions become radically disproportionate. If you're consistently giving away five times as much as the other side, you may have some difficulty settling near your target. Neither escalate nor shave your concessions in order to improve your position (Rule 3). Instead, resort more and more to krunching.

If you've opened and made some concessions on an issue but the other side still hasn't opened (or has opened but hasn't moved much), it's time to apply the brakes. Stay almost exclusively with krunches until they start to move. Consider one more concession. If they still refuse to move, temporarily abandon the issue and go to the next.

Whenever you stop making progress on an issue, change the subject (Rule 5). Skip it and move on to something else. Conversely, while it may appear that there's no further disagreement, you must not unequivocally settle any issue until the end of the negotiation

(Rule 5). If, when you attempt to change issues, the other side says something like, "Wait! We haven't settled issue X yet. Let's resolve issue X before moving on," respond truthfully: "I don't think we have any further differences on issue X, but I can't firmly agree to it until I see how the other issues work out. Let's leave it where it is for now, and then wrap everything up as a package at the end."

If there are other issues, move on to the next (more important) one: "Let's take a look at issue Y." Repeat the above procedure: Try to get the other side to open on the issue, krunch that opening, keep krunching until they stop moving, then counteroffer. If no headway can be made on the issue, move on to another: "We're not making much progress on this. Let's skip this one for now. Where do we stand on issue M?" Return to the stuck issue later. If progress is being made, continue krunching and counteroffering, bringing the issue into near-resolution, then setting it aside and progressing to the next (still more important) issue.

Continue the process of narrowing and/or moving on, working your way through the remaining (larger) issues. You've now completed your first pass or circle through the agenda. Keep circling, performing additional passes as necessary to bring most of the issues into near-agreement. After the first pass the "smaller matters first" idea becomes completely superfluous. Thereafter, direct your attention to where it's needed as you shepherd all of the issues toward an agreement: "Let's take another look at issue Z. The last time we discussed this, you were at A and I was proposing B. Where do we stand on this now? What can we do to wrap this up?"

Your counterpart will often show increased resistance to concessions when he approaches, and particularly when he reaches, his target on an issue. However, this does not mean that he has reached his bottom line on the matter. While his statements that he is at his bottom line should routinely be ignored (Rule 10), if he fails to move further on the issue after repeated krunches and counteroffers from you, he may genuinely be at his bottom line. Patience and persistence are the only ways to confirm this.

If your steeply tapered concessions don't produce a tentative agreement by the time you reach your target, you're going to have to move below your target on the issue. Concessions below your target, toward your bottom line, are made in the simplest of patterns: the smallest increments justifiable under the circumstances, with lots of reluctance. As always, each should be traded for an "if." A legitimacy device such as "split the difference" or "round it off" (Rule 16) may be particularly useful at this stage to provide a medium for an agreement.

In time, the circling process of multiple passes through the agenda will have winnowed down the discrepancies on most matters, leaving only one or a handful of issues where there's still a substantial gap between the parties. When you feel you're getting close to an agreement—with perhaps one or two larger issues still actively in contention—it's time to propose a final "package" that settles everything.

Link all of the issues in a final, let's-settle-everything proposition: "I think I see a basis on which we can wrap this up. We've got two issues still unsettled, and a bunch that are settled—tentatively, of course, pending resolution of the two open issues. Let's review what we've conditionally agreed to. This is a long list. Tell you what. I'm willing to firmly commit to them if you'll just lean my way on those last two unresolved issues. What do you think? That seems eminently fair to me. Let's wrap it up on those terms and go home."

This "package" approach uses the tremendous leverage of the many nearly settled issues to resolve the few unsettled issues in your favor. About half the time, the other side will simply accept your package proposal, as is. When this happens, you can't nibble (Rule 6) because the deal's already closed. The rest of the time the other side will either nibble on your package proposal ("We're very close. Throw in A and B and I'll do it") or, less desirably, they'll propose a package of their own ("I can't settle it on those terms, but I would be willing to settle it this way . . ."). This late in the talks, you won't get a simple, flat rejection of your offer.

If the other side nibbles, nibble back ("I'll throw in A if you'll do C") and close. If they propose their own package, don't reflexively reject it just because it's not yours. If it's close to acceptable, nibble on it and close. If it's not close to acceptable, add a small concession to your earlier package proposal and offer it again. Continue to exchange packages until agreement is reached—or the deadline arrives. At the deadline, if you have an offer in hand from the other side that's within your Envelope, nibble and close. If not, declare your bottom line; this should be the first time you've used that or an equivalent expression. If this doesn't work, you did the best you could with what you had. No matter what, try to end on an upbeat note.

Independence Day

That's how it's done. If it seems like I've tried to make the process somewhat mechanical and formulaic, you're absolutely right. The more formulaic (and less artistic) the techniques, the more reliable and usable they'll be. Most of us are not particularly artistic, and we shouldn't have to be in order to negotiate with skill and confidence. If negotiating is artwork, my goal is to make it "paint by numbers" artwork. In this way it becomes predictable and replicable. Even more importantly, it's freed from the tyranny of emotion that has always had such a profound effect. If you negotiate as I suggest, the outcome will be virtually immune to the vagaries of emotion and personality. It won't matter if you or your counterpart are having good days or bad ones. It won't matter if the other side is sweet or sarcastic, nice or nasty, delightful or despicable. You're still going to do the same things: Your first concession will still be roughly halfway to your target, and so on. In the last analysis, you've got your Envelopes, and you've got a clock. And when it comes to negotiating, that's pretty much all that matters.

PART · THREE

THE PRACTICE OF
NEGOTIATING

10

Ethics

After a brief conference, the client prepared to leave his lawyer's office. Expressing his thanks for the lawyer's assistance, he inquired as to how much he owed. "A hundred dollars should take care of it," replied the lawyer. The client produced a crisp new hundred-dollar bill, and departed. Alone in his office, the lawyer was absentmindedly playing with the hundred-dollar bill when suddenly he discovered that he had received not one, but two hundred-dollar bills, stuck together. "Now I have an ethical dilemma," said the lawyer to himself. "Do I tell my partner or not?"

A lawyer-negotiator writing about ethics? What's wrong with this picture? I freely admit that my qualifications to preach on this topic are no better than anyone else's. In good conscience I can only tell you what my ethical standards are, and what principles I have observed, over the years, to work successfully in negotiating. I would be honored if you found these standards suitable for you.

Whereas most negotiations are conducted ethically, I regret to say that there are frequent glaring exceptions. My impression is that the overall level of ethics in negotiating is on the decline. There's an amazing amount of dishonesty out there. Even those who want to do the right thing are often hindered by unprecedented economic pressures and the lack of a well-developed ethical compass.

The subject of ethics has never received much attention in the United States. A fortunate few Americans have had parents or mentors who instilled in them the habits of identifying the right thing to do in a given circumstance, and then doing it. Some have a strong religious faith or cultural tradition that has given them ethical guidance. A handful have actually had formal training in ethics. But most of us have been left to sort it out on our own. Even with the best of intentions, it is startlingly easy to make ethical mistakes.

This is compounded by the traditional, casual acceptance of a certain amount of deviousness in bargaining. Rightly or wrongly, negotiation is routinely associated with trickery, sharp practices, and subterfuge. The roguishly beguiling Artful Dodger–type character who lives by his wits and hoodwinks his rivals is, for many, the archetypical negotiator.

Financial demands, amoral stereotypes, and anemic scruples are a volatile mixture. In negotiation (as in any other human activity), opportunities abound for the brigand. Every negotiator has been, or will be, tempted by deceit. Many will succumb.

The Ethics of Win-Win Negotiating

Win-win negotiating is synonymous with ethical negotiating. Like win-win negotiating, ethical negotiating isn't the right thing to do, it's the only thing. Like win-lose negotiating, unethical negotiating is unsuccessful in all but the shortest of runs. Whatever short-term friction there may be between ethics and pragmatics always disappears in the long term.

**Ethical negotiating isn't the right thing
to do, it's the only thing to do.**

In anything but the simplest one-shot deal, an agreement that is grounded in connivery will ultimately fail. It will either collapse as soon as the deceit is revealed, or will require around-the-clock surveillance in order to enforce compliance. Even if such an agreement survives to completion, the damage wrought by duplicity will destroy the relationships between the organizations and the negotiators. The reputation of the dissembler will be diminished or destroyed. Messy, expensive, and very public litigation may ensue.

Mistakes

Never attempt to take advantage of an obvious, serious error made by the other side. If your counterpart makes a mistake that might affect the deal in a meaningful way, politely call it to her attention. A deal based on a major mistake may not be legally enforceable, and is almost certain to be a win-lose proposition (with all the problems that foretells).

Lying

Diogenes with his lamp still searches for an honest man. Everybody lies. Ordinary conversational etiquette permits—even requires—a certain amount of dishonesty. We've become so deadened to the low rumble of falsehood that it takes a real whopper to even get our attention anymore. In bargaining, untruthfulness runs the gamut from sociable "white lies" to material, fraudulent misrepresentations. The temptation to lie can often be overwhelming, and in general, the short-term risks are not very great.

Lying has absolutely no place in quality negotiating. True partnerships are based on trust, not law. However small, each promise kept builds trust and each one broken undermines it. Not only do you do not need to lie in order to negotiate successfully; if you lie you *cannot* negotiate successfully. A lie discovered will ruin the problem-solving enterprise upon which win-win agreements are based. Even bluffing—hinting at or actually threatening an action that you have no intention of taking—is too close to the ethical line. Like threats, bluffs are climate-killers. And bluffs are sometimes called, damaging your credibility. If you say "I've got better offers" when you haven't, you've crossed the line. Krunches like "We're looking for a better number," or "I'd like you to sharpen your pencil," are, by comparison, absolutely true and appropriate statements.

Depending on how they're phrased, assertive, "high" opening offers can quickly put us in an ethical danger zone. The more words we tack onto our openings, the more trouble we're likely to get into. Opening the negotiation by saying "I need X," or "X is the least I can accept," or "I've got to have X," when your real bottom line is something less than X, is untruthful. Nothing should ever be called a bottom line unless it really is the bottom line. Besides being unethical, such a misrepresentation is also very foolish: If your counterpart believes your ultimatum, yet truly can't give you X, she'll simply leave. Your negotiation will be over almost before it's begun. If you're quick enough to offer a deal-saving concession before the door closes behind her, she may stay—but you will have compromised your present and future believability. All of this can be avoided by sticking with simple, truthful openings like "X makes sense to us," or "We're looking for X," or "We want X," or just "X."

Lying is sufficiently common in negotiating that a prudent player must be wary. Your counterpart may not even know that her statements are false—her organization may be keeping her in the dark. Always be on the lookout for lying by the other side. If possible, test your counterpart occasionally by asking questions to which you already have answers. Check things out. Making final agreements conditional based on the verification of outcome-significant facts is a very good habit that will dramatically reduce your risk of being victimized by a lie. If the other side objects to such verification, be suspicious.

Full Disclosure

Although what you say should always be truthful, you don't need to say most things. Discretion in the making of disclosures isn't lying. Negotiators, in general, talk entirely too much. Being an ethical negotiator doesn't require you to make a full disclosure of all your information about the matter at hand. If you were selling a business for $30 million, it would be neither necessary nor advisable to tell a potential buyer that the sale was to generate cash to pay off a $20 million bank loan coming due immediately. Say only what needs to be said and can be said honestly.

THOMAS'S TRUISMS

Negotiators, in general, talk entirely too much.

THOMAS'S TRUISMS

Withdrawing Concessions

Rule 5 says that all concessions should remain tentative—and thus withdrawable—until the final handshake. Trading a concession for one received is the standard (and preferred) form of "if," but withdrawing a concession you've already tentatively made is an acceptable alternative. However, don't expect your counterpart to be overly pleased with this approach, as he may already have counted the now-withdrawn concession as "his." Regardless of what he may claim, you haven't violated your integrity by taking it back.

In order to avoid any misunderstanding about the transient nature of your concessions, it may be wise to advise your counterpart early in the discussions that nothing is firm until the final handshake. And don't forget that Rule 5 works both ways. Your counterpart may want to renegotiate issues on which tentative agreement had already been reached. Having had some time to think about it, she may have changed her mind.

Renegotiations

To a win-win negotiator, contracts must always remain elastic. Things change. Agreements must be continually reevaluated in light of current circumstances. A win-win negotiator never hides behind the terms of the contract. He would never say something like "The agreement is clear on that point, so we're going to hold their feet to the fire" (or "The agreement doesn't cover that, so we're free to do whatever we want"). Legally, that might be 100% correct—but it's 100% irrelevant. The important question, for win-win purposes, is "What is the spirit of the contract?" No matter what the contract says, you're *never* free to do whatever you want in a forward-looking relationship. If one side is discontented, simply brandishing the terms of the contract won't make their unhappiness go away. If an athlete proves to be worth considerably more than he's being paid, a smart coach will quickly renegotiate the guy's contract—ideally, *before* being asked to—so that he's happy.

If the current situation has changed significantly from when the deal was struck, perhaps the agreement too should change. A word to the wise: I've never yet seen a truly "ironclad" contract. It's a myth nurtured by lawyers. And even if there's no loophole, an unhappy party can be "maliciously obedient"—or endlessly disobedient—to the terms of the agreement. Or they can just breach the agreement. "Sue me," they'll say. Years—and tens of thousands of dollars—later, you may win. Then again, you may lose. And meanwhile, the contract is producing no work and no revenue for anybody.

Attempting to enforce an agreement that has become genuinely onerous to one side is (1) destructive of the relationship between the players; and (2) an invitation to resistance, noncompliance, and litigation. Given the new circumstances, is a renegotiation fair? If so, proceed—but make it clear to the side requesting the renegotiation that any changes will have a substantial price. Meaningful *quid pro quos* should be exacted in order to deter frivolous renegotiations.

If you decide to initiate a renegotiation, keep in mind that you may be impairing your credibility. You gave your word, and now you're attempting to recant. Seek to renegotiate only if something genuinely unanticipated and extraordinary has made compliance impossible or profoundly difficult. Be sure the new situation more than justifies your requested change. Offer some concessions to help make the proposed new arrangement more attractive to the other side. Above all, never agree to a deal that you can't do, or don't really want to do. Such deals are renegotiation-bait.

A "buy-in"—first cousin to a lowball offer—is often the first step in an unethical, premeditated renegotiation. A buy-in occurs when a seller offers an exceptionally attractive deal that a buyer accepts. The unethical part comes later, when items normally within the scope of such an agreement are suddenly declared by the seller to be "changes" or "extras" requiring substantial additional payments by the buyer. If the buyer is to meet her deadline, she must capitulate.

Buying-in, by itself, is perfectly ethical. If a seller wants to invest some of his working capital in a below-cost deal designed to showcase his capabilities to a potential long-term customer, both sides may benefit handsomely. By buying-in now, the vendor hopes to profit in the future. The customer receives an excellent price on the current job, and can "qualify" a new vendor for future work. But if the buy-in is part of a calculated plan by the seller to generate unfair profits by demanding renegotiation after the buyer is committed and vulnerable, then the practice is clearly unethical. The best defense against an unethical buy-in is to investigate the vendor's reputation before negotiating. Then write detailed specifications into the agreement, and resist unwarranted changes thereafter.

Amateurs and Pros

Who's more likely to behave unethically—an expert or a novice? I think you're far safer when negotiating with a pro. It would be unusual for a veteran bargainer to knowingly negotiate unethically. The expert knows that her very livelihood may be at stake. Among professionals, reputation is everything—and she's not going to risk her reputation for a single-deal blowout.

The amateur or occasional negotiator may not feel so constrained by matters of reputation and relationship. Novices sometimes lack the long-run perspective that acts as a moderating influence on the pros. Rookies see the immediate advantage to be gained by a lie, and may not think ahead to the consequences. They also sometimes underestimate their counterpart's intellect, and assume that their own conduct will go unnoticed.

Recognizing and Dealing With Unethical Behavior

Be sure not to let your guard down at the last minute. A few moments of carelessness can squander the results of a long and otherwise successful negotiation. This is especially true when it's time to sign the final agreement. Regardless of who prepared it, check the fine print, line by line. Don't assume anything.

How do you determine if an action you're contemplating, or something that's been done to you, is ethical or unethical? And if someone does something unethical, what should you do about it?

Some of the negotiating techniques we've discussed—lying and lowballing, for example—are clearly unethical. Others, including renegotiation and buying in, are sometimes ethical and sometimes not. Even some old and well-respected bargaining tactics such as legitimacy, limited authority, and good guy–bad guy can be employed unethically. There are many cases where it's just not clear what's ethical and what isn't. There is no Little Golden Book of Ethics in Negotiating. While many organizations have published excellent general codes of ethics for their personnel, they rarely provide specific guidance about negotiating. The line between "good faith" and "bad faith" bargaining is still vague.

Let me offer up a handful of ethical tests that have kept me off the reef more than a few times. The old Golden Rule, in particular, is probably still the most useful guide: How would you feel if the thing you're considering was done to you? Would you think it was a justifiable negotiating move? If not, don't do it. Another test: Would you take the contemplated action with a friend or a family member? Or, how would you and your behavior be viewed by your neighbors if a detailed account of it appeared on the front page of the local newspaper? Would your family be honored or ashamed? Or, would you be proud to tell your children about what you did? If you have any serious misgivings about the ethics of a given action, you already have your answer: Don't do it.

If your counterpart behaves unethically during the negotiation, your problems are only just beginning. She has revealed her true nature to you, and she's not likely to become rehabilitated any time soon. Unwittingly, she has done you a favor. Seriously consider whether continuing with the negotiation makes sense. Is this the sort of person you want to be doing business with? Are you prepared to question, and subsequently verify, every assertion she makes? If you reach an agreement, are you ready to police it around the clock? If you elect to press ahead notwithstanding, guard your posterior with special diligence thereafter.

> **"Always do right; this will gratify some people and astonish the rest."**
> Mark Twain

11

International Negotiating

International business activity is increasing spectacularly. Our hottest markets are often offshore, and opportunities abroad are immense. As nations grow more interdependent, the number of purely domestic issues dwindles. All of these trends are accelerating. Organizations that ignore the international arena—or stumble there—may find themselves on the commercial sidelines. Improving our global awareness has become a matter of the utmost practical, dollars-and-cents importance.

Negotiators from different cultures bargain across a gulf of incongruous world views, conflicting patterns of reasoning, even dissimilar notions of space and time. With their newfound economic clout, our foreign business contacts are insisting that we adjust to their ways. While some U.S. companies complain that foreign markets are closed to outsiders, more progressive players are listening to their offshore partners and busily making the necessary adjustments.

A traditional solution to the problem of American intercultural myopia has been to hire only foreign nationals for overseas bargaining. The result is that ineffective cross-cultural negotiating still occurs, only now it's wholly inside the organization: between the negotiator and his manager. And this strategy leaves unresolved the continuing problem of American managers making short negotiating forays abroad. The fact is that most successful executives in multinational companies will, at one time or another, negotiate across cultural lines. We simply must learn how to negotiate better with people from other countries.

Even if you never negotiate overseas, you'll inevitably—and increasingly—find yourself bargaining with people having cultural backgrounds very different from yours. The United States becomes more culturally diverse all the time; the fabled melting pot doesn't melt like it used to. There has been a considerable lessening of the traditional eagerness of newcomers to assimilate by mimicking the stereotypical American style. Cultural groups within the States are less willing than ever to submerge their distinct heritages in the classic American cultural mainstream.

What follows are some miscellaneous observations on intercultural bargaining. No attempt has been made to present a complete or balanced picture of this vast subject. A thoughtful analysis of the nuances of cross-cultural negotiation would require hundreds, if not thousands, of pages. My goal here is more to help the reader ask the right questions than to provide all the answers. I have tended to emphasize Japanese examples, both because of that country's importance as a global trading partner, and because much of my own international negotiating work involves Japan.

Language

If international negotiating success requires an understanding of our counterpart's culture, then her language is certainly the window to that culture. While it is true that English is the language of international commerce, it is also true that competency in the other side's language is an enormous negotiating asset. Nevertheless, Americans continue to expect our counterparts from other cultures to know and use English. We make little effort to learn other languages beyond a few obligatory, long-forgotten high school classes. How many Americans do you know who speak passable Japanese? How many Japanese do you know who don't speak passable English?

The unmistakable message this assumption-of-English sends to the other side is that we don't think their culture is very important. And if our competition knows the language and culture of the other side, we are put at a great disadvantage.

Ideally, the negotiator should speak the local language competently. While fluency is rarely practical, at a minimum the negotiator should take the time to learn a few basic phrases in the local tongue. Your foreign counterparts will be delighted by any attempts you make, no matter how inept, to use their language. Occasionally throwing even simple words like "hello," "goodbye," "please," and "thank you" into the conversation will be taken as a sincere compliment by the other side.

Large foreign organizations will usually have a number of fluent English-speakers to serve as spokespersons or interpreters. However, smaller organizations may not, and an outside interpreter will be required. Beyond whatever translation services your host makes available, it is desirable for you to find and retain your own translator if circumstances and budgets permit.

Good translators are not easy to find. Translation is alchemy; mere fluency in both languages isn't nearly enough. The translator must combine words and ideas with their associated implications, tone, and cadence; and in converting the whole package to a different language, he must make it understood as the speaker intended it by somebody whose mind may operate very differently. Hire only a professional translator who is a native speaker (a local is preferable to an émigré), and who translates regularly. If the subject of the negotiation is very technical or jargon-filled, the translator should already know the field.

The U.S. Embassy or Consulate nearest the venue of the negotiation will usually be able to suggest some competent translators. If the negotiation will be chiefly scientific or technical, a nearby university may be a better source. Both must be contacted well in advance of your trip. As insurance, ask the nearest Stateside diplomatic office of your host's country for some translator referrals. A candidate's skill can be quickly tested using previously translated text.

Operating in a different language is exhausting and tricky. Translation takes extra time (doubling it at a minimum, since everything must be said twice), and demands considerable patience from negotiators and translators alike. A translator isn't a machine, and the entire process is rife with opportunities for mistakes. Subtle shades of meaning may attach to certain words and phrases, requiring more than a split second to explain. Words often lose—and gain—much in the translation.

Get to know the translator before the meeting. Provide a list of the names of the participants and their organizations, and any technical terms that may be used. Make it clear that you're much more interested in your counterpart's ideas than in a literal translation of his words. A good translator will explain the nuances of the other side's statements, and will listen in on side conversations for you. Never assume that the other side's use of an interpreter means they don't understand English.

Remember to always look at, and talk to, your counterpart and not the translator. This may be facilitated by having the translator sit behind you. Even though you don't understand a word the other side is saying, the accompanying gestures and facial expressions are communicating things you need to know.

Whether or not an interpreter is used, remember to speak slowly and clearly. Short sentences are helpful. Go over important points a second time, rephrasing them, to confirm the other side's comprehension. Speak in "offshore English" that avoids slang and jargon. Common expressions like "That's a whole new ballgame" and "We can't put up with that" are meaningless to people for whom English is a second language; slang phrases like "blow them away," "scream their heads off," and "take our best shot" will at best cause confusion. Jokes almost never translate well and should probably be avoided.

Westerners are often troubled by what they see as their non-Western counterparts' lack of directness. We like "yes" or "no" answers, and we're impatient with our non-Western counterparts' tendency to talk around the issues. But to the ears of many non-Western negotiators—Asians and Arabs in particular—Westerners converse with shocking bluntness. Speakers in Asian and Arab cultures prefer a certain "civilized ambiguity" to their words. Indirectness and muted terms are revered. They allow for graceful retreat from positions, and help keep doors open for future dealings.

While their Chinese and Korean neighbors are beginning to speak with more directness, the Japanese are still notoriously careful to avoid causing embarrassment with blunt words. For example, Japanese particularly dislike saying "no" or having it said to them. If necessary, a Japanese will say nothing at all in order to avoid saying "no." You're expected to be sensitive enough to grasp his meaning without his having to spell things out so plainly. If you press too hard, he may laugh—but out of embarrassment, not amusement.

Your Japanese counterpart's frequent "hai" (yes) and nod don't indicate assent, only that he's following the conversation—very much like "I see" and "uh-huh" in English. His smile represents neither happiness nor agreement with what you're saying, but merely an effort to appear cheerful. Westerners find it especially disconcerting when a sunny Japanese visage accompanies verbal bad news. What we see as insincerity, our hosts intended as thoughtfulness. If your Japanese counterpart changes the subject, asks a question in response to your question, or tells you that he'll "think about it," "make concrete efforts," or "do his best," he's actually trying to politely say "no way." You would be wise to let the matter drop for now.

While silence in the midst of a conversation often makes Westerners uncomfortable (and would be unimaginable among garrulous Brazilians), it is quite natural in many other parts of the world.

Silence allows for the careful consideration of positions, and, if appropriate, the making of concessions in a patient, face-saving manner. It's also a tactful way of changing the subject or saying "no." Be prepared for lengthy silences when negotiating in the Middle and Far East.

Negotiating journals are full of horror stories of Americans who made huge concessions in response to the other side's silence, having mistaken it for rejection. Resist your Western urge to fill the conversational gaps with reiterations or worse, concessions. Join your host in a long, silent cup of coffee or tea. Wait for him to continue when he is ready.

Lies and Lawyers

Westerners sometimes accuse their foreign counterparts of bargaining with less than complete honesty. As evidence, they cite specific statements to which the other side assented but later disavowed, and apparently "done deals" that kept being renegotiated.

One answer to this problem lies in the intermingled issues of indirect language and truth-telling in general. As was noted in the previous section, in many parts of the world it is considered rude to openly refuse another's request. In public one is expected to respond agreeably or ambiguously, but never negatively. Dissent is signaled discreetly so that face isn't lost on either side. Americans relying on a literal translation while overlooking the accompanying explanatory signals would receive an altogether incorrect impression that a deal was close, or closed.

Diplomacy aside, the veracity of even direct statements made during negotiations may have to be discounted from culture to culture. Regional customs may allow negotiators to "put their best foot forward" in their statements. The speaker may assume that the truth will ultimately reveal itself through the dialectic of the negotiation, and that, in any event, it is each party's responsibility to verify everything that is said. A party claiming he was lied to would be told that he had no right to rely on the other party's statements and should have done his own homework.

For some cultures, a handshake is as firm a bond as any written contract. For others, nothing but the most minute documentary precision will suffice. The international negotiator must walk a fine line between formalizing an agreement sufficiently to confirm that an understanding actually exists, and giving the impression of distrusting the other side.

Few countries are as legalistic as the United States. We naturally resort to attorneys and legal documents even for simple agreements. Not so in other cultures. With legal systems sometimes less accessible and dependable than in America, negotiators elsewhere rely more on direct, personal relationships with their counterparts to insure compliance. The inclusion of attorneys in the negotiating process—and in some cases merely asking for a formal contract—may be regarded as a signal that the other side isn't trusted. While the Japanese admire precise contracts, they see the typical American bodyguard of lawyers as a poor alternative to genuine sincerity and trust in business dealings.

This isn't to suggest that lawyers should not be involved. On the contrary, the complicated legal ramifications of international business transactions make competent legal help a necessity. The appropriate legal structure for the deal (such as license, joint venture, and the like) must be chosen. Political and commercial risks must be evaluated. In some cases financing must be obtained and intellectual property rights protected. All of this takes time, effort, and lots of money.

Nevertheless, strive to keep the lawyers in the background. Direct contact between your lawyers and the other side should be minimized, and you should always be present when it occurs. Counsel should be discouraged from even writing directly to the other side; letters should be to you, with a copy subsequently sent to the other side under an explanatory cover letter from you. In most cases it isn't

necessary that your lawyers physically attend the negotiation. However, make any agreement subject to "corporate formalities" to provide an opportunity for legal review.

Other areas of potential conflict between negotiators from different cultures are the concepts of contract scope, contract flexibility, and the propriety of renegotiation. A signed contract means very
different things in different parts of the world. Westerners, particularly Americans, value compliance with the exact terms of a deal and
feel little obligation beyond those terms. "Good" people, in the
American view, keep their word—to the letter. Germans, Russians,
mainland Chinese, and to a lesser extent Japanese also fall into this
"legalistic" group.

Negotiators from many Latin American, African, Middle Eastern, and some Far Eastern cultures have a much less formal view of
contracts. They may feel bound more by the overall spirit of an undertaking—in some cases short of the precise language of the contract, but in other cases well beyond it. Particularly in the Middle
East, India, and Indonesia, even when a formal agreement has been
reached there may be a certain casualness about compliance. In their
enthusiasm and desire to be positive, negotiators from these cultures
may make promises that are wildly optimistic, are superseded by
other events, or are just forgotten.

These cultures put their faith more in long-term coopera-
tion and trust than in legal documents. They believe that it isn't the
paper that binds the parties, but their broader mutual objectives and
duties—and it naturally follows that if circumstances should
change, so too should the deal. Adjustment to the other side's changing needs and feelings is seen as a measure of integrity. To be inflexible would be immoral—it would allow individuals to hide behind
mere legal prescriptions and avoid their broader, ongoing societal
responsibilities.

When a contract-informal "Easterner" requests a renegotiation
from a contract-formal "Westerner" and the above-described views

collide (as they almost certainly will), each side may end up viewing the other as deceitful.

Time and Patience

Domestic notions of time often do not travel well. Western Europeans, Japanese, and North Americans are highly punctual, and expect everyone else to share their "time is money" attitude. But most other places on the globe have a much more laid-back approach to schedules. "The end of the day" may mean sometime this week, while "a few weeks" may mean next year or possibly not at all. Without particular concern, an African, Arab, Southeast Asian, or Latin American executive may reschedule a meeting at the last moment, arrive an hour or two late, or continue to negotiate for hours beyond the scheduled wind-up time. In some cultures age and status determine punctuality: Bosses may be late, but underlings must be on time. Your counterpart would be astonished if you showed any unhappiness about such practices. His "lateness" in no way indicates laziness or a lack of interest, but merely demonstrates his unsegmented and highly flexible view of time. He regards your incessant hurrying and clock-watching with a mixture of suspicion and pity. He sees your dogged attempts to comply with arbitrary schedules as a sign of misplaced values.

Latins and Africans are very fatalistic about events, believing that things will begin and end when they should. They are like Middle Easterners in putting a far higher value on family and social matters than do North Americans, for whom business issues are often paramount. Negotiations must wait upon family affairs in these societies. In Spain, Latin America, and Italy, commerce generally halts for lunch, which is the principal meal and often includes numerous courses. The intermission may also include a post-lunch siesta, with discussions resuming in late afternoon and continuing into the evening. Only in North America, Western Europe, and Japan is business routinely discussed during meals.

Unending patience is a most important virtue for offshore negotiating. The Japanese and mainland Chinese are famous—some would say notorious—for negotiating until the other side is simply worn out. In Japan, it routinely takes three to five times as long to reach an agreement as it does in the States. Numerous meetings are required to accomplish anything. Throughout Asia it will take sellers longer to conclude negotiations than buyers. Sellers will frequently find themselves waiting days for appointments, only to have them canceled at the last moment.

In Japan, every decision must be passed upon by multiple levels of management. Attempts to accelerate the process are futile, and may be counterproductive. Minds are rarely changed at the negotiating table. Concessions are decided upon privately, in harmonious consultation with colleagues. Consequently, if an impasse is reached on one point, you should politely move on to the next point. If the impasse is on the only remaining issue, cordially recess the negotiation for a while. Allow the other side some private time. Never press for an immediate decision; this would be seen as rude and overbearing.

Particularly in Africa, Southeast Asia, and the Middle East, meetings will be interrupted constantly. Family and friends will regularly drop in unannounced. Telephone calls will intrude. The demands of higher-ups will require immediate attention. Showing frustration at these distractions is pointless and will serve only to emphasize your foreignness.

Getting Acquainted

"We only do business with friends" is a common theme from Africa to Latin America. Particularly where the players have never met, a personal bond—in particular, a certain amount of trust—must

first be established before successful business discussions can com-
mence. Without trust, there is no reason to talk about business.
The get-acquainted period, with its seemingly insignificant social
niceties, will determine whether your business mission succeeds or
fails. If you change negotiators, this "schmoozing" process must
begin anew.

North Americans and Germans customarily hurry through the
small talk (or skip it altogether) so they can "get down to business."
Five or ten minutes of chitchat is more than enough. But if the other
side is from some other nationality, a full morning or half a day
of small talk is called for—or even more; and the bigger the deal,
the longer the schmooze. In Japan, the entire first meeting is often
nothing more than a get-acquainted session. Subjects discussed—
current events, flowers, golf, the weather—will include anything but
the issues to be negotiated. In other countries several meetings may
pass without discussion of business issues.

Be prepared to spend as much time getting acquainted as the
other side may desire. Let your counterpart be the one to initiate
the business discussions. The small talk—and the negotiations that
follow—must be done face to face. Outside of North America and
Western Europe, telephone negotiations are almost always unsuccessful.

In Europe, Latin America, and the Middle East, begin the meeting by shaking hands with each person in the room. A gentle handshake or a simple grasp of hands is far more common than the solid
North American squeeze. Most Asians do not care for such direct
contact, so a nod (in lieu of a bow) is usually sufficient. However,
the Japanese (who study bowing their entire lives) will genuinely appreciate any effort you make toward mastering the subtleties of the
bow. A correct bow is made from the waist, with the arms held stiffly
at the sides. Pause at the bottom of the bow, and bow longer and
deeper to people who outrank you.

Spaniards and Latin Americans are sometimes very demonstra-
tive in their greetings. Their embraces, pats on the back, and arms

around the shoulder can surprise and embarrass unprepared North Americans. Latins share with Southern and Eastern Europeans the custom of mock cheek-kissing among acquaintances, male and female. When hugged, kissed, or otherwise palpated, try to go with the flow.

Polite, individual greetings are appropriate. A broad "Hi, guys" would be considered rude almost anywhere. Greetings (and farewells) should take place in descending order of rank. Canadians and Australians appreciate first-name informality. In Asia, Latin America, the Middle East, Germany, France, Spain, Italy, and Britain, where formality is the norm, last names and titles such as "Doctor" and "Professor" should be used until you are advised otherwise. When in doubt, always stand on ceremony.

A number of cultures—particularly the Japanese—judge virtually every relationship in terms of rank. These rank differences determine who behaves to whom with greater deference and respect. Because of this system, the Japanese are most interested in immediately assessing their counterpart's rank. The rituals of the get-acquainted period, especially the exchange of business cards, assist them in this determination. You and your team members are expected to cooperate by explaining your positions and organizational rankings so that your Japanese hosts will know how they compare to their own. Any uncertainty will lead to embarrassment and inertia.

Your business cards are as important as your passport in international dealings. They should be exchanged with those of your counterparts' during all business introductions. Bring ten times as many cards as you would for a domestic trip, and have your hotel imprint a local translation on the reverse side. Present the card with both hands, with the translation facing toward your counterpart. Study the other side's card for a few moments before setting it down. In some countries it is acceptable (even desirable) to scribble notes on the back of the card. In others—Japan, for example—this is considered rude. There, do any writing on the card after your counterpart is gone. Leave the other side's business cards on the table during the meeting; it's a sign of respect, and it will help you remember who's seated where. Never offer the same person a card at a subsequent meeting—that would indicate that you had forgotten him.

In Latin America, small talk should always include questions about the other side's family. However, such personal questions—particularly if they relate to female members of the family—must be avoided in the Middle East. There, expect to drink several small cups of coffee during the schmoozing period. Chat about sports, history, exports, or tourism. Compliment the local flowers or weather. Exchange travel notes about interesting destinations, good restaurants, and the like. Stay clear of controversial topics like politics or religion.

While the Western workday generally ends at five o'clock (particularly in Germany and England), after-hours socializing is an integral part of doing business in many other societies. In Japan and elsewhere, business continues after work and such gatherings are considered mandatory. This is when business relationships are cemented. If you routinely make an early night of it, you may find that your negotiating accomplishes little.

Much has been written about the lavish business entertaining that is commonplace for the Japanese. They spend more of their GNP on such entertainment than on defense, and the expense account of a Japanese businessperson may exceed his salary. After a few rounds of drinks in the local nightclub, your Japanese counterpart may slowly begin to reveal his true feelings to you. This will signal his growing acceptance of you as a colleague, and give you valuable insights into the progress of the talks.

Status

With their egalitarian social orientation, North Americans assume that anyone selected by an organization to negotiate should be fully acceptable to the other side. In many cultures this assumption is fundamentally erroneous. The bargainer's organizational rank must be at least equal to the importance of the issues being negotiated. Western Europeans and Latin Americans, for whom social classes retain a degree of importance, share with Asians a sensitivity to the perceived rank and prestige of the other side's negotiator.

Women may encounter extreme difficulties negotiating across certain cultural lines. On the Japanese ladder of status, women are on the bottom. They are substantially excluded from Japanese management. Further, a foreigner's status will always be lower than that of a Japanese of equivalent age and rank. A female foreigner, therefore, has a double status whammy. A woman with a responsible position on a negotiating team presents her Japanese hosts with an unwelcome, embarrassing dilemma. She "doesn't compute"; she is a contradiction toward whom they have little idea how to behave. Her position on the team is all but certain to reduce its chances for success.

Right or wrong, an organization preparing to negotiate in Japan should carefully consider the wisdom of having females in senior team positions. This also applies to Latin America, where the culture of machismo still predominates, and to the Islamic world, where women and men are often segregated. Women in these cultures are substantially excluded from management, and a female negotiator may encounter special problems.

Age is given great respect in Asia, and executives under 35 should probably not serve as principal negotiators. Also, larger organizations have greater status in Asia than do smaller ones, and buyers have higher status than sellers. In negotiating with foreign government representatives, it would be well to remember that while businesspeople are often accorded more respect in North America than government personnel, in most other parts of the world this distinction is reversed. Elsewhere, government bureaucrats are authority figures and must be treated accordingly.

Authority

American negotiators pride themselves (mistakenly, as we point out in Rule 17) on the broad grants of authority they take abroad, and often feel deceived when their foreign counterparts reveal that a given decision must be cleared with the "home office." Strict limits on bargaining authority are the norm overseas. They are virtually automatic in Japanese organizations, which rarely have a Western-style top decision-maker. Instead, a series of management groups make decisions in an elaborate, ritualized, time-consuming process. The Chinese also employ broad-based group decision-making procedures. By comparison, French corporations often have extremely centralized authority, in which a handful of top executives make most of the choices for their negotiators. In India and Pakistan, the number-one executive makes all the decisions, so nothing can happen if he is unavailable.

In many parts of the world, the host government is a silent participant in commercial negotiations. To a degree unthinkable in the United States, there is a close, almost symbiotic relationship between Japanese business and government. Some of the many delays Westerners complain about are caused by their Japanese hosts' need to periodically consult with the government about the ongoing discussions. This is true throughout Asia and to a lesser extent in Western Europe. Ascertain early the extent to which the host government will be a force in the bargaining, and take steps to establish and nurture a beneficial relationship with this important tacit participant.

Teams

Cross-cultural negotiating is the major exception to the "keep teams small" suggestion of Rule 20. For a variety of reasons, the American inclination to "go it alone" may be unwise in offshore negotiations.

The overall strain of negotiating through a translator, taking notes and making mathematical calculations, working in multiple currencies, communicating with the main office, battling mystifying legal and tax issues, and facing what is usually a large group on the other side of the table, can be debilitating to all but the most capable negotiators. A few extra team members will significantly ease these burdens. However, as in domestic negotiations, strict team-management rules apply.

A larger team sends a signal of earnestness to the other side. It bolsters the perceived status of the lead negotiator. And it's an opportunity to begin educating the next generation of bargainers. In Asia, the Middle East, and parts of Latin America, the size of your team will be viewed as an indication of how serious you are about the talks and the overall relationship. In these societies, your counterpart could well regard your tiny team as a slight.

The Japanese tradition of consensus, in which every management level must join in a deal, is reflected in the size of their teams. Small Western negotiating teams are often surprised to find themselves confronting Japanese teams of five to twenty members. Equally disconcerting, the membership of this platoon changes constantly as different issues come up on the agenda. Each member represents a separate corporate interest, and acts as a "precinct captain" to build support for the agreement within his designated group back at headquarters or the plant. Prior to the negotiation, a well-prepared bargainer should request information about the position and background of each member of the other side's team.

Gifts

Except in mainland China, where they may be considered bribes, small gifts are required in Asian business situations and appropriate almost everywhere else. In Japan, gift-giving has reached epidemic proportions. It seems as if almost no occasion is too small to warrant a gift. A quality brand-name item will always be well-received there. Since many items that are relatively inexpensive in the United States (designer scarves, specialty teas, leather goods, and liqueurs, for example) are both costly and greatly appreciated overseas, it's smart to purchase such gifts before traveling. Have them professionally wrapped after your arrival. Flowers are a welcome gift everywhere, but because the number, color, and variety of flowers denote different things in every culture, be sure to obtain and follow good local advice. In the Islamic world, avoid gifts that contain alcohol or that depict humans or animals, as they are considered sacrilegious.

In Asia, gifts are presented at the initial meeting. Elsewhere, they are exchanged later in an informal setting. Present the gift slowly, with two hands. Open your own gifts later, in private. Send a prompt thank-you note for any gift or favor. And be cautious when admiring an Arab's possession; if your host is a more traditional Arab, such a compliment will obligate him to give the item to you. If you then refuse the gift, you will have insulted him.

Miscellaneous customs

Conservative business dress is always appropriate. In some countries this may be shorts, so it pays to know the local dress code before you go. Arabs and Asians alike consider it offensive to be shown the soles of another's shoes. The Western male habit of crossing the leg—thereby revealing the sole of the shoe—may be taken as an insult.

Anti-smoking sentiment is still largely confined to American shores, and at times it will seem as if everyone outside of the United States smokes. "Smoke-free" areas are virtually nonexistent abroad, and on local flights your aircraft will quickly fill with clouds of cigarette smoke. If you are bothered by this, you have neither law nor popular opinion on your side, so accept the situation as gracefully as you can. In China, not only do most people smoke, they also spit: copiously, loudly, and publicly.

Westerners and Japanese have a very large (30-inch) spatial envelope that we consider our personal "turf." Unless we're being intimate, we don't like anybody inside that spatial envelope. When others invade it, we attempt to reestablish it by backing up. Arabs, by comparison, like to converse at extremely close range (as close as 12 inches). Since any retreating by you may be seen as an attempt to be evasive, you must try to hold your ground. The accepted spatial envelope in Latin America (and within some Hispanic communities in the United States) can be less than one foot. Latins get right up into each other's faces when they bargain. It's considered a sign of respect if your counterpart can feel your breath *on his face*. (How about *that* after a nice spicy meal?)

Picture your Latin American counterpart closing in on you to get within a comfortable speaking distance, while you frantically back up, courageously defending your spatial envelope. You think he's being pushy. He thinks you're being evasive. Negotiating hasn't even begun and cultural differences are already interfering.

In the Pacific Rim and India, direct eye contact—especially with superiors—is considered impolite and insensitive. Looking down or away is a sign of respect, not shiftiness. With Arabs and Europeans, however, direct eye contact demonstrates honesty and sincerity, and should be maintained. One never eats, gestures, or offers anything with the left hand in the Middle East; this hand is considered dirty. The North American "O.K." sign, with the thumb and index finger forming a circle, should be avoided almost everywhere outside of North America; it means the same thing as a raised middle finger in the United States, or worse.

Homework

While experiencing another culture is the only way to truly learn it, good homework will speed and enrich the learning process. There are a host of consultants, workshops, books, CDs, tapes, and magazines available to help educate you. Cross-cultural "training camps" offer short, intense "immersion" experiences. Industry groups, trade associations, and numerous federal and state government agencies will provide counseling, referrals, and an abundance of information about overseas business transactions. The U.S. Department of State's *Area Handbooks* and *Background Notes* for individual countries are particularly useful. The International Trade Administration of the U.S. Department of Commerce has information and advice about trade opportunities, and the Office of the U.S. Trade Representative publishes reports about the trade and legal practices of other nations.

Study some of the history, economy, politics, geography, literature, and customs of the host country. Aside from making your subsequent journey more enjoyable, a demonstration of your interest in the finer points of some aspect of the local culture will greatly flatter and impress your hosts. Practice a few basic conversational phrases in the local language. Try to read a work by a major literary figure of the host country. Don't overlook everyday practical matters like currency, tipping, transportation, weather, business hours, time zones, and food. While you cannot possibly learn all the in's and out's, do's and don't's of the local culture, you can begin to see the world more like your hosts do.

Local agents or consultants are often the best source of information about social and business etiquette, including greetings, gifts, entertaining, social hierarchy, and other important issues. They are also helpful for initiating business contacts and introducing you to the right people. Although their services are sometimes costly, these individuals can act as a vital bridge across the cultural gap. Your local representative can also help insure successful contract performance. He can regularly inquire as to the status of the project and confirm that it is receiving the necessary attention. Hire the very best local help you can afford; this isn't a place to economize. Select your agent carefully, and only after speaking with a number of impartial references.

12

Quickies

Whenever I talk with people about negotiating, a handful of topics, concerns, and questions seem to come up again and again. In this chapter we'll look at some of these everyday negotiating issues. I won't treat anything exhaustively, my goal being only to offer some ideas that you might find useful, provocative, or entertaining. Enjoy!

1. What if the other side won't negotiate?

If your otherwise amiable counterpart is unwilling to enter into a give-and-take with you on an issue, briefly try taking a very firm lead—dancing for him, in effect. Let's say the first issue is quantity, and your counterpart—a person of few words—says, "200 units." You ask if he's sure about that number, and he says, "Yup." Gently krunch his position again: "What can we do to raise that number?" If his response is still indifferent or negative, it's time to play Fred Astaire. Imagine dancing with a totally limp partner. You'd have to pick him up bodily and muscle him here and there around the dance floor. Negotiate similarly: "If you could go to 300 units, I'll bet I could get you 90 days on the invoice and maybe a better price. Would that be of interest?" [Heave.] See if anything happens. If not, try another robust by-yourself dance step: "All right, could you do 275 units if I got you a price under $500 each?" [Heave.] Each one of these moves is the next step along your steeply tapered concession curve.

If there's still no progress after these two concessions, move on to other issues. Periodically revisit the stalled item, krunching and perhaps making another small concession or two. If the other side remains firm (or nonresponsive), that issue will eventually become the only thing standing in the way of final agreement. If it's a very important item to you—and you have the luxury of a little time—put the talks on hold. Reconvene the discussions closer to the deadline. If the pause hasn't inspired a concession from your counterpart, he's probably at or very near his bottom line on the issue. If his offer is within your Envelope, nibble and close; if it's not, politely declare your bottom line. If that's unacceptable to him, end the meeting on the most upbeat note you can manage.

2. What if the other side is difficult or sensitive?

Let's deal with difficult (angry, hostile, ornery, generally disagreeable) first. Aside from the obvious fact that they're unpleasant to work with, difficult people actually negotiate pretty much like everybody else. They think rationally most of the time, and they're motivated by the usual carrots and sticks. If you can manage it, the best approach is to try to ignore their obnoxious behavior and keep to your game plan. Be pragmatic: Your goal is to reach an agreement, not to give the other side a lesson in manners. Slap a smile on your face and keep it there until the job is finished.

Be particularly careful not to change your concession pattern because your counterpart is acting like a jerk. It's amazing how the other side can pull our strings where concessions are concerned. When otherwise competent negotiators suddenly adopt particularly self-destructive concession patterns (escalating, shaving concessions, or stonewalling, for example) their explanation will usually be, "Well, that's what the other side is doing!" Surely there must be a better standard than the worst behavior at the table. Don't let the other side's stinginess tempt you to adjust your concession slope.

Strangely, a very effective way to deal with a difficult person is to apologize. Apologize even though you didn't do anything wrong, and keep apologizing until they stop yelling. Apologizing won't hurt your bargaining position, and most people find it almost impossible to continue berating someone who's apologizing.

If someone is totally irrational, don't bother trying to negotiate with him. You can't bargain with a lunatic. The usual prime directive—enlightened self-interest—isn't operating. Carrots and sticks are of no interest.

Especially sensitive people (or normal people dealing with especially sensitive issues) require patient and solicitous negotiation. The opening offer is particularly dangerous in high-sensitivity situations, and should be approached with extreme caution. An assertive but realistic offer—one that would be entirely appropriate under ordinary circumstances—may so shock a sensitive counterpart that she will simply refuse to negotiate further. Some negotiations particularly prone to opening-offer hypersensitivity include domestic-relations matters (divorce, custody of children, support, the division of marital property), the sale of a personal residence or a family "heirloom," and the sale of any item on which the negotiator has invested considerable personal time and effort (a car she customized, a work of art he created).

3. How do you negotiate with children?

Kids are born with the ability to negotiate. They have Rule 11: Never accept the other side's first offer imprinted in their DNA. Kids always make counteroffers: "What about tomorrow?" "How about if I promise to clean up my room?" Parents often misread this nascent bargaining behavior as uppity, and try to stamp it out: "Stop talking back." I love it when my kid asks me to double his allowance. Where other parents might see a greedy brat, I see a child starting high.

Kids instinctively understand, respond to, and participate in bargaining. It gives them a way to assert some control over their lives. By the time they're teen-agers the negotiating spark is usually gone, and persuasion (or, in the case of teenagers, whining) has become the dominant influence technique. I suspect that the signals we send our children when they try to negotiate are at least partially responsible for this. Walk into any toy store and you'll overhear a variation of the following conversation:

PARENT: You can pick out one thing.
KID: Can I get two if they're small? Or if I use some of my own money?
PARENT: You're so selfish! You'll get one present and like it. If I hear one more word you won't get anything.

What does a kid learn from this approach? He learns to be submissive, to keep his mouth shut, to be passively accepting of whatever's offered, to trust that people will be fair with him. In short, he learns to not negotiate. Even if the parent doesn't want to negotiate now, wouldn't a response like "That's an interesting idea, but we had an agreement that it would be one thing," or "No, but thanks for asking," help reinforce the idea that it's O.K. to negotiate sometimes?

Although they're natural-born negotiators, kids are often embarrassed when their parents negotiate. I believe it is the responsibility of all parents to be a grievous embarrassment to their children. Mortifying our kids is one of the few universal nurturing rituals. Our parents did it to us, we do it to our kids, they'll do it to their kids. It's tradition. In keeping with my parental embarrassing responsibilities, I like to demonstrate negotiation to my children. One such demonstration is the annual purchase of the Thomas Family Christmas tree. I get the kids out there on the tree lot, in the freezing cold. Everybody's bundled up. "Come on, Dad," they say. "Can we get this over with?" There's the ever-present teenage salesperson, warming his hands over the fire in the oil drum. In front of me are a bunch of gnarled, dead shrubs with preposterous prices, which everyone knows were purchased wholesale for a few cents each. One of the less repulsive specimens is priced at $80. It's got a price tag on it that's about a foot across. This tag is so big I've got to lean to one side to even see the tree.

I call the teenager over. "How much for this tree?" I ask him. He replies, "They're all marked, sir. That one's eighty dollars." Time to go to work. Let's lead with a krunch. I gasp—the gasp is important. "Eighty dollars? For this?" The teenager looks at me, uncomprehending, saying nothing. I continue krunching: "You can't be serious. Are you going to *decorate* it for me?" The children are staring fixedly at the ground. The teenager still says nothing; his expression is a mixture of surprise and confusion. Krunching may not work with this kid. Time to counteroffer: "I'll give you five dollars for it." The teenager's jaw drops, and at the same moment, my kids run away! "We don't know him," they say over their shoulders as they flee. "Who is that man? He's no relation to us. We've never seen him before."

I wind up paying, oh, $78, $79 for the tree. But what entertainment! Also, I get a free tree stand. That's my nibble. Every year, I get another tree stand. I've got 30 tree stands in my garage. I write the year on it and throw it in the stack. It's my way of keeping score.

One other thing about negotiating with kids is that *they don't keep their deals*:

PARENT: Everybody downstairs!

KID: [on sofa, watching television; part of before-school wake-up-get-ready ritual]: Let me see the end of the show! It's only got five more minutes!

PARENT: [having read *Negotiate to Win* and now attempting to bargain]: You can watch till the end if you promise to turn the TV off and come downstairs as soon as it's over. O.K.?

KID: Sure!

Twenty minutes later, no action. Kids don't keep their deals.

4. How do you negotiate with your boss?

We'll consider the question that immediately comes to mind—salary—in the next section. But the vast majority of boss-subordinate negotiations have nothing to do with salary, so let's deal with them first.

Subordinates don't negotiate enough with their bosses. There's lots of blame to share on this, but the important thing is that everybody—and the organization—is worse off as a result. Subservience leads to low morale, poor decision-making, and reduced productivity.

In a typical case, a boss will give a subordinate a task that—unknown to the boss—exceeds the subordinate's readily available resources. The subordinate, who prides herself on being a team player, salutes and says, "Yes, sir!" She knows she's got a problem, but she doesn't want to complain; besides, it's an opportunity to show how valuable she is. The boss hasn't a clue that the subordinate must work nights and weekends to complete the task, and thus expresses no gratitude for these extraordinary efforts. The result is (1) an employee who feels overworked and unappreciated; (2) slipshod work; or (3) both. Of course, if the work is deficient, the boss will let the employee know immediately. Each time this cycle is repeated the employee becomes more unhappy and less productive.

Most bosses don't want to make poor decisions, give unreasonable assignments, or embitter their employees by requiring them to sacrifice their personal lives. But yes-people unwittingly encourage their bosses to do all those things. By refusing to speak up, sycophants deprive their bosses of information they need to manage intelligently.

The ideal time for boss-subordinate negotiations is when the boss first gives an assignment. If the project is well-considered and within your capacity, negotiating isn't called for. But if you believe it needs to be rethought, or if, given its deadline and priority, it clearly exceeds readily available resources, you have a responsibility to negotiate it.

First, make sure you fully understand the project. This is a very important step from which you mustn't be deterred, either by your timidity or the boss's impatience. It's even O.K. to be a little pushy about this, if you must. If you jump into an assignment with a flawed understanding of what the boss really wants, you'll look bad, the boss will be angry, and everybody's time will be wasted. Get agreement on the overall outline, the tasks and subtasks, and the desired outcome. Discuss the anticipated short- and long-term effects. If you see public relations, political, ethical, or legal issues that the boss may not have noticed, raise them.

Next, if the project seems to exceed the available resources, point this out and attempt to discover where there might be flexibility. Krunch each of the task elements. Is every individual report necessary? Is the deadline flexible? Must everything be completed before the deadline? Could some elements be delivered later? Would a preliminary draft by the deadline be sufficient, or must the work be in final form? Krunch the resources, as well. Is assistance available from within the organization? Can outside help be obtained?

Armed with this information, make your offer to the boss. Propose a package—or better, alternative packages—that provide for successful completion of the assignment: "If you can let me have an additional programmer, I can get it done on time," or "If we can get Tom's group to take over my current project, I can get this one done on time," or "If you can give me two more weeks, I can get it done," or "I can give you subtasks A and B by the deadline, and subtask C a week later." Your timeframe proposals should be a little high to allow for unanticipated events, and to provide some flexibility if the boss should wish to negotiate further.

If the boss regularly refuses to negotiate assignments that are ill-considered or require out-of-your-hide personal time to complete, the next section may help you negotiate a salary high enough to make the situation tolerable. In the long run you'll probably be happier if you negotiate yourself a new job.

5. How do you negotiate your salary?

Whether you're a job seeker or a current employee, salary negotiations will probably rank right up near the top of your "most stressful meetings" index. Certainly we should enjoy and be proud of our work, and certainly some very fortunate people have such terrific jobs that they'd do the same work as a volunteer if they could afford to. Still, a portion of what we feel about ourselves and our employers is tied to our compensation. So many plans, hopes, and expectations revolve around salaries and raises. But despite the crucial importance of how much money we make, most of us approach our salary negotiations as victims. We walk in, we're given "the number" by the boss (accompanied, perhaps, by a few words of explanation), we feel joy or disappointment, and we go back to work.

My students complain that they have no power to negotiate salary with their bosses. As a boss myself, I must respectfully disagree. If you're a crummy employee, you have little or no power. But if you're a good employee, you have a great deal.

What power do you have? You have the power to be more cooperative or less, to do outstanding or merely competent work, to be resourceful and creative or spitefully compliant. You have the power to make your department look good or bad, to help your boss succeed or fail. That's a *ton* of power.

Those employees who aren't held back by the typical employee-as-victim mentality, and who actually do attempt to negotiate their salaries, often do it so poorly that the results are disastrous. As they watch their former colleague's belongings being packed, the remaining employees are strongly reinforced in their belief that you either take the pay that's offered or you leave.

Here are a few suggestions that may help you get the salary you want without having to change employers:

A. Don't expect your employer to negotiate for you. Where money is concerned, your interests diverge somewhat from your employer's. To your employer, you're an expense. The more he pays you, the less profit he makes. Smart employers spend as little as possible to get (and keep) the talent they need. Trusting your employer to "take care of you" in the salary department could be a costly mistake indeed.

B. Do your homework. Prior to a salary discussion, make a comprehensive list of your accomplishments. These are what determine your value as an employee. What specific contributions did you make to organizational goals? What savings did you bring about? What additional revenues did you generate? Where did you increase productivity? Write these things down. Don't assume the boss knows, or remembers, your contributions.

Be informed of your boss's and your organization's situation. Is your boss up for a promotion? Will she be needing an assistant? What are the company's numbers? When asked for a raise, bosses sometimes paint bleak pictures of flat or declining revenues. Know the facts. Have major contracts just been signed? What's happening in the industry? What are the prospects for the future? If the company is really in bad shape, it would be foolhardy to ask for a raise.

C. Be realistic. In salary negotiations, the 900-pound gorilla of supply and demand is both your ally and your enemy. On one hand, it generally prevents individual employers from paying talented people significantly less than the going rate for their services. On the other hand, unless you're a relative of the boss, it will generally prevent you from negotiating a salary significantly higher than the market.

Know what comparable jobs are paying elsewhere. Have some hard evidence. Many professional and trade groups publish salary statistics for their industry. Check the employment sections of newspapers and trade publications. Ask colleagues and employment agencies. Salary reference guides are always available online.

D. Your needs are irrelevant. Emotional appeals ("I need the money") are worse than useless in salary negotiations. From management's perspective, they're proof that not only do you not understand business, you can't even manage your own finances. To management, only the organization's needs matter, and only the organization's needs should be discussed. Focus entirely on how important you are to the company. Review the list of accomplishments you prepared. Show how you saved, or made, money for the company. Don't be shy.

E. Never threaten. The ultimatum ("If I don't get the pay I deserve, I'm going to have to start looking") is the nuclear weapon of salary negotiations, and it always blows up in the employee's face. Don't even *think* about it. Your right to work elsewhere is an implied condition of every employment relationship. You gain nothing by reiterating it to your boss. Threatening to leave smacks of disloyalty, and nothing's worse than a disloyal employee. If the boss says "no" to your threat, your only remaining choices are to back down (and lose face) or quit. Even if the boss says "yes" and you get the raise, you'll immediately become an outsider, someone who cannot entirely be trusted. If your threat reveals that you've been talking to a competitor, you're history.

Never, ever announce your intention to leave your current position unless you have a firm, written offer from your new employer. Before accepting the offer, you owe your current boss an opportunity to bid for you. Explain the situation as tactfully as possible, and give him time to prepare his response.

F. Change your job description. Merely doing your job—even doing it well—doesn't entitle you to a raise. To get anything more than a cost-of-living adjustment, you're going to have to do more or different things. Discover things the boss needs done, and suggest expanding your job responsibilities to include them. Make yourself indispensable. These additional tasks are the necessary *quid pro quos* that will let your boss save face when she gives you more money. They will also help you escape from the standard legitimacy arguments (such as salary freeze, increases limited by formula or percent, official salary range, one increase per year, or departmental limit. Because this is a job change, it's an exception.

G. Krunch, then start high. The standard procedure of trying to get the other side to open, then krunching their opening, is best. When you finally do open, start high. Use your research about what is paid elsewhere as a reference point for your opening. Remember that your first number freezes your upside, and people tend to undervalue themselves. Your proposal will probably be rejected, but you'll have room to back down and let the boss save face. Rehearse before a mirror until you can say the number with confidence.

Don't forget nonsalary and "quality of life" incentives like stock options, flexitime, health-club membership, child-care expense reimbursement, a choice assignment, a better office, more vacation, graduate or continuing education, and the like.

H. Look for trade-offs. If you're already covered by your spouse's medical plan, consider asking for a higher salary or other incentives in lieu of participating in your employer's health plan. If you meet firm resistance on salary, suggest additional vacation time instead. Signing bonuses are increasingly popular and are frequently negotiable.

I. Timing can be everything. If you're a potential new hire, hold off the discussion of money, benefits, and perks as long as possible. Try to have the employer offer you the job first. Your leverage goes way up the moment they decide they want you. If the employer attempts to bring up money too early, finesse the issue with a statement such as, "Let's first decide if I'm the person you're looking for. Once that's settled, I'm sure we'll have no problem working out the details."

Always seize a good opportunity. If you've just done something spectacular, it's a good time to negotiate. Immediately after you win the sales award, complete the major project, or develop the new product, your leverage is at its maximum. Your boss will feel grateful and somewhat obligated, and your importance to the organization will never be clearer. This leverage fades quickly, so don't dawdle.

J. Don't take "no" for an answer. If you get a "no," don't give up. It's only "no" for now, not forever. Push for a commitment to an early, specific date for a performance/salary review.

6. How do you negotiate your termination and severance?

You've been deinstalled. Decruited. Downsized. Canned. Fired. The first thing to do is negotiate a better severance deal for yourself.

A. Behave. Take a deep breath. Of course you're distraught; don't make the situation worse by mishandling the most important meeting you're likely to have for a while: your termination meeting. Be a rock. You're making an impression on everyone you see. Be sure it's a good one. Don't let them see you sweat. Be smooth and serene. Don't say an unkind thing about anyone or anything.

B. Get the details. Find out exactly why you're being let go. Take careful notes. If you genuinely believe that you have a valid legal claim—that your employment contract was violated, for example, or that you were fired because of your race or age, or that your firing is prohibited by a whistleblower statute or the like—you should talk to an employment lawyer discreetly but promptly.

C. You have leverage. Why, you may wonder, might your former employer be willing to negotiate your severance arrangements? Because you still have a lot to offer. In particular, the organization doesn't want any trouble from you. They just want you to go away quickly and quietly. They don't want you talking to employees, the press, the Board of Directors, or the government. They certainly don't want any negative publicity. Although litigation may be the farthest thing from your mind (and you may not have even the slightest grounds to sue), they don't want to worry about the aggravation and cost of a possible lawsuit—even a frivolous one. They may want you to sign a release saying you won't take any legal action against them, or a nondisparagement promise not to badmouth the organization, or a noncompetition agreement restricting (for a period of time) who you can work for, what you can do, and where.

A number of factors will increase your leverage. If you're a long-term employee with significant accomplishments, or if you're likely to encounter special economic or other hardships, or if your termination was grossly unfair or potentially illegal, you've got added bargaining clout.

Two things will significantly shrink your leverage. If your termination is part of a general downsizing or mass layoff, you're not likely to be able to negotiate a special deal. Ditto if you were fired for misconduct.

D. Don't automatically take the standard deal. Get a detailed, written summary of the organization's severance benefits: pay, vacation and sick time, health and life insurance benefits, reemployment assistance, and any other compensation. Read the employee handbook or check with Human Resources.

It you're not offered anything and your organization doesn't have a written severance policy, call some former employees and find out what they received. Learn what is standard in your industry. Mention these to your former employer. Point out your many contributions and the financial hardships you're facing. Paint a grim picture of the current job market.

If you're still not offered severance, consider asking to talk to someone higher up in the organization. If that doesn't work, see item F, below.

Set an Envelope. Your opening should be assertive but not unreasonable. The opening, target, and bottom line should all reflect industry standards, the organization's practices, and your needs. The company will open with a package that includes, say, three months' severance pay. After krunching, you should open with a year or even more. Don't forget the important nonsalary issues such as continued health, disability, and life insurance coverage, outplacement assistance, the temporary use of an office, telephone, and secretary. Be sure to negotiate how your departure will be explained to potential future employers. This will come in handy when interviewers ask you why you left your job.

A note of caution: Never tie your receipt of extra severance to your keeping mum about something (such as not telling the SEC about a deceptive accounting practice). That's conspiracy and/or extortion; both are serious crimes.

E. Don't be hurried. Don't be pushed into immediately signing a release or a nondisparagement or noncompetition agreement. Ask for a reasonable amount of time to review the proposed agreements with your advisers. Don't be intimidated if your former employer says you must sign by a deadline. Such deadlines are almost always negotiable. Trade off signing such agreements for a more generous severance package. In addition, the duration and scope of the noncompetition agreement can (and if appropriate, should) be negotiated.

F. Do you need a lawyer? If there's no potential legal claim, there's not a lot of money at stake, and your former employer is behaving decently, you don't need a lawyer. Bringing a lawyer into such circumstances would likely do more harm than good, especially to your future relationship with your former employer.

On the other hand, if you're being treated inexcusably, or lots of money is involved, or you've got a potential legal claim, you should be represented by counsel. Even the suggestion that you're thinking about bringing in a lawyer will often be enough to generate some extra concessions from your former employer.

7. How do you negotiate a house purchase?

Even though there are reams of excellent material on this topic, questions about buying and selling houses come up so frequently that it's obviously very important to people. Let's approach it first from the buyer's perspective, then from the seller's.

Buyers

Agents. Most house-buying projects start in a real estate office, so the odds are that you'll be working with a real estate agent or broker. This agent (the "selling agent") will probably be a very nice person who will work diligently, driving you hither and yon, to find you the house of your dreams. Once a candidate dream house is located, the agent will help you draw up an offer (somewhat below the house's asking price, in order to "test the water") and will present your offer to the "listing agent" who is marketing the house for its owners. You may have confided to "your" agent that because you truly love the house you would be prepared to raise your offer, if necessary—up to the asking price, even—in order to get it.

Shortly after this conversation, "your" agent will pick up the phone and tell the listing agent that you just said you'd be willing to pay the asking price if necessary. Surprised? Don't be. The agent was legally obligated to make that call. It comes as a real shock to would-be house buyers to learn that the friendly agent with whom they have worked so hard to find a home isn't "their" agent at all. They don't have an agent. In the majority of residential real estate transactions, nobody works for the purchaser. Both the listing and selling agents are paid by the seller (they split the 6–7% commission), work exclusively for the seller, and owe their undivided fiduciary loyalty to the seller. Any relevant confidences (your maximum price, for example) that you might disclose to either agent must be reported immediately to the seller. Purchasers have good reason to be paranoid. They don't have a friend in the world.

There are two solutions to this problem. One is to deal more effectively ("guardedly" may be a better word) with the selling and listing agents. The other is to consider getting your own agent—a buyer's agent or broker.

It may seem rude, but you really shouldn't give the agent much more information than your name, the kinds of houses you want to see, and whether or not you're financially able to buy them. Most lenders are quite happy to "prequalify" you for a mortgage up to a certain size, and to confirm it in writing. This letter is all the financial information the agent needs. The more you reveal about how much you make, your anticipated raises, bonuses, and promotions, the location of your office, the sale of your current residence, why and when you're moving, the schools you'd like your children to attend, and how much you cherish the seller's house, the more bargaining power you give the seller. Be especially skeptical if an agent promotes a house that is listed with the agent's own firm. This situation is known as a "dual agency." Since the firm stands to get the entire commission, their own agents are often given extra money in dual agency situations.

In the past few years, so-called "buyer's brokers" have become more popular in certain parts of the country. If you're a first-time buyer, new to an area, or have little time for house-hunting, a buyer's broker or agent may be an especially good idea. Buyer's agents will help you through the entire process, giving you advice about candidate properties, helping you determine a negotiating Envelope, suggesting contract terms, helping you find financing, and assisting with inspection and settlement.

The loyalty of the buyer's agent belongs entirely to the buyer for one very important reason: The buyer pays him. As a practical matter, having a buyer's agent costs the buyer little or nothing out of pocket. A simple addendum to the purchase contract "authorizes" the seller to pay the buyer's agent's fee (half of the commission offered by the seller) at settlement.

Referrals from satisfied friends are your best source for qualified buyer's agents. Interview several before selecting. Some buyer's agents ask for an agreement obligating you to only buy a home through them for a three-to-six-month period. Others request a nonrefundable, up-front deposit of as much as 0.5% of the anticipated price of the home, which is later credited against their fee when—and if—the buyer finds and buys a house. I recommend against lengthy "exclusives" and upfront fees. If you and the buyer's agent don't get along, if you're unhappy with his work, if you'd like to go out and do some looking on your own, or if you want to use a number of brokers, you should be able to do so without penalty.

Although the data are very preliminary, it appears that buyers with agents do about 5% better than those without. On a $300,000 house, that's a $15,000 saving with no associated cost. Makes sense to me.

Dealing with FSBOs. My advice is to avoid buying a FSBO (For Sale by Owner, pronounced "Fizz-bo") home if possible. FSBO deals regularly have more problems than those where licensed real estate agents are involved. FSBO sellers often have very inflated ideas of what their homes are worth. They can be quite greedy (they are, after all, trying to avoid paying a sales commission) and difficult to negotiate with. While licensed agents are required to disclose known defects in homes they sell, FSBO sellers may not be. However, any good buyer's agent will know how to deal with a FSBO.

If you choose to buy a FSBO house, be sure to obtain a price discount for the additional legwork you will be taking on. At a minimum, you will have to obtain your own financing without the valuable assistance—and contacts—of a real estate agent. Don't use a sales contract purchased from a stationery store, as they usually aren't as good as those used by agents. I'd recommend having an experienced real estate attorney prepare the contract. Insist that the property pass a professional inspection and require the FSBO seller to disclose in writing all known defects in the house.

New construction. A newly constructed house in a development or subdivision presents a tough negotiating problem. The terms of the builder's construction loan may preclude her from lowering prices. Also, because mortgage loan appraisals are based on "market value," if she reduces the price of your house, it will instantly lower the appraised value—and the maximum mortgage loan amount—of every similar unsold house in her development. A single price break could cost her again and again. Still, some residential developers will bargain on price, particularly if the market is slow and the competition is cutting prices. If the builder says she doesn't negotiate price, ask to take a look at the contracts for houses sold in her development within the past couple of months.

With new construction you're much more likely to be successful getting "in-kind" concessions than price concessions. Negotiate for no-charge (or builder's cost, as a fallback) extras: a finished basement, a deck, an extra bathroom, additional landscaping. The builder often has the crew and materials on site, and can do this work at a small incremental cost. Upgrades—on carpet, appliances, and lighting and plumbing fixtures—also make excellent concessions when buying a new home. Finally, the builder may be willing to pay some or all of your closing costs or help "buy down" your mortgage rate.

The closer an unsold house is to completion, the more it costs the builder to carry and the more flexible he is likely to be. Because bankruptcy is so common in the building industry and developers regularly disappear, be sure your builder provides a comprehensive home warranty from an independent warranty company.

Offers and counteroffers. While houses are usually overpriced, there is no set percentage of the seller's asking price that you should offer. Except in the most unusual circumstances, never offer the full asking price. If you do, the sellers will know they could have sold it for more. This may spell trouble later if problems arise before settlement.

Have the real estate agent prepare a detailed, written market evaluation, and establish your Envelope around that evaluation. Ignore the asking prices of the comparable homes, focusing instead on recent sales prices. Offer an assertive figure reflecting prices for similar properties, factoring in the pluses and minuses of the target property, the strength of the current real estate market, and your relative strength as a purchaser. The lower your proposed down payment and the more contingencies in your offer, the less leverage you will have in negotiating price. The weaker the market or the more desperate the seller, the lower the price you can offer without offending the seller. Even if the market analysis shows the property to be a steal at the full asking price, offer three to five percent less.

Buyers should remember that a very low offer for the seller's residence says—inadvertently, of course—that he's living in a dump. When you make somebody an offer on his castle, he always takes it personally. The seller may be so insulted by your aggressive opening that he'll refuse to deal with you further, no matter what you might subsequently offer. If the target property isn't the seller's residence, he'll have less emotional attachment to it and you can be more assertive with your opening. Counteroffer using the classic steeply tapered concession pattern. Because real estate offers and counteroffers are almost always in writing, krunches are pretty much out of the picture.

You'll always increase your negotiating leverage by being pleasant. When you tour the property, spend some time establishing a personal rapport with the seller. Praise the property profusely. Keep your criticisms to yourself. Sellers like people who like their house. If the seller dislikes you, he'll view your offer more critically, reject it more easily, and be less inclined to counteroffer.

As in any other sort of negotiating, face-to-face is best. You're far more persuasive in person than you are acting through an agent. Agents typically discourage direct buyer-seller contact. It may surprise you to learn that you have the legal right to be in attendance when your offer is presented to the seller. Absent compelling reasons to the contrary, you should take advantage of this right.

Don't negotiate the purchase of a residence with the same cool objectivity as you would an ordinary investment. There is a certain romance to buying a home that, in many cases, should take precedence over textbook hard bargaining. Buy the house you love. If it's priced appropriately (or nearly so) and you can afford it, don't lose it over price. However, don't let yourself get into the position of wanting a property so much that you can't walk away from the deal if it doesn't measure up to your original requirements.

Other contract issues. Price is only part—and sometimes not the most important part—of the negotiated deal. Your offer should be contingent upon at least two things: your obtaining mortgage financing, and a successful professional inspection of the property. You may also make your offer contingent upon the sale of your current home.

The mortgage financing contingency should specify the rate and terms that you could afford to pay. If the mortgage market goes up beyond those terms, you have the option of being released from the contract. The inspection should show the house to be in satisfactory condition. If it reveals problems, the seller must repair them before settlement. If he refuses, you have the choices of canceling the deal or using the problems as leverage to negotiate a better deal.

If the contract requires you to demonstrate to the seller your ability to obtain financing, make sure that the demonstration is "reasonable." That way, the standard, heavily hedged lender's letter of intent will be satisfactory. If the demonstration must be satisfactory "in the seller's sole discretion," it gives the seller the absolute right to terminate the contract. You don't have a contract to buy the house, you have an option—exercisable by the seller.

Negotiate for a generous closing date. Bargain for any fixtures (an attractive chandelier, for example) or appliances you desire. Things that are "attached" to the property (a kitchen range, a ceiling fan, wall-to-wall carpet, window blinds, for example) are considered "fixtures" and usually convey to the buyer upon sale; however, to avoid misunderstandings, the contract should spell out in detail exactly which appliances and fixtures stay or go. If you'll need a riding lawn mower and the seller has one, why not nibble for it?

Try to keep the earnest money deposit as small as possible, and insist that it be kept in a separate, interest-bearing escrow account. Get the seller to agree to pay as much of your closing costs as possible. Closing costs generally include loan fees, attorney's fees, termite report, survey, title search, and local and state sales, recording and transfer taxes and fees.

Lenders and other players. Don't forget to negotiate with the bank. Best strategy: Pursue back-up financing. Let both banks know there's competition, but don't tell them who. Also, don't be discouraged by the inherent legitimacy of the bank. Their "standard" rate, fees, and other terms are often negotiable.

The other players—the home inspection firm, the moving company, the surveyor, the settlement attorney—also provide excellent negotiating opportunities. Since it's unrealistic for you to learn enough about each of these markets to make assertive but sensible offers, krunches are the best bet.

Sellers

Agents. When you select an agent to sell your house, you're hiring a professional, just like a doctor or a lawyer. Interview several agents before making a choice. You will be working together closely, so select someone you like and trust. Have each candidate prepare a written analysis of the local market and their recommended listing price for your home. Ask each agent how many listings he has. If the answer is more than 15 or so, you'd be better off selecting someone else. Speak with some recent clients of the leading candidate to find out how satisfied they were. When you've decided on an agent, commit only to a short listing of no more than 90 days. If the agent wants a longer listing, insist on an unconditional right to cancel the listing at any time without cause. Don't advertise in the listing your willingness to pay closing costs.

Current sales commissions are 6 or 7% of the purchase price. The agent's commission is negotiable, but it's probably not a good idea to negotiate it. A reduced commission reduces the agent's incentive to quickly find you a buyer. A lower commission is appropriate if the seller assumes the responsibility of showing the property and holding weekend open houses. It is also quite proper to negotiate an adjustment of the commission if the agent produces an offer that is considerably lower than his projected selling price.

Selling as a FSBO. I don't recommend it. Selling a house today is just not an amateur undertaking. Every "no-money-down" and "make millions in real estate" seminar teaches its students to target FSBOs, because they're so vulnerable. FSBO sellers generally attract bargain-hunters and not much else. A professional agent will almost certainly sell your house faster, at a higher price, than you can. The agent will also help the buyers get a mortgage and handle the many other details leading up to settlement.

Offers and counteroffers. Never accept the buyer's first offer. If you do, he'll know he could have bought it for less. His unhappiness may show up in a host of presettlement disagreements.

It's a mistake to assume that because the agent's commission is tied to the price, the agent will automatically fight for the highest figure. The agent will fight for a reasonable price, but with the earliest closing date and the strongest buyer. In all likelihood, you alone will be fighting for the highest price. Another mistake is to assume that agents know anything more about negotiation than you do. I have had the pleasure of working with a number of major real estate firms and associations, and I've learned that while most agents are experts on real estate, they are no better or worse than anyone else in the negotiating department. You are your own best negotiation consultant.

Other contract issues. The larger the earnest money deposit, the more serious the buyer is about going forward. As a practical matter, the deposit is the buyer's maximum risk if he backs out of the deal, and it is your maximum restitution. Don't take your house off the market for a dinky deposit. If the buyer defaults, the agents will be entitled to some of the deposit in lieu of their commission, and only what's left of it will be yours.

The standard "contingencies" in a purchase offer are (1) purchasers' ability to obtain financing; (2) successful professional inspection of the property; and, less frequently, (3) purchasers' sale of their current residence.

While the buyer's offer will almost always have a financing contingency, it should be limited to terms that are reasonable in the current mortgage market. If the rate specified is unrealistically low, the buyer will have a free "out" from the contract. The contract should also require the buyer to obtain a loan commitment promptly, within 30 days. If financing cannot be obtained, you can quickly get your house back on the market. Ask for complete financial information, including a credit report or other satisfactory demonstration of the buyer's financial ability to qualify for the mortgage. If you're considering holding some or all of the financing yourself, this is mandatory.

If the buyer's offer contains a sale-of-their-current-house contingency, insist that a 72-hour "kick-out" clause be included in the contract. This clause provides that until the sale contingency is removed, your house will remain on the market. If you accept another ("backup") offer on your house, you will notify the original buyers and give them 72 hours to delete the sale contingency and give you satisfactory evidence that they will be able to obtain financing. If they are unwilling or unable to do so, you may terminate their contract and sell to the backup buyers. The clause should also provide that the buyers must start marketing their house promptly, within a week at the most.

Because so many contracts don't settle for one reason or another (usually involving the failure of one or more contract contingencies), prudent sellers and their agents should continue to show the house to potential purchasers, and accept one or even two backup contracts, even after the first contract is accepted, at least until all contingencies have been removed. Backup contracts help combat "buyer's remorse" by confirming the buyer's opinion about how wonderful the property is.

8. How do you get the best deal on a car?

Everybody wants to learn how to do better car deals. I can't give a talk on any aspect of negotiation without getting at least one question about car deals. It's a little depressing to deliver a brilliant, witty, and insightful lecture on trade negotiations with Asia, only to discover that what everybody really wanted to hear about was car deals.

In truth, there is very little I can add to the many excellent books and articles that have been written about car buying. Nevertheless, because this is a negotiating issue of such fervent interest—it touches almost everybody's pocketbook, after all—this book would be incomplete without a discussion of car deals. Let's bow to popular pressure and take a whack at it.

New cars

We love new cars, but we hate buying them. Survey after survey has confirmed that consumers loathe the rug-bazaar atmosphere of most dealerships. In response, automakers constantly experiment with programs—"no-haggle" dealerships, "value-priced" cars, and warm-and-fuzzy sales approaches (giving salespeople sensitivity training; calling them "customer-assistance representatives" or "associates") designed to make new-car buying less of an ordeal.

No-dicker car pricing (also known as standardized, one-price, single-price, haggle-free, no-haggle, no-hassle, no-negotiation, and non-negotiable pricing) certainly isn't new. In addition to its standardized parts, Henry Ford's Model T had a standardized price. General Motors reincarnated the practice in 1990 when it introduced its Saturn line with an interesting twist: a discounted, but basically non-negotiable price. GM's no-haggle experiment with Saturn has proven extremely popular, and now each of the Big Three American automakers sell some models with no-haggle prices.

Alas, the comfort of no-dicker pricing is purchased at a considerable cost to the consumer. Customers at haggle-free dealers pay more for their cars than buyers who bargain skillfully. And no-haggle dealers can, and do, boost profits by cutting staff, adding inflated fees, pushing expensive extras, offering costlier financing and leasing, and paying less for trade-ins.

Is the sun setting on new-car haggling? Don't count on it. Even though automakers have spent millions trying to persuade their 20,000 U.S. dealers to be nicer, it hasn't worked so far. The manufacturers' charm-school reforms are defeated by their own incentive systems that reward volume and turnover—"moving the metal." The most successful dealers know that what really moves the metal is the hard sell: creating feelings of excitement, desire, and urgency in their customers. Protected by state laws that greatly restrict manufacturers' ability to dictate sales practices, dealers stand on their right to use every hard-sell trick in the book. Less than 10% of the nation's new-car dealerships have experimented with fixed-price selling. Many who have tried it have reverted to more traditional practices. For the foreseeable future, haggling for new cars won't end. The dealers won't let it.

Let's briefly explain how car dealers make money when they sell new cars. There are five main sources of potential profit: markup, trade-in, financing, "packs," and fees. Just like any other business, car dealers buy low (from the factory, at wholesale) and sell high (to consumers, at retail). Markup is the difference between wholesale and retail. They can do the same thing when they take a car in trade. They buy low (from you, at wholesale) and, after cleaning up the car, spraying protectant all over the interior and silicone on the tires to make them shine, they sell high (to other consumers, at retail). If the dealership arranges financing or leasing for you, it gets a hefty referral fee from the bank actually making the loan or lease. The longer the term and the higher the rate, the bigger the fee. "Packs" are the small but especially profitable items that dealers push late in the negotiation, when customers have that new-car smell deep in their lungs. They include extended warranties, vehicle protection packages (paint sealant, rustproofing, fabric protection, and door guards), tinted windows, anti-theft systems, and other extras. Finally, a host of mock-official "conveyance," "document preparation," "dealer preparation," and "advertising" fees are added and the deal is totaled up.

Getting the best price on your new car boils down to a four-step process:

1. Decide on the car you want.
2. Find out what the dealer paid for it.
3. Commit yourself to paying no more than a few hundred dollars above that.
4. Avoid the gauntlet of ingenious dealer gimmicks (trade-in, financing, packs, and fees) designed to get you to pay more.

The first step, deciding on the car you want, isn't as easy as it sounds. There are hundreds of models to choose from, most of which are available in a number of different trim lines. Each trim line, in turn, has a different set of standard and optional equipment. You should visit the showrooms twice: once to shop, and once to buy. For now, you're just shopping. Ask the receptionist at each dealership for the name of the top salesperson, and work only with that person each time you visit. The best salespeople make extra money on the dealer's bonus plans, which reward the largest number of cars sold, irrespective of profit. The prospect of this bonus money will encourage the salesperson to be a little more generous on your deal.

Take lots of test drives, ask lots of questions, eyeball some window stickers (but don't take them seriously), and collect lots of glossy brochures. The more time each dealership invests in you, the more flexible it will tend to be later during the negotiating endgame. Don't answer any questions about when or why you need a car, how much you're willing to pay (monthly or in total), other models you're looking at, other dealers you're visiting, whether you'll be trading in, or if you'll be needing financing. Don't leave any deposits for any reason, and don't even think about buying at this stage. When you've collected enough information, make a leisurely choice.

Now that you've selected your car, your next task is to find out how much it cost the dealer. Before we go further, let's define a few terms. The "window sticker" is the suggested retail price sheet that the manufacturer glues to the new car's window. This number is sheer fantasy and should be disregarded for negotiating purposes. The "factory invoice" or "dealer invoice" is the confidential bill sent by the manufacturer to the dealer for each new car. Sometimes a dealer will reveal this invoice to a particularly tenacious customer with the explanation: "I'm not supposed to do this, but lemme show you what I've got in this car." The official dealer invoice is widely assumed to be the dealer's actual wholesale cost for the vehicle. But dealers of most domestic and foreign cars actually pay less than the dealer invoice. This discount is known as "holdback" in the car business. When you deduct the holdback from the dealer invoice, you get the true "dealer cost" for the car.

It is imperative to learn the dealer invoice, or better, the dealer cost, of your target vehicle before you begin to negotiate. There are various sources of this information, but the best I've found is the Consumer Reports New Car Price Service. Any issue of *Consumer Reports* magazine will explain how to use it, and you can access it online at www.consumerreports.com. For a small fee, *Consumer Reports* will tell you the actual dealer cost for any make and model of new car, as well as the individual dealer costs for every option and option package the factory can stick on the car. They'll also tell you about any factory-to-consumer and factory-to-dealer cash rebates available with the vehicle, what low-cost factory financing might be available, and what options are especially desirable. *Consumer Reports'* April car-buying issue includes some excellent car-buying tips (not that you'll need them). Another good car-pricing Web site is www.edmunds.com. New ones spring up all the time.

On a separate worksheet, add up the individual dealer costs for the basic car, the options, and delivery. Subtract any factory-to-dealer rebates in effect. The total is the dealer cost for the car. Your goal is to pay from $300 to $500 above this figure, inclusive of everything except sales tax and vehicle registration fees. The only exceptions to this "$300 to $500 over" goal are the top-end luxury vehicles on which you can expect to pay as much as $1,000 over, and the high-demand "hot" models that are considered separately below.

How, you may wonder, can a dealership survive selling cars at $300 over their actual cost? They work the averages. Your $300-over deal will be balanced by another deal at $2,700 over, for an average of $1,500 over. The trick is to be the $300 person, not the $2,700 person.

If you're considering selling or trading in your current car, this is an excellent time to find out what it's worth. Used car prices fluctuate constantly and even vary from region to region. Local classifieds are helpful and used car price guides can be found online, but once again *Consumer Reports* seems to have the best data. For a small fee, their Used Car Price Service (accessible through their Web site at www.consumerreports.com) will give you accurate, regionalized prices.

Visit the banks or credit unions offering the best rates on new car financing (or leasing, if that's your plan), and find out how much they will let you borrow for the car you want. If possible, get preapproved for the loan or lease. Don't sign any legally binding documents yet. If you're financing, try not to borrow for more than 36 months. With longer loans, there's a real possibility that the car's value will depreciate faster than the loan is paid down, resulting in your being "upside down"—owing more than the car is worth—until the last year or two of the loan. Until then you'd have to come up with extra cash just to sell or trade the car. We'll consider leases in a separate section below.

It's now time to return to the showrooms to buy. Try to purchase as close to the last day of the month as possible. You'll benefit from the dealers' month-end sales quota and inventory financing ("floor plan") pressures. Work with the same salesperson you did on your "shopping" visit, thereby adding to the time already invested in you. Since you have little negotiating leverage on cars that must be ordered from the factory, try to select a car from the dealer's on-the-lot inventory. If the car you select has any options that differ from those on your worksheet, refigure the total dealer invoice.

It's time for the games to begin. Your immediate goal is to get a firm but "shoppable" offer from this dealer. Show the salesperson your dealer cost calculations, and tell him, (1) you're prepared to buy the car immediately from the dealer who gives you the best price, and (2) you want *his* best price, now. Make it clear that you will be taking bids from other dealers.

Be prepared for some aggressive "you can't be serious" krunches when you reveal your number. Here are some other standard responses from salespeople, to which you should reply as indicated:

1. **"Your numbers are way out of line."** Ask the salesperson to show you the dealer invoice and the holdback amount. Ask him to point out your errors. It won't happen.

2. **"What would be a fair profit for me to make on this car?"** or **"What would you be willing to pay for this car?"** or **"What sort of monthly payment do you think you could afford?"** Each of these questions asks you to make an offer. You're there to *receive* offers, not make them. Reiterate your request for a firm quote. Never discuss monthly payments with a salesperson. Only the cash price matters.

3. **"If I could get it for you at $500 over cost, would you buy today?"** Notice he isn't making an offer, he's trying to get you to make one— and making offers isn't what you're there to do. Ask him if $500 over is a firm offer. If it isn't, continue to insist on a firm offer. If it is, tell him that if none of his competitors can beat it, you'll buy at that price before the end of the month.

4. **"I'll sell to you at $500 over cost, but only if you buy it right now."** You need an offer you can shop. "Right now" isn't shoppable, so it isn't a valid offer. The "today only," "tonight only," "one-time only,"

"right now," and "this car probably won't be here tomorrow" dead-line is a time-honored sales technique to create urgency and keep you from shopping the deal. Car salespeople know that if you leave without buying, you'll shop, and if you shop, they'll probably lose. In spite of what the salesperson says, at a minimum the price will be good until the end of the month.

5. "Shop the competition, get your best price, and I guarantee I'll beat it." You're not going to give anybody "last look." You need to compare everybody's best number on equal terms.

If the salesperson still refuses to give you a firm offer, tell him that if you leave without one he'll be out of the running. Stick to your guns and you'll get your quote. Move on to the next dealer and repeat the process. As you move from dealer to dealer, check your answering machine frequently for calls "improving" earlier quotes.

Note how many dealerships seem designed to be intimidating, with the sales managers holding court on an elevated platform over-looking the sales floor (called "the tower") or in a glass-walled room. Remember that dealers have been known to eavesdrop on customer conversations when the salesperson is out of the room. The walls may have ears.

Keep alive—in the dealer's mind, at least—the prospects of your trading in, financing through the dealership, and loading the car with packs. Don't close these doors yet, as they're powerful induce-ments to the dealership to give you an especially attractive price. If you're asked whether you'll be financing and/or trading, say "maybe" and leave it at that. There's no need to disclose that you've already shopped for financing. Better to play dumb. If the salesperson wants to appraise your potential trade, let him, but make it clear that you want separate offers for the new car and the trade. If you're so in-clined, you may express your admiration for extended warranties and protective coatings. Watch the salesperson's eyes light up. Re-fundable or not, don't leave any deposits—for "good faith," "earnest money," to "lock in the quoted price," or for any other reason. Sales-people ask for such deposits because they subtly entangle the customer with the dealership.

When the lowest-price dealer emerges from your auction, krunch the next-lowest. Tell him that he's close but that you have a better quote. Don't say what the lower number is or who it's from. If he drops his price below the other dealer, krunch the former leader. Tell him that he was the lowest but you now have a better quote. Continue krunching until there are no further concessions being made by anybody.

If the best quote is within your Envelope—no more than $500 above dealer price—it's time to close the deal. If it's not, and the car you're after is neither an exceptionally high-demand or luxury model, a mistake's been made somewhere. Abandon your efforts for this month, refigure your numbers, and start again next month.

Revisit the lowest-price dealer. If the salesperson makes any attempt to renege on his earlier quote and raise his price because (a) a math or clerical error was made in the quote; (b) a higher offer was received for the car, which you must match; (c) unknown to the salesperson, the car you wanted was already sold, and now only more expensive models are available; or (d) the sales manager wouldn't approve the deal as quoted, you have been "lowballed." Any questions about whether you're dealing with a shyster have been answered. Your choices are two: Ignore the attempted increase and negotiate against the dealer's earlier lowball quote, or leave immediately and try to close a deal with your second-place dealer. If the number-two dealer's quote is within your Envelope, leaving is probably your best bet. You may still have time to close a deal before the end of the month. If it's not, you may wish to stick around and work on the number-one dealer a little longer.

Offer to buy the car at dealer price. Your offer will be rejected, perhaps with some vehemence. It's O.K.; car salespeople are trained to always reject the customer's first offer. Move toward your "$300 over" target in steadily decreasing increments. Only if absolutely necessary should you move past your target toward your bottom line.

As you move toward closure you'll be treated to a special private performance of the time honored ritual of good guy–bad guy. Pay close attention, as you will rarely see Rule 18 demonstrated with such consummate skill. The salesperson will disappear each time you make an offer, ostensibly to carry it to the lair of the hardhearted sales manager and beseech his acceptance. Sadly, each of these valiant efforts will fail and the salesperson will return, defeated and apologetic, with the sales manager's counteroffer. "I couldn't get him to go for it," he'll say. "He was really upset with me for even bringing it to him. Here's what he says he'll do." Written in large red letters with lots of exclamation points, these counteroffers from the sales manager will often display some thinly disguised indignation.

If the salesperson has not yet had your potential trade-in appraised, he will do so now. Remind him that you want the purchase price of the new car calculated independently of the allowance for your trade. Dealers will sometimes "overallow" on trade-ins to tranquilize customers who are being hosed on the price of the new car. You're not in this group. Because price negotiations are not going well with you, the dealership will be trying to make money on your trade. When your appraisal comes back, the news will not be good. "Woo-eee, it's got some miles on it, doesn't it? And that looks like a pretty bad wreck you were in a while back. Hope nobody was hurt. The car's a little dirty, and it's got a few rust spots. We're going to have to wholesale it. But we want to be completely fair with you. Let's look it up in the Blue Book and see what it's worth."

The "Blue Book" is the Official Used Car Guide, and while it's got tremendous legitimacy, it's perceived as a work of fiction. The numbers in the Blue Book are low, and the principal users of the Blue Book—banks, insurance companies, and car dealers—are people who *want* low numbers. The Blue Book is published by the National Automobile Dealers Association, the acronym of which is

"NADA"—almost exactly what the book says your trade is worth! Your salesperson will find the Blue Book's average wholesale number for the year, make and model of your trade, and write that number on the worksheet. The number is almost certainly much less than the car's actual worth. That's exactly what you want; the lower, the better, in fact. Don't debate it. Tell him you're interested, but remind him that you don't want to finalize the trade until you've settled on a price for the new car.

The salesperson will also introduce the idea of financing or leasing through the dealership. Ask for his rates and terms. While dealers sometimes have below-market loans and leases, they often make them available only on slow-moving cars or to customers who are overspending. Don't be surprised if your quote is far less attractive than the ones you've already gotten from other lenders. Again, that's exactly what you want; the worse, the better. Handle your financing the same way you handled your trade: Express interest, but defer further discussion until after the price for the new car has been settled.

It's also time for the salesperson to try to "pack" the deal. Salespeople are trained to work each deal for maximum profit, and since it's now apparent that not much money will be made on price, he'll try particularly hard to "get well" with high-profit packs. Be careful. Many customers, suffused with new-car aroma and already resigned to spending lots of money, become inattentive free-spenders in the waning moments of the negotiation. You don't want the extended warranty (it offers little more than the manufacturer's standard new-car warranty). Pass on the rustproofing, undercoating, paint and fabric protection. The factory has already applied them, and refills are available at most drug stores. If you genuinely want pinstripes, door guards, side molding, mud flaps, tinted windows, an alarm system, or an upgraded radio, buy it later from a specialist. You'll get more and pay less. No matter how much the salesperson may discount their prices, say "no" to the packs. If the dealer has already installed an item, treat it as a freebie. Ignore it in figuring your deal. Try to close the deal with a nibble or two on items like free floor mats, touch-up paint, shop manuals, a full tank of gas, oil changes, and a full-sized spare tire.

Once the price is agreed to, you have just one more challenge to overcome: the "F&I" (finance and insurance) guy. While he may resemble an accounting clerk, the F&I manager is really another salesperson. He sells loans, extended warranties, fabric protection, anti-theft systems, and extra fees to customers who are "in the box" with him.

The F&I guy will inquire how you'll be paying for the car. Ask him to review the trade-in allowance the dealership is offering. While it almost certainly won't be your trade's full retail value, if it's good enough to offset the hassle of selling the car privately, krunch it a few times, then take it. More likely, it won't be nearly good enough. Withdraw the trade from the deal. Tell him, "I think I'll just keep my old car."

Next, the F&I salesperson will ask about financing or leasing. Have him requote his best available financing options. Don't discuss monthly payments; concentrate strictly on rate and term. In the unlikely possibility that his loan is better than the quotes you received from outside lenders, krunch it a few times, then take it. Decline the credit life insurance and be sure there are no hidden charges, especially in the event the loan is paid off early. If his quote isn't competitive, tell him you'll be using your own prearranged financing. This may trigger a new better offer. If so, keep krunching him until he stops moving, then finance with whoever's lowest.

The F&I manager will also give the extended warranty and other packs another try, perhaps cutting the price even further than the salesperson did. You may be honored with the famous (and very effective) "If you only use it once, it's paid for itself" closing line. As before, pass. He will then prepare the sales contract. Read it very carefully before signing. Make sure that everything that's supposed to be in or out, is. Eliminate or sharply reduce any "conveyancing," "document preparation," or "dealer preparation" fees. All of this work is supposed to be included in the basic price of the car. Any "advertising" fee should be supported by an invoice to the dealer. Even if it can be documented, negotiate it aggressively. Advertising is a cost of doing business, and it should come out of the dealer's markup. He doesn't charge you a "rent" fee or an "electricity" fee, does he? Besides, you hate his ads. He should pay *you* to suffer through them. If the dealer won't cut a particular fee, try to get floor mats, oil changes, or something else in exchange.

When the sales contract is finished and checked, go ahead and sign. Make sure the finance or sales manager signs also. After the paperwork is signed the dealership will usually let you take the car home. Sometimes they'll request a personal check or a promissory note, which will be returned or destroyed when your bank settles up. That's fine. Within the next day or two, take the contract to your bank, pick up the check, and give it to the dealer. Pat yourself on the back; *you did it!*

By the way, let me assure you that the dreaded "revenge of the service department" is one of the biggest myths in the car business. A surprising number of consumers are intimidated from negotiating assertively—and may even deliberately spend extra—because they believe that somehow their behavior on the sales floor will be reciprocated later by the service department. "If I'm good to them, they'll be good to me," the reasoning goes, "and if I'm not, they won't."

Nothing could be further from the truth. They're going to hose you on service whether your deal was generous or not. Service is where most dealerships make their real money. On the other hand, the service guys usually dislike the sales guys (because they always seem to have some "emergency" requirement), have as little to do with them as possible, and would do nothing to help them out. When the service guys find out that you're the person who hosed that sales guy a few weeks back, you'll be a hero in the service department. "Hey, here's the guy!" they'll say. "Give him a free tune-up. He's one of us!" If you're still worried, remember that you never have to go back to the original dealership for service. Warranty work can be performed at any authorized dealer.

"Hot" Car Models

Every year there are a handful of new models that are so popular the manufacturers can't keep up with demand. Other cars, including limited-production and some luxury models, are manufactured in such small quantities that they're always scarce. You'll know almost immediately if the car you're after is one of these "hot" models: Nobody will have any in inventory. Or they'll have one—in purple— and they're going to auction it off to the highest bidder.

Market forces can wreak havoc on the best-laid negotiating plans. High demand and/or low supply naturally makes dealers less willing to bargain. If a dealer can sell his entire inventory of a model at full list price, he'd be crazy to negotiate with you. When the same car enjoys both high demand and low supply, its dealers can actually command a premium—selling it for more than list. This isn't price-gouging, it's free enterprise. If your heart is set on a hot car, you'll probably have to abandon the "$300 over" target suggested above. Depending on the car, the date, and the region, prices from $500 or $1,000 over dealer cost, all the way up to full list and beyond, may be commanded.

The local "auto row" may be fine for buying most cars, but your best hope of getting some kind of a deal on a hot car is to get way out of town. Urban and suburban dealers of these vehicles, swamped with orders from affluent and impatient customers, are the least inclined to be flexible. About three hours from the city ought to do it.

Used Cars

In three short years, the typical new car will have lost half its value. But much of its useful life will still remain. Escalating new-car prices and better quality standards have created an exceptionally strong used-car market. Smart consumers looking for transportation value are turning in record numbers to the used-car market—a market that is often the epitome of pricing-by-haggle.

If you're buying, a good starting point is the April issue of *Consumer Reports*. It lists the frequency of repair experience of many recent models and suggests, by price range, especially desirable and undesirable models. It also gives excellent advice on picking winners and avoiding dogs when you get down to shopping. Once you have a particular model in mind, figure out its current market—"retail"—price. This process is described earlier in the section about valuing a potential trade-in. Next, try to figure out the car's "wholesale" price—what a dealer would pay for it. Call the managers of a few used-car dealerships and ask what they'd give for a car of the model and vintage you have in mind. If you know people in the business, ask them. Make the wholesale price your target, and the retail price your bottom line. (If you're selling, these numbers are reversed.)

Now it's time to actually find the car. You've got two main choices of sellers: dealers selling new and used cars, and individuals. I'd stay away from independent used-car dealers, banks, finance companies, rental car companies, and service stations. The new-and-used dealers generally offer decent-quality cars, service, and maybe even a warranty (typically limited and brief, but better than nothing). Governmental oversight and concerns about reputation generally restrain them from the more flagrant used-car rip-offs. The bad news: You'll pay more. You'll probably get a better price from a private seller, but you'll also run a higher risk of being swindled.

Whoever you buy from, be guided by your head, not your heart. Before a final price is negotiated, ask to see the paperwork—including receipts—documenting the car's complete maintenance and repair history. Contact the former owner to find out if it was in an accident or had any other problems. And have the car inspected by a mechanic. Use this information, along with the car's mileage, options, and overall cosmetics, as bargaining leverage. If the seller hasn't got the service history or won't let you have the car checked over, don't buy it.

Leasing a Car

Either leasing or financing a vehicle will almost always be more expensive than simply paying cash for it, and in the long run, leasing usually costs more than financing. But the steadily increasing cost of new cars has made the principal advantage of leasing—low monthly payments—more attractive than ever. While you won't actually own it, you can usually lease a nicer car than you can buy for the same monthly payment.

Shop for a lease like you would for a loan: before you buy the car. Get various quotes and, ideally, preapproval. Next, negotiate the price of the car as explained above, without disclosing your intention to lease. Consumers who focus their attention on the monthly lease payment instead of the purchase price are routinely duped into signing "full pop" leases at up to 110% of the sticker price. Once the price is set, have the finance manager quote you his "best" lease. Take your time and read the lease document carefully. While the rate is all-important in financing, in leasing the rate and the terms (the legal provisions) are equally important. The lease rate is called the "money factor" and it's a small number like .0035. The dealer isn't obligated to tell you this number, but if he won't, go elsewhere. Multiply the money factor by 2400 and you have the effective "interest rate" of the lease.

The lease should be "closed-end" (you neither have to buy the car nor guarantee its value at the end of the lease), and no more than four years in duration. Three-year terms are standard. Under no circumstances should the lease be longer than the manufacturer's new-car warranty.

Look carefully at the yearly mileage allowance and the charge for extra miles. Be certain the allowance will cover your expected use.

Push for the largest annual allowance and the lowest excess-mileage charge. Note the definition of "ordinary wear and tear" because you'll be responsible for any damage beyond this. Clearly spell out what constitutes "excess" wear and tear. "Gap insurance"—to cover you for any deficiencies if the car is stolen or totaled—is a must. It should be included at no extra charge; if not, pay only up to $200 for it. If you have to terminate the lease early, you should be responsible only for the difference between what you've already paid and the car's then-current value. Remember that early in the lease, this is likely to be a pretty large number. "Acquisition fees" and "disposition fees," if any, are sometimes negotiable.

The finance manager usually has various lease packages he can make available, depending on how hard you negotiate. Rarely will he lead off with his most attractive offering. Individual lease provisions—including the factor, security deposit, set-up fees, and mileage allowance—are also negotiable.

9. How do you negotiate with airlines?

There are three principal areas where you can negotiate with airlines: delayed or canceled flights, overbooking and "bumping," and lost, damaged, and delayed luggage.

A. Delayed or canceled flights. If your flight is canceled or delayed, Rule 240 says that the airline must provide alternate transportation on another of its flights or on another carrier, at no additional cost to you. All you have to do is request this service from the airline.

The airline isn't required to do anything else. Airlines used to automatically provide meals, lodging, and telephone calls when flights were canceled or significantly delayed. These amenities are often still available, but you must ask for them—nicely but insistently. Remember: The airline has no obligation to provide them. Never be confrontational with airline personnel!

B. Overbooking and "bumping." Airlines routinely overbook flights because of anticipated last-minute cancellations and no-shows. As a result, sometimes more people show up than the plane can hold and some passengers—even those with confirmed reservations—must be "bumped." The U.S. Department of Transportation requires the airline to ask for volunteers who will give up their seats in exchange for monetary compensation or other benefits. The amount of this monetary compensation or benefits is negotiable, and the negotiation between the airline and the volunteer takes place right there at the gate. If the volunteer doesn't like the offer, she doesn't have to take it.

If there aren't enough volunteers, the airline must bump people involuntarily. In that case, unless the airline arranges a substitute flight that gets you to your destination within one hour of your originally scheduled arrival time, the Department of Transportation requires that you be given "Denied Boarding Compensation." The amount of this compensation is set by law, and it's pretty small. More importantly, if you don't like what's offered, you have the right to attempt to negotiate a larger compensation from the airline.

C. Lost, Damaged, and Delayed Luggage. If your bags are lost, damaged, or delayed, you've got some negotiating to do. If your luggage is delayed, you can sometimes negotiate small sums from the airline for personal necessities, such as toiletries. If your bag is lost, or the contents damaged, the airline will compensate you for the depreciated value, not the original purchase price or current replacement cost, of the items. Whatever the offer, you can usually bump it up through negotiating. If your bag is damaged, the airline may push for repair instead of replacement; this, too, is negotiable. Make sure the luggage is examined, and a damage report filed, before you leave the airport.

10. How do you negotiate with hotels?

Every night, approximately one-third of all hotel rooms in the country are vacant. Hotels are more negotiable on rates than ever before.

You're better off negotiating directly with the hotel instead of the chain's toll-free reservations line. As with most negotiating, being shy isn't helpful. Don't accept the first rate you're offered. Hotels have dozens of rates for their rooms, and they usually quote from the top (referred to as the "rack rate") down. Ask what the corporate rate is, and what special or promotional rates are available. Krunch that the rate given is just too much. If the rate won't move, ask for a suite at the regular room rate, or a room on the concierge floor. Hotels know that any revenue from a room is better than none, and reservation agents and front-desk staff are increasingly being trained not to let customers get away because of price. If all else fails, ask to speak with the manager. He may give you a deal rather than let the room go vacant. Your leverage is highest when reserving your room, but even with a reservation you can still negotiate for a better rate or a room upgrade when you check in. Of course, any kind of a problem (you reserved a king-sized bed but none are available, for example) calls for a nice concession from the hotel.

Organizations with even moderate hotel usage (as little as 50 person-nights per year) can negotiate attractive discounts with hotel chains. The more usage you can show, the better the deal you can negotiate. You can negotiate directly with the hotel chain, or have your corporate travel agency handle it.

11. How do you negotiate with rental car companies?

Once again, what you don't ask for you won't get. Rental car rates have always been negotiable, but most customers don't negotiate.

Rental car negotiations are best conducted at the rental counter. Like hotels, car rental companies have many rates for their cars, and the first quote is usually the highest. Begin negotiating from there. Find out what the corporate rate is and what specials are available. Krunch even those rates ("We've got to be able to do better than this"). Nibble for a car-class upgrade. If you have real chutzpah and some time, you can go counter-to-counter and auction your business to the lowest bidder. In addition to the foregoing, any goofs by the rental company (for example, they haven't got the model you reserved, or you'll have to wait for it) should always fetch suitable concessions.

12. How do you negotiate with retail stores?

My students are routinely surprised, amused, and more than a little skeptical when I tell them that the prices of many everyday items they buy at retail—furniture, jewelry, appliances, mattresses, antiques, electronics, clothing—are negotiable. Even those who acknowledge that retailers will bargain, or who have friends or family members who are devoted dickerers, often say they'd be too embarrassed to do it themselves.

I'm fascinated by the continuing, widespread acceptance of the idea that bargaining is somehow undignified. Retailers have exploited it forever. Whoever coined the expression "If you have to ask the price, you can't afford it," must have been a retailer. What's going on here? When did it become chic to overpay? Perhaps I'm missing something, but I just can't see any benefit to paying full retail for something I can get—with only the slightest additional effort—for less.

Yes, many retailers will flat-out refuse to bargain. Others will bargain only occasionally, or only in special circumstances, or only with great reluctance. And yes, price flexibility is most common on the purchases that are least common: expensive things. But so what?

The risk-to-reward ratio makes retail bargaining a no-brainer. Your downside—that you'll be told "no"—is negligible. Your upside—saving a slew of bucks, having some fun, and reinforcing your at-work negotiating—is outstanding. The inescapable conclusion: It makes sense to ask.

It may help put some fire in your belly to know that the standard markup from wholesale to retail is 100% (called "keystone"). That means a $1,000 sofa might have cost the store $500; a $50 shirt, $25. Luxury items are marked up even more. As a very general rule, the more the markup, the more flexible the price. On the other hand, high-volume retailers (grocery stores, for example, and discounters like Wal-Mart) thrive by moving huge quantities of goods at very low markup. These are less likely—but by no means impossible—venues for bargaining. Retailers of every stripe agree on one thing: All markup is good markup. Keystone or more is wonderful, but "no sale" is doom.

While there are no special tricks for negotiating retail purchases, here are some suggestions that may help.

- **Do your homework.** Try to learn what other local retailers are charging. Check the Internet or newspaper, call, or drop by. Study the price guides for antiques, other collectibles, and cars. The single most persuasive—and, for the consumer, most comfortable—argument for a price cut is that the same item is being sold elsewhere for less. Merchants never want to admit they're uncompetitive. Many will match or beat the competition's price—some even guarantee it—if that's what it takes to make the sale. Be knowledgeable and truthful—but not unnecessarily specific—about the other prices.
- **Be nice.** Retailers are no exception to the rule that we concede more to people we like. The sweetie gets more concessions than the screamer.
- **Lead with a krunch.** A gentle krunch is the perfect open-

ing: "I love it, but it's just so expensive. What can you do on the price?" It requires no preparation, avoids opening-offer angst on both sides, and lets you keep all of your options open. Remember: You have no idea how low the merchant will go.

- **Ask about the sale price.** "Sale price" krunches—asking when the item will go on sale, and what the sale price will be—are comfortable and effective. If you like the merchant's answer, offer to buy now at the future sale price. If the item's already on sale, or it's a "special purchase," the price is even more negotiable. A sale price is a signal that the store wants to move the item out, quickly. No matter how attractively it may be priced, "special purchase" merchandise—things the store bought especially cheaply—almost always carries a higher profit margin than regular merchandise.

- **Ask for a volume discount.** Whenever you buy more than one item, and especially if you're buying multiples of the same item, you're entirely justified in asking for a volume discount. Play your hand by degrees: "It's $100 for one, but what if I bought two? $190? How about three? $280? How about five? $450?" Respond to the proposed discount with a nibble ("O.K., if you throw in a box of widgets"), a counteroffer ("I'll give you $400 for five"), or a krunch ("There must be something more we can do"). If you're not getting any discounts, just simple multiples of the price for one, boost your hypotheticals to the extreme. "What if I bought 1,000? How about 10,000?" If these numbers yield a discount, ask that it be applied to you: "So the price is negotiable. Well, I'm not buying 10,000, but I am prepared to buy five, right now, if you'll give me that price." If you're still having no luck, try dealing with a manager (see below).

- **Exploit all flaws and problems.** It's easier for everybody if you can find a pretext for the merchant to give you a deal.

Be on the lookout for the tiniest defect—a scratch, a loose thread, a ripped seam—and exploit to the fullest the bargaining leverage of any such flaws. Never disparage the item ("How can you ask this price for such a piece of junk?") and be careful to preface any criticism with a compliment ("I love the dresser, but I'm troubled by that scrape on the front leg"). Regardless of its condition, if the item is a display or a demo model, a discount is called for. If the merchant is out of stock on the model you want, he's given you a hammer for a discount on the more expensive model.

- **Time is money.** The more time you spend with the salesperson, the more the store has invested in you, the more it stands to lose if you don't buy, and the more flexible it will tend to be. You'll encourage this investment by looking like a serious buyer.

- **Deal with the manager.** Don't fool around attempting to negotiate price with a sales clerk; you're wasting your time and the clerk's. Only managers have pricing authority. Ask to speak with a manager as soon as politeness permits. And the smaller the store, the easier it will be to reach the ultimate decision-maker: the owner. That's why you'll usually have a better chance of bargaining in a smaller establishment.

- **Don't forget to nibble.** Whether or not you've gotten a price concession, you may be able to get some free or reduced-price sweeteners as the deal is getting ready to wrap up, on things like delivery, assembly, alterations, installation, batteries, and speaker cable. Or ask the merchant to take care of the sales tax.

- **Cash has clout.** If you charge your purchase, the merchant instantly loses a 2 to 3% "merchant fee" to the card issuer. This means that if he's still willing to take plastic at the end of the deal, he's still got room to move. If paying cash is an option, leave the cash-or-credit payment issue open during the negotiations. At the end, offer a credit card, then hesitate and ask, "What's your merchant fee on this? Three percent? For two percent I'll write you a check."

13. How do you negotiate with lawyers?

The recently departed lawyer was delighted to be greeted by St. Peter at the gates of heaven. "Welcome, Mr. Jones," said St. Peter. "We're thrilled that you'll be joining us. You're the first lawyer we've ever had up here. And we're especially impressed that you lived to be 200 years old." "200?" said Jones. "I was 80. How did you figure 200?" Replied St. Peter, "We added up all the hours you billed to your clients!"

At the risk of being expelled from the bar, let me say straight out that consumers have considerable bargaining power when shopping for lawyers. The critical issue is the complexity of the legal matter.

Most everyday legal transactions—wills, real estate closings, contracts, traffic tickets, bankruptcies, probating of estates, uncontested divorces, incorporations—are (from the lawyer's perspective, at least) simple. Almost any competent general practitioner can handle these matters. In fact, such work is so routine that many lawyers flat-rate it, charging, for example, $500 for a standard real estate settlement or a will. Comparison-shop a few lawyers (the initial consultation should be free) and buy strictly on price. You may be able to win some further concessions with the suggestion of an ongoing relationship. The lawyer knows that a startup business or a new family may provide a growing, increasingly profitable stream of future legal work.

For legal issues of moderate difficulty—child custody, contested divorces, drunk driving and other criminal cases, personal injury matters, and commercial cases—I'd suggest a two-step process.

First, call and visit a number of lawyers and do a "rough cut" on the basis of competency, rapport, and price. For this initial step, keep in mind that bigger firms, downtown firms, and firms with fancy offices charge the most and negotiate the least. Second, sit down with one or two finalists and talk turkey. Negotiate subtly. Present the lawyer with a problem: I want you, you're the greatest, you're worth every penny you charge and more, but I'm just a poor individual with a family to feed. Will you help me get justice? Always ask the lawyer to take the case "on contingency." If she will, you won't have to pay unless—and until—you win, but the lawyer will get a third or more of the proceeds. Accident cases are customarily handled this way, and contingent-fee arrangements are not unheard-of in other matters. They are not permitted in criminal cases, however. If your case is unique or newsworthy, you'll have extra leverage. Also, be aware that lawyers can't help reckoning the affluence of their clients, and may, consciously or unconsciously, reflect that assessment in their billings—so dress and speak modestly.

If you're in serious legal trouble, or there's a great deal of money at stake, or the issue is very sophisticated (a complex trust, securities, estate, or tax matter, or an intellectual-property question, for example) this isn't the time to economize. Get yourself a specialist, the very best you can find. A real star has the tremendous advantage of being known and respected by the key players in the system. And an expert will have a far shorter learning curve than a generalist, so you won't have to pay for your lawyer to "get up to speed" on the matter.

Always keep your lawyer on a short leash. For anything more than a small, fixed-fee matter, agree on a detailed budget at the outset. Insist on itemized, monthly billing thereafter. Regularly compare budgeted numbers to actuals. Require weekly or semiweekly telephone status reports. Make it clear that you're extremely sensitive to costs. Close (but not offensive) oversight will help prevent misunderstandings and keep legal expenses down.

14. How do you negotiate with doctors?

Medical and dental fees are more negotiable than ever. Nevertheless, doctors are easily affronted by direct haggling; grace and decorum are essential.

If the procedure is covered by your medical insurance, negotiating is relatively straightforward. Ask your carrier how much it will pay for the procedure. If it's less than your doctor is charging, tell him; doctors are often willing to reduce their fee to the amount the patient's insurer will cover.

If your procedure isn't covered by insurance, some shopping and then some haggling are in order. Get at least three opinions. Shop not just for price, but also experience, disposition, and therapeutic strategy. Negotiate—diplomatically—with the top one or two candidates. Remember that like lawyers, home contractors, and other service professionals, doctors inevitably take the measure of their patients and adjust their charges accordingly. If you're wealthy, don't flaunt it. Remember also that likable patients tend to be charged less than difficult ones, and for future reference, long-standing patients pay less than new ones. Always negotiate directly with the doctor, not the snippy no-authority receptionist/office manager who would appreciate payment now, thank you.

Even if you can't get the fee lowered, extended-payment arrangements can sometimes be worked out. Some doctors will even barter medical work in exchange for goods or services.

15. How do you negotiate with contractors?

You can almost always hammer a contractor for a lower price. And it's *not* always wise to do so. The first question is, how big is the job? If it's tiny—fixing a leak, repairing an appliance, installing a lock—

just krunch. You don't have time to get estimates, and the contractor isn't making much money on the work anyway.

If the job is small or entirely straightforward—replacing a sink, building a fence or a simple deck, painting a room, refinishing a hardwood floor—negotiate assertively, pick the lowest-priced competent contractor, and define the work carefully in the contract so that nothing can be avoided.

If the work is more elaborate—new construction, an addition, remodeling—greater discretion in bargaining is called for. While it's unlikely you'd have a "payback" problem from too-aggressive negotiating with lawyers or doctors (can you imagine a plastic surgeon's revenge?), home contractors are a different story. On larger jobs, contractors have an overwhelming number of ways to cut costs and add extras. The more mistreated or financially squeezed they feel, the more inclined they will be to do so. And because anybody who provides labor or materials for improvements to your property can file a mechanic's lien (which can, in the worst case, lead to foreclosure), they can do a lot of mischief. Concentrate on finding a contractor who will do your job right. Getting the work done for a reasonable price is an important but secondary goal. Set aside all thoughts of vanquishing the contractor. If you get what you've paid for, you've scored a resounding triumph. Remember that bad construction is like a bad haircut: The discomfort continues long after the work is done.

Always get at least three quotes on anything more than a small repair. Some contractors have begun charging for estimates, so determine beforehand if there's a fee. Don't look for contractors in the Yellow Pages; referrals are the best source. Ask neighbors and friends who have had similar work done and were pleased with the outcome.

Have the most prestigious contractor bid first. With this contractor's assistance, define the specifications of the job in detail. Be sure each subsequent contractor bids on the same specifications.

Insist that each contractor itemize his bid. The more detail provided in each estimate, the better the job is likely to turn out—and the more negotiating power you'll have. If you're only given a price for the total job, you can't do much more than a simple auction among bidders followed by some krunching. Itemization reveals the soft spots in each bid. With itemized prices you can better compare each contractor's appreciation of the difficulty of each element of the work. You'll know the quality of the materials each plans to use. You'll be able to spot potential misunderstandings and corner-cutting. If you decide to take on some of the work yourself—for example, painting—you'll know how much to deduct.

The bids you receive may vary dramatically. Larger outfits tend to charge more because of higher overhead. Individuals and family firms may not have to pay workmen's compensation insurance, so they can bid lower. If you live in a better neighborhood or have an expensive car out front, you'll be charged more. If you're friendly, you may be charged less. A very common reason for a low bid is that the contractor has a gap in his schedule. If he has no work for his crew, he can't pay them and they'll leave. He may bid a job at cost just to keep his crew together. But a surprising amount of pricing is plain guesswork.

Once you've got your bids, it's time to negotiate. Never simply choose the low or middle bidder. The lowest estimate is rarely the best deal. The workmanship or materials may be inferior, or the bid may be a lowball on which the contractor plans to profit through expensive "change orders" after the work starts.

Start with a little cherry-picking between contractors. Compare the bids on a task-by-task basis, and have the higher bidders either justify or reduce their price for each task. A contractor who refuses to reduce a bid may have figured it scientifically—even by computer. On the other hand, a contractor who bids on the spot or concedes too quickly may just be pulling numbers out of the air.

At this stage many homeowners, suddenly confronted by bids bigger than budgets, start thinking about doing some of the work themselves. If you have the time and the competence, it's possible to save some money this way. However, choose your tasks carefully. It's tempting to try to economize by buying materials yourself, but it rarely pans out. Contractors mark up the prices of their materials, but they usually buy them cheaper than you can. They also find them, select them, get them delivered, inspect them, and pay for them. For example, you can probably save a few bucks buying the lumber yourself, but unless you're prepared to learn not just the different types of wood but the different grades of the different types, to be able to recognize them on sight, and to be present to inspect each delivery and reject any inferior lumber, you'd be much better off leaving it to the builder. Painting, on the other hand, is often a good do-it-yourself choice. So is cleanup. Rather than having the crew periodically stop work to drive small loads of debris to the dump, it may be considerably less expensive for you to rent a dumpster and have it picked up when the work is done. If you're interested in doing some of the work yourself, don't hesitate to ask the contractors for their suggestions.

When you've finished your rounds of negotiating with the bidders, discard bids that are radically high or low. From the bids that are fairly close, pick the most competent contractor. If you haven't already done so, check the contractor's references. Ask about timeliness and attention to detail. Find out if the price increased during the job and if so, why. How has the work held up? If the references check out, call the local consumer affairs office to confirm the contractor's license and check on any complaints filed against him. Touch base with the Better Business Bureau as well. Before any work is done, have the contractor's insurer give you a certificate of liability and workmen's compensation insurance coverage.

Your negotiations are by no means over. Now it's time to negotiate the contract. Good contracts make for successful projects; never turn over any money until you have a signed contract. Get everything in writing, and include as much detail as you can. Not just the color of paint, but also the brand, sprayed or brushed, and how many coats. Identify manufacturers, model numbers, grades, and so on. Define the contractor's responsibilities at each step of the project. Don't be embarrassed about what seems like nit-picking. A little nit-picking at this stage will help establish a conscientious tone for the entire job, and may avoid big hassles later. If the contractor's written agreement is too skimpy, the Internet and many office and legal-supply stores sell contracting forms to help you beef it up. There are also a number of software programs for managing larger remodeling and construction jobs.

The payment schedule set forth in the contract may be a subject of negotiation. Building projects generally call for partial payments as the work progresses. Be sure your agreement specifies exactly when payments are due; tie each payment to the completion of a specific, easily identifiable milestone. Never let the payments get ahead of the work. Remember that each payment you make reduces your leverage. Retain at least 10 to 15% of the total price as a final payment, due when all work is complete. Never pay for work that isn't done, no matter what sob story the contractor gives you, and resist pressure to pay for tasks early—"almost" done isn't sufficient. On the other hand, deserved progress payments should be made immediately.

Even with a detailed, signed contract, a few bumps in the road to a successful project must often be negotiated: changes and extras. These are the source of some of the most serious disagreements between contractors and clients. There are two black-letter rules applicable to changes. One, the contractor must supply all labor and materials necessary to complete the job in a "workmanlike manner." That means he must fulfill the plans to the letter, furnishing everything—hardware, fixtures, trim, whatever—unless specified otherwise in the contract. Second, any changes to the plans must be approved by you, in writing, before being undertaken. That would seem to cover all the bases, but it doesn't. What happens when rotten studs are discovered under sound drywall? Or granite is encountered instead of the expected soil? Or any one of a thousand other significant, unanticipated problems crops up that wasn't specifically provided for in the contract? Is it fair for the contractor to eat the whole cost? Sure, you could demand that he do so. And you could throw him off the job if he refuses, hire another contractor, and file suit. You may even win. There's even the tiniest chance you may actually collect some money before the next Ice Age. This may give you some satisfaction, but it won't get your work done. And meanwhile, your house is going to be awfully hard to refinance or sell with an unsettled mechanic's lien.

If the matter is unambiguously covered by the contract, firmly but diplomatically insist that the contractor perform as agreed. Maybe you could offer some trivial but face-saving accommodation. But if it's in a gray area, negotiate. Keep your eyes on the prize. Is the issue important enough to cause the whole project to collapse? A concession from you—perhaps in exchange for some additional low- or no-cost work by the contractor—may keep things together. If necessary, offer to pay half. Or more. Try to get *quid pro quos* for whatever you give, but don't let the job bog down.

Here are a few more contracting tidbits you may find useful:

- Never hire a contractor selling door to door.
- There actually isn't much real gouging in home repair, but it happens more often on siding, window replacement, driveway sealing, and basement waterproofing jobs.
- Roofing jobs produce the widest range in bids. That's because in roofing work, the decision to repair or replace is very subjective. Surprises often lurk under old shingles. Repairing is initially less expensive than replacing, but can be more expensive if the repairs only last a year. Give extra weight to a roofer's reputation.
- Your zip code will show up in your bids. Contractors bid jobs higher in better neighborhoods. The affluent pay more, but also tend to be harder to work for and quicker to sue. If you live in an especially nice house, try to get a preliminary quote over the phone—before the contractor

visits. If you have a Mercedes, put it in the garage. Leave your kid's junker in the driveway.

- Clear the work area before you get bids. Contractors love access. Inside or out, spruce up the job site.
- Budget for contingencies. Include an extra 5 to 10% in your budget for the project, especially with renovations. Until the walls are torn out, the final cost is only an educated guess. Don't tell the contractor about this contingency fund.
- Get lien releases. If your contractor will be using subcontractors or laborers, make sure each one signs a waiver of mechanic's lien rights. Try to get the principal suppliers, such as the lumberyard, to sign waivers also. If they don't, and your contractor doesn't pay them, they can slap a lien on your house and go after you for the money they're owed. It doesn't matter that you've already paid your contractor; the unpaid sub or supplier can make you pay *again*. Don't laugh; it happened to me.
- If you're nicer, things will go better.

16. How do you negotiate with auto mechanics?

A little background, first. Distinguish the small jobs (tune-ups, brake pads, mufflers) from the big jobs (collisions, transmissions). The real negotiating—and money-saving—is on the big jobs. Second, forget about parts and concentrate on labor. The amount of money that garages make on parts is negligible; labor is a different story. The labor charge is the garage's hourly rate times the hours required for your job. So far so good; but now it gets weird. The hours usually aren't the actual hours, they're the "book time"—what the published labor-time guide used by the garage says the job should take. There are a number of these labor guides, they estimate the time required for almost any auto repair down to the nearest tenth of an hour, and most importantly, they're all different. None are low, some are pretty accurate, and some are high. Most garages charge book time, not actual time. If the job was estimated to take 2.2 hours but Randy Rapidwrench gets it done in an hour, you'll be charged for 2.2. (To be fair, if it takes 10 hours, you'll probably still be charged for 2.2.)

On small jobs, the best technique by far is a simple krunch: "$400 for a tune-up? I'm stunned. The whole car isn't worth $400. Let's try to come up with a better number." You can take it from here.

With larger jobs, have the garage holding your busted car (the "admitting garage") give you an estimate. When you get it, call at least two other reputable garages for estimates. Insist that each garage specify the time required (call it "the book time" if you want to sound like a *cognoscento*) and the hourly rate. If the admitting garage is significantly higher, ask them to match your best quote. They probably will; it's a cutthroat business. If they won't, have the other garage come get your car (nibble for a free tow, of course). But if the admitting garage is competitive, krunch their quote a few times and then give them the go-ahead.

13

Concluding Thoughts

There will come a time when you believe everything
is finished. That will be the beginning.
Louis L'Amour

You've come to the end. Now it's time for you to begin. Before you
jump into the Big Bazaar, please allow me a few final words of advice.

1. Focus. It's all about the Critical Rules. Don't even think about
doing the rest of them. It's not possible, and even if it were, it would
be completely unnecessary and profoundly counterproductive.
Focus all of your attention on the Critical Rules, and let the rest slide.
Anything that distracts you from them will make you less effective.
You'll remember the lesser Rules when you need them. Trust me on
this—when the right time comes along, they'll pop into your mind.

2. You'll make lots of mistakes. That's O.K. Remember: Good decisions come from experience, and experience comes from bad decisions. The perfect negotiator hasn't yet been born. All of us get
outwitted sometimes, and confused, and tired. Don't let a few mistakes cause you to lose confidence in your ability to bargain well.
Embrace your blunders; resolve to do your best not to repeat them,

and then move on. Learn from the mistakes of others. You won't live long enough to make them all yourself.

3. Sometimes you'll lose. Periodically you'll be dealt a negotiating hand that can best be described as hopeless. You've nothing they want, there's no time, management is desperate, the other side knows your bottom line. The best negotiator who ever lived couldn't succeed. You'll lose. Maybe you'll lose big. Go easy on yourself. It wasn't that the Rules didn't work or that you're not a perfectly competent negotiator. You just got crummy cards. You'll do better next time.

4. Take it easy for the next couple of days. The newly trained nego-tiator, enthusiastic to shake off old habits, has a nasty tendency to try hitting the first couple of pitches out of the park. Please be careful not to overnegotiate your first deal or two after you finish reading *Negotiate to Win*. You're hazardous to yourself and your organiza-tion for at least the next 48 hours. Within a few days, you'll have mellowed out and you'll be fine.

5. You have an ace in the hole. If you still find yourself questioning your bargaining potential ("I'm such an American. I'll never get this stuff right!") you may be comforted to know that you have an ace in the hole so powerful it will virtually insure your negotiating success. Here it is: You'll usually be negotiating against Americans! I know you're going to do well.

6. Celebrate your humanity. Do you remember way back in Chapter 1 when I told you that among animals, only humans negotiate? It's part of our heritage, our patrimony. Sooner or later, someone will tell you that negotiating is becoming obsolete—that the way of the future is instantaneous, computerized commerce in a global marketplace. Humans will be out of the loop, and negotiating will be a dinosaur.

Sit down with this person, and help him. He has lost sight of some of the unique gifts of his own humanity. It'll never happen. Let me tell you why.

First, only the tiniest fraction of human interactions take place within a context that could even remotely be called a marketplace. These are hugely outnumbered by noneconomic interactions that are inherently free of market forces.

Next, neither market forces nor computers can produce the original, subtle intermingling of interests that a good negotiation can. Only humans are capable of the sudden insight, the intuitive leap, the *ad hoc* measure, the makeshift arrangement, the spur-of-the-moment decision, the bold move, or the masterstroke. Humans alone experience the warm satisfaction of mutually flexing positions and trading interests to reach agreement, of weaving high-payoff/low-cost creative options into a final deal.

With great difficulty, computers can be instructed to behave in ways that resemble what we call "forgiving," "forgetting," and "showing a little flexibility." But the logic of the heart—"gut instinct"—staunchly refuses to be programmed into them. And our finest passions—love, friendship, courage, loyalty, gratitude, humility, honor, humor, sympathy, good will—are utterly and forever absent from their circuits.

These are unique and irreplaceable virtues. The agreements of just and principled people have always reflected them, and always will. For however long humankind endures, we'll be negotiating.

14

Thomas's Truisms

What goes around comes around. Sooner or later, you have to pay for your sins.

■

For the Japanese, the only difference between a yes and a no is the size of the "if."

■

How do you get agreement when persuasion doesn't work? You negotiate.

■

When you can't sell 'em, you can usually buy 'em.

■

Always persuade first.
Negotiate only when persuasion fails.

■

Face is humankind's third rail. Touch it and die.

■

Win-win negotiating is mandatory because the other
side survives the talks.

■

Don't make a concession without seeking something
in exchange.

■

Try to avoid saying "no" to the other side.
"Yes, if" is better.

■

If you ask for more (within reason) you'll get more.

■

Your opening offer should be assertive,
but never ridiculous.

■

The moment of the opening offer is the most important,
and most stressful, in the entire negotiation.

■

Never dignify an unreasonable offer with a concession.

■

The swiftest negotiator can never outrun
supply and demand.

■

With enough trust, negotiating becomes unnecessary.

■

Never make a concession that's larger than
the one preceding it.

■

Make your concessions in a skewed
Rule of Halves progression.

■

Never escalate unless you have no alternative.

■

Never shave a concession. Either make the whole
concession that you're supposed to make,
or don't make any concession at all.

■

The krunch is the simplest and most frequently used
tool in negotiating.

■

A krunch is the only way to respond
to an unreasonable offer.

■

Every concession has a price,
but krunches cost nothing.

■

Only the final handshake seals the deal.
Until then, all issues remain open.

■

Never stick with an issue that's not working.
Skip it and move on to something else.

■

The nibble is negotiating's equivalent of a layup.

■

Nibbling is part of doing a complete job as a negotiator.

■

Sometimes people find satisfactions in strange places.

■

Creativity is the most fickle and capricious tool
in negotiating.

■

The value of the concession to the other side
is what matters.

■

Setting your Envelopes is your most important
homework task.

■

Separate the people from the problem.
Be hard on the problem but soft on the people.

■

We make more concessions to friends.

■

Climates tend to persist.

■

The wise negotiator frequently chooses not to negotiate.

■

"It's my bottom line" is the biggest lie in negotiation.

■

Only when the other side doesn't move any more can
you be sure they're truly at their bottom line.

■

Never say you're at your bottom line unless you are.

■

Nobody likes having their first offer accepted.

■

Schmoozing is the last refuge of the weak negotiator.

■

It's better to bring things up now, when you've got some
leverage, than later when you don't.

■

The quicker the deal, the greater the risk.

■

The more authority you have,
the more concessions you'll make.

■

Always negotiate with the highest-authority person
you can get access to.

■

Bosses give away the ranch.

■

It's where you open, not when, that matters.

■

Teams are inherently dangerous, and the bigger
the team, the greater the risk.

■

Being outnumbered means you're in a
target-rich environment.

■

The caucus is the solution to the dangers
of negotiating teams.

■

Ethical negotiating isn't the right thing to do,
it's the only thing to do.

■

Negotiators, in general, talk entirely too much.

■

INDEX